As a jou... sent on h... aged twenty-nine. His career was ...upt...y ...t short by militiamen who kidnapped and held him captive for five and a half years.

Since his release he has written four books prior to this one: *Some Other Rainbow* (with Jill Morrell), about his hostage years; *Island Race* (with Sandi Toksvig), an account of their circumnavigation of Britain; *Between Extremes* (with Brian Keenan), a journey through Chile; and *A Ghost Upon Your Path*. He continues to work in both radio and television.

Praise for *You Can't Hide the Sun*:

'John McCarthy takes us on an unforgettable journey through a tumultuous and complex landscape. His passion and humanity are all the more remarkable in the context of his own brutal experience of the dark side of its political context.'
Tom Bradby, Political Editor, ITV News

'John McCarthy's excellent book focuses in on Palestinian citizens of Israel, who sometimes get ignored as a complexity too far. McCarthy doesn't hide his sympathy for the human beings who have been battered by Middle East conflict. Perhaps that's because he was caught up in it too when he was held hostage in Lebanon for more than five years between 1986 and 1991. Like Palestinians, and Jews, he longed for the sanctuary of home. McCarthy made it home. But in his journey through Israel and the occupied Palestinian territories he finds Palestinians who are still waiting, hoping and struggling for their homes more than 60 years after Israel was created. Fascinating and timely, and written with the charm of a man who's still determined to explore the tempestuous region that for five years was just a dream on the other side of his locked cell door.'
Jeremy Bowen

'From a man who knows much about human spirit's refusal to be cowed comes a beautifully written, compassionate and insightful account of Israel's non-Jewish population. *You Can't Hide the Sun* does not just champion a people too long bullied, marginalised and ignored – it drives home that without heeding their voice no long term solution of Israel-Palestine is possible.'
Tim Butcher, author of *Blood River*

'A powerful account of the Palestinians of Israeli citizenship as told in their own words. Eloquent and moving, this book is essential reading to understand the full complexity of Palestinian-Israeli relations.'
Eugene Rogan, author of *The Arabs: A History*

Also by John McCarthy

Some Other Rainbow (with Jill Morrell)
Island Race (with Sandi Toksvig)
Between Extremes (with Brian Keenan)
A Ghost Upon Your Path

You Can't Hide the Sun

A Journey through Israel and Palestine

John McCarthy

BLACK SWAN

TRANSWORLD PUBLISHERS
61–63 Uxbridge Road, London W5 5SA
A Random House Group Company
www.transworldbooks.co.uk

**YOU CAN'T HIDE THE SUN
A BLACK SWAN BOOK: 9780552774475**

First published in Great Britain
in 2012 by Bantam Press
an imprint of Transworld Publishers
Black Swan edition published 2013

Typeset in 11/14.5pt Times New Roman by Falcon Oast Graphic Art Ltd.
Printed and bound by Clays Ltd, St Ives plc.

2 4 6 8 10 9 7 5 3

For the Azbarga family, with the profound hope that soon their right to a secure home will be assured.

For Lydia, for whom I pray this right will never be in question.

Contents

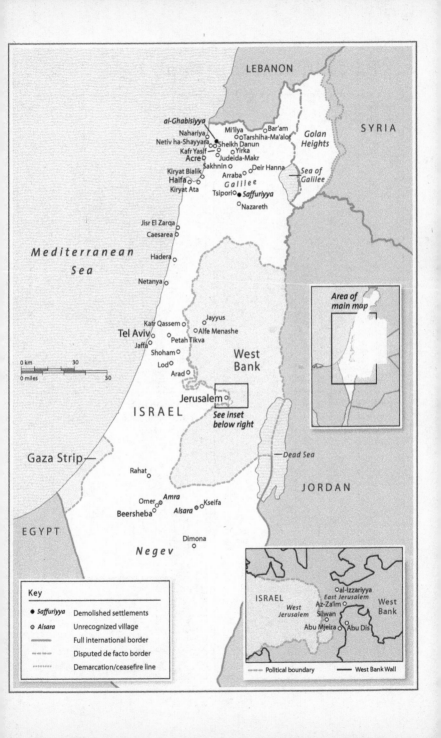

LEBANON

SYRIA

al-Ghabisiyya
Mi'ilya   Bar'am
Nahariya   Tarshiha-Ma'alot   *Golan Heights*
Netiv ha-Shayyara   Sheikh Danun
Kafr Yasif   Yirka
Acre   Judeida-Makr
              Sakhnin   Deir Hanna
Kiryat Bialik   Arraba   *Sea of Galilee*
Haifa   *G a l i l e e*
Kiryat Ata
              Tsipori *Saffuriyya*
                 Nazareth

Jisr El Zarqa
Caesarea

M e d i t e r r a n e a n
S e a

Hadera

Netanya

Area of main map

Jayyus
Kafr Qassem   Alfe Menashe
Tel Aviv   Petah Tikva
Jaffa
        Shoham   West
        Lod   Bank
        Arad

Jerusalem
ISRAEL   *See inset below right*

Gaza Strip

                    Dead Sea

Rahat   JORDAN

        Omer *Amra*
Beersheba   *Alsara* Kseifa

EGYPT   Dimona

N e g e v

Key

● *Saffuriyya*	Demolished settlements
○ *Alsara*	Unrecognized village
———	Full international border
----	Disputed de facto border
········	Demarcation/ceasefire line

al-Izzariyya
East Jerusalem
Az-Za'im
ISRAEL
West Jerusalem   Silwan   West Bank
        Abu Mjeira   Abu Dis

---- Political boundary   —— West Bank Wall

0 km   30
0 miles   30

Palestinian loss of land, 1946–2008

Palestinian and Jewish land, 1946

Halfa
Tel Aviv
Ramalah
Jerusalem
Gaza Bethlehem
PALESTINE

- Palestinian land
- Jewish land

UN Partition Plan, 1947

Halfa
Tel Aviv
Ramalah
Jerusalem
Gaza Bethlehem

- Palestinian land
- Jewish land

Palestinian and Jewish land, 1948–67

Halfa
West Bank
Tel Aviv
Ramalah
Jerusalem
Gaza Bethlehem
ISRAEL

- Palestinian land
- Jewish land

Palestinian and Jewish land, 2008

Halfa
West Bank
Tel Aviv
Ramalah
Jerusalem
Gaza Bethlehem
ISRAEL

- Palestinian land
- Jewish land (military and civil control)

Author's Note

Although it incorporates detailed research from written histories and documents, this is not an academic work; nor is it intended to be a comprehensive account of the conflict between Palestinian Arabs and Jews before and since the creation of the state of Israel.

My aim is to shed light on an often overlooked community: the Palestinian citizens of Israel. So while there are, of course, Jewish people in the book, they are not the main focus. It is the remnant of the Palestinian people who had, prior to 1948, been the indigenous majority who take centre stage.

The main source of the information included here has been my meetings with ordinary people. The book reflects my journeys around Israel to hear the testimony of these people in their home landscape. There are first-hand accounts from those who remember the end of British control of Palestine and the formation of Israel and the consequent displacement of Arab inhabitants, the time Jewish Israelis celebrate as bringing independence, but which the Palestinians remember as the Nakba, or Catastrophe.

These voices are followed by others to paint a picture of the life of an ethnic minority in a state established as a homeland for another people. I met and interviewed dozens of people, yet have selected only a few to be exemplars of their community.

At the heart of the book is the idea of home: the need to have a place where we feel we belong and in which we feel safe. This need is shared and understood by all people. It is the tragedy of Israel and Palestine that it has led to brutal and, so far, unending rivalry. I hope this book will bring to light the human stories of a hidden side to this conflict.

1

One in Five

I CANNOT BELIEVE THAT ANYONE COULD CALL THIS PLACE home.

What might once have been houses are now piles of shattered concrete, baked by the stifling mid-morning heat. Spires of twisted metal glint rust-red in the fierce sunlight, and weeds fight for a foothold at their base. A breath of wind chases torn newspaper into the debris. As it settles, so too does a silence as oppressive as the heat.

High above my head, jet fighters' vapour trails etch the blue sky. On the ground I feel as though I'm walking through the aftermath of a battle. Clambering over one of the demolished buildings, I set off an avalanche of rubble. As its echoes die away I peer beneath a slab of concrete at the wreckage of a bathroom: shattered washbasin, torn shower curtain and broken mirror, their bright colours turning grey under thick dust. A few feet away a crushed suitcase spills a tattered dress and shoes among shards of broken glass. Shock – and something close to fear – moves me. Not so long ago, this was a home. Who lived here? I wonder. And where are they now?

'*Ahlan wa Sahlan!*' The friendly welcome rings round the debris and then a man appears, walking quickly and balancing a tray of cold drinks. Smiling broadly he introduces himself as Moadi Azbarga.

As we stand sipping in the sticky heat, I have the chance to observe him more closely. Tall and lean, with dark, swept-back hair, Moadi reminds me of Daniel Day-Lewis. I'm struggling to reconcile his cheery Arab hospitality with the devastation that surrounds us. I ask him what happened here.

Moadi's mood changes. Our eyes meet occasionally as we talk, but most of the time he looks over my shoulder. Standing very still and upright, he tells me that he and his neighbours are locked in a long-running battle with the council about the redevelopment of their land as an industrial zone. His jaw tightening, he explains that this is really about their wish to exile the inhabitants who have lived here for generations.

Moadi and his family are Bedouin, part of the indigenous Arab population of Israel. Until now my images of the Bedouin have been drawn from a mix of colour-tinted pictures in my primary-school Bible, and finer paintings by the likes of John Singer Sargent. I've always imagined them as free spirits roaming the desert with their camels, sheep and goats, dressed in flowing robes and pitching their black tents under shade-giving palm trees. This idyllic vision bears no relation to the scene in front of me.

'At night I go to my mother's or brother's place but,' Moadi says, pointing to a bivouac in the rubble, 'this is my home. I stay here during the day.'

It may look like a war zone, but we are standing in the outskirts of a town right in the heart of modern Israel. Just a few miles from Ben-Gurion Airport and Tel Aviv, we are less than an hour's drive from my comfortable hotel in Jerusalem. Lod has been inhabited for thousands of years and is reputed to be the birthplace of St George. Now a predominantly Jewish community, it was exclusively Arab when the modern state of Israel was established in 1948.

I have come here to make a television documentary about the role of religion in Israel's internal politics. Travelling around the country, I am becoming very much more aware that there are two sides to Israel: the Jewish homeland, which sees itself as a modern European democracy with nice hotels and beaches on the Mediterranean shore and close links to international, Western culture and commerce; and the Arab homeland, which cannot ignore its Middle East location and heritage. I've been thinking about where that leaves the Arab community within Israel, people like Moadi Azbarga and his neighbours. What is their relationship to the state, and what is the state's relationship to them? More and more questions form in my mind. In every direction, the landscape is littered with building sites, yet here, just a few miles from booming, bustling Tel Aviv, a community is being destroyed.

Adopting the role of genial host once more, and

seeming to shrug off the terrible story he has just told me, Moadi takes us round the corner to meet his brother. Saud Azbarga's house – a whitewashed breeze-block and concrete single-storey building – is one of a handful that is, miraculously, still standing. A shoulder-high wall running round its parched yard affords some relief from the sunlight.

Saud, a pharmacist, is stockier than his brother. Clasping his hands to his chest he bows us into his home and invites us to sit on cushions spread around the floor. His wife Rania, a nurse, offers us sweet black tea and small cakes. She is smartly dressed, her pretty face framed by a light pink headscarf, and her eyes smile behind gold-rimmed glasses. The couple's three young children, two girls and a boy, play around us. On the wall a picture of a waterfall is draped with prayer beads, and an elaborate clock, featuring the al-Aqsa mosque in Jerusalem, sits on a shelf.

Once they begin telling their story, I can see the same tension and frustration sweeping through them that I'd felt with Moadi. Their eyes flit between each other and me. They seem distracted, almost broken. They tell me that there is a demolition order hanging over their home, and armed men, police and military, had already stormed in early one morning.

'At first I thought I was dreaming,' Rania says, her eyes now brimming with tears. 'Ten soldiers came right into my bedroom, even though I was still in my night clothes. I fell to the floor, shaking. Saud was away and the children were terrified.'

Outraged at the intrusion and shamed by her state of undress, Rania says she was desperate to comfort the children, who were crying in another room, cowering from the throng of uniformed strangers.

I find myself glancing across to the children. Jenna and Nowa are around six and seven, and their brother Annis is two. The girls, in smart frocks and with their hair neatly plaited, sit close by their parents, listening intently. The little boy plays with some bricks on the floor. I think of my daughter, Lydia, playing at home just like this, carefully stacking her building bricks and laughing when they topple over. Not quite a year old and on the cusp of walking, she is constantly on the move, pulling herself upright on any available piece of furniture. Suddenly my eyes fill with tears and my throat tightens. I have to swallow hard before I can look again at Rania, who has fallen silent.

Saud tells me that this dawn raid was just a warning, aimed at making it clear that the security forces and demolition crew would be back in a few months to carry out the job. 'We built this house,' Saud says, shaking his head in frustration. 'It's on the site of our old family home. It was falling down. They wouldn't give us planning permission for this new building, so now they say it is illegal.' He shakes his head again. 'What were we supposed to do? Our children need a roof over their heads. This is where we live. This is our home! But now the authorities are telling us it is not.'

The Azbargas, like their neighbours, have tried every avenue of legal appeal but so far to no avail. While Saud speaks, Rania sits very still and looks across at her children. Then she speaks again, so softly that I have to lean towards her to hear.

'When we ask where they expect us to go, they just sneer and say, "You can go to the desert with all the other Arabs."'

My romantic image of Bedouin life is rapidly evaporating. There is no romance in Rania's nervous exhaustion or Moadi's bivouac conjured from a scrap of tarpaulin.

'It's like living in a kind of suspended animation,' Saud says, as little Annis starts pulling at his shoelaces. 'You cannot reach for the sky, you cannot touch the ground. The children have nightmares about the soldiers coming to knock down their house. I think the Israeli authorities want to terrorize and terrify us so that we'll all run away.'

He describes the atmosphere in the community when the demolition notices were first served. They were in a state of emotional exhaustion as the day of reckoning approached. When the demolition crews, backed by hundreds of police, finally went to work, the families were forced to watch as the bulldozers destroyed their homes. Some owners, like Saud and Rania, were told theirs would be left standing – but only for the time being.

The focus in the media, at least in the UK, has always seemed to be on the conflict between Israel and the Palestinians living in the territories of the West Bank and Gaza, or in Lebanon, Syria and Jordan. It's only now that I'm beginning to appreciate there are deep tensions present within Israel's borders, between the Israeli authorities and the Arab citizens of the state.

I hit the highway back to Jerusalem and the early-evening rush hour. With me, in the passenger seat of the car, is a woman named Suha Arraf: I've been working with her on the documentary. A light breeze coming from the Mediterranean Sea, a couple of miles to the west, has taken the edge off the heat of the day. Ahead, the rocky summits of the tree-covered hills around the city are bathed by the setting sun, and I am excited, as always, to be heading towards that beautiful but tragic place. So holy to so many, yet that very holiness has been employed to justify thousands of years of hatred and violence. For as long as I can remember, the conflict between the Israelis and the Palestinians, in all its brutal complexity, has never been out of the headlines.

During this visit Israel has once again become embroiled in conflict on two fronts with its Arab neigh-bours. The jet fighters that have been decorating the sky today are not on manoeuvres. They've been making bombing runs either to Palestinian positions in Gaza in the south-west, or north to the Hezbollah forces in Lebanon. Suha keeps up a running translation of the news on the car radio, hopping between Arabic and Hebrew stations. The latest round of fighting between Israel and her Arab neighbours inevitably dominates all other stories on today's news, and the headlines tell of rocket attacks from Hezbollah across the northern border and clashes with Palestinian militants in Gaza.

Like the Azbargas and their neighbours, Suha is an Arab citizen of Israel. Over the years, our paths have crossed on various journalistic projects in which she has worked as a translator and local producer. She pauses only when her mobile phone rings. It's her mother. She lowers her head and starts speaking intently.

I think back to our meeting with the Azbarga family. Though trapped and worn down by their terrible circumstances, they radiated a fierce pride in, and determination to hold on to, the place they call home.

'How many Arabs are there in Israel?' I ask, as Suha ends her call.

'Around one and a quarter million.'

'But that's, what, twenty per cent of the population?' It takes a moment to sink in. 'One in five?' Although I have been following the news most of my life and coming here regularly over recent years, I just hadn't realized how significant a proportion of Israel's population is Arab. I confess my stupidity.

Suha chuckles. 'If you feel stupid, what do you think it's like for me?'

'What do you mean?'

'I didn't know I was Palestinian until I was twelve years old.'

The traffic is stationary so I can turn and stare at her. Suha begins laughing, a deep, rolling laugh, clearly delighted by my surprise. 'Yes, I didn't even know the word "Palestine". I'm from a Christian village in the north, and I was reading a book from the little library the nuns ran at the village school. I saw the word but couldn't work out where this place was. When they told me, "It is here," I was amazed.'

I am amazed too. With some rapid mental maths, I manage to calculate that this bombshell had landed in Suha's vocabulary while I was at university. Now we are both laughing. A horn blares behind us; the traffic is moving. I put the car in gear as Suha's phone rings again.

The history of the Jewish struggle has been written about at great length, as has the formation of modern Israel. A great deal has also been written about the Palestinians outside Israel, fighting for their homeland and a place to live. But not much has been written about the experience of Arabs who stayed in the territory that had formerly been Palestine, after the formation of Israel in 1948.

Driving now on this familiar road, I am filled with a desire to learn more about this other side of modern Israel's history. I want to explore and understand the experience of the Arabs who remained here in 1948 and who the state claims are today classed as full citizens of Israel.

Sitting in the house in Lod this afternoon, and now hearing Suha speak to members of her family, I realize what has touched me so much about these people. It is that at the heart of a huge political and national conflict lie their intimate, personal stories. I know I must discover the human history of the past sixty-odd years.

I glance at my watch. My daughter Lydia will be tucked up in bed already. A wave of homesickness washes over me as I picture my wife, Anna, tidying up after the bedtime routine and checking that our little girl is sound asleep. Throughout today I have been thinking of home, mine and those of the people I've met. Bricks and mortar are important, of course, but so is the knowledge that your right to be there is accepted by those around you.

As the evening light thickens over Jerusalem, toning down the sky's blue from the light end of the palette to the darkest shades and then to black, my mind fills with memories distant and fresh. The threat to the Azbargas' home takes me back to the time when I first appreciated our profound need to know that we have a place where we belong. Their confusion, weariness and fear, mixed with hope and determination, provoke echoes of my first experience of the Middle East twenty years ago.

2

Not a Way

EVEN AS A BOY I WAS FASCINATED BY THE MIDDLE EAST. I longed to see the deserts and oases, the Crusader castles clinging to their rugged mountainsides and the wonders of the Holy Land. My interest in the region, and particularly in Palestine, had been sparked by my father. Patrick McCarthy had served his last posting there, as a Royal Engineer in the 6th Airborne Division, at the end of the Second World War, and the excitement of his brief immersion in its culture and landscape never left him.

My father loved life; he never felt it owed him a thing, and despite some extraordinary personal ordeals, the sparkle never left his eye. History and travel ranked high on the list of his many enthusiasms, and he took every opportunity his business activities presented to engage in both. He made frequent forays into Europe and Scandinavia and added the US and Australia in later years. On his return, he would delight my mother, my brother Terence and me with tales of his experiences. Business acquaintances became lifelong friends, and he recalled places and conversations so vividly that you'd think you'd been there too, enjoying them as he had done. He'd mimic voices and mannerisms to perfection: the jazz-loving cab driver in Chicago and the wheedling Romanian businessman in an airport lounge (asking and then demanding that my father give him his state-of-the-art calculator) came to life in our sitting room.

There was something about Palestine that really touched him. He went as a young man, lucky not to have been scarred by close combat during the war. The British Empire was creaking heavily, but he and his friends were on the winning side – and safe. I still have pictures from his time there – all of them small, some barely passport-sized – showing tanned and carefree young men in sailing dinghies or buttoned up in uniform. Whether they were crossing the River Jordan to Petra, the 'rose-red city half as old as time', exploring Jerusalem or sailing on the Dead Sea, their adventures lived on for all of us. Sometimes they were able to take a jeep out into the desert. I listened enthralled as my father talked of making camp in wadis and gazing up at the starlit sky. I wanted such adventures. One New Year, while discussing plans for our summer holiday, the family sat down to talk about the possibility of mounting such an expedition. Sadly it came to nothing; we rented a cottage in the Scottish Borders instead.

We never talked in detail about his military duties or the violence that was increasingly besetting Palestine during his time there. I knew that the situation had been highly volatile and cost the lives of some of his friends, but because he had come home safe, the exotic atmosphere and sense of adventure were what caught my imagination.

They did again in early 1986 when, at the age of twenty-nine, I was offered the chance of being WTN's acting bureau chief in Beirut for a month. As a TV news journalist, hungry for experience and excitement, I was eager to get out to Lebanon, where civil war had raged for a decade.

I announced my forthcoming mission to my parents over pre-lunch drinks one Sunday and was rather deflated by their reaction. They both went quite still and silent. My mother's sweet face seemed to crumple for a moment. Always keen to encourage her boys to do whatever they wanted, she was struggling to be positive, I could see, but all she could say was, 'Why does it have to be *you*?'

I tried to reassure them that all would be well, that there had been little fighting of late, that mostly I would be living and working in a confined area of Lebanon's capital, that my local colleagues would look after me . . .

The conversation moved on to our plans for the summer, but I knew they were still anxious. My trip to Lebanon wasn't their only worry: my mother had been diagnosed with cancer again. The prognosis at that point wasn't too frightening, but radiotherapy loomed.

As I hugged her goodbye later she seemed as strong as she had always been, and just as jolly. Nothing could really threaten our 'camp', as she sometimes referred to us all. 'Don't worry,' I said. 'I'll be back here in mid-April – it's only five weeks.' That was the last time I saw her.

My father kissed me at the station and gave me a big smile. Then he paused and said, 'Be careful out there, boy. It's more dangerous now than it was in my day.'

Danger was not something I knew about then. If I thought about it at all before leaving for Lebanon, it was in terms of testing myself, of wanting to prove my worth to others. Embarrassingly, I also thought I was off to join the glamorous pantheon of war correspondents. Not so embarrassing, perhaps, was the feeling that there was something profoundly glamorous about Lebanon itself, whose location had cast it as a commercial and intellectual hub of the ancient world. Before the civil war it had also been renowned as the Paris of the Middle East, where you skied in the mountains before lunch and lazed by the Mediterranean in the afternoon.

This landscape had been annexed by a dizzying array of warrior bands of every faith and political persuasion. Druze, Christian, Sunni and Shia Muslims, Communists and nationalists, Lebanese and Palestinians had forged a melting pot of unsurpassed brutality.

It wasn't until I was frisked at Heathrow that I began to feel anxious. I wasn't going on holiday: I was going to a place where security was a bigger issue than I'd ever known. After take-off I glanced self-consciously around the cabin of the Middle East Airlines jet and realized that I was the only Westerner aboard. As we came in to land a few hours later, Beirut, bathed in afternoon sunshine, looked reassuringly peaceful – but men with guns policed the endless queue through a terminal building scarred by more than ten years of civil war.

A Lebanese in front of me presented his passport at the immigration desk. A dollar bill floated out as it was opened. The duty officer grimaced and pushed the offending currency back towards its owner with the tip of his index finger. My father had spoken of 'baksheesh' and bribery: here was my first glimpse of that complex world.

WTN's office manager met and escorted me into town. Ghassan Salem was a slim, good-looking Palestinian with dark hair and moustache. We had spoken often on the phone, and now hit it off immediately. We headed through the poor and sprawling southern suburbs, home mainly to Lebanon's Shia Muslim community and many Palestinian refugees. This area was controlled by the Shia militias – including the rapidly growing and pronouncedly Islamist Hezbollah – and a no-go district for Westerners. Shadowy groups like Islamic Jihad were known to operate here, ready to pick up foreigners and use them as pawns in the murky and Byzantine chess game of Middle Eastern politics.

That I could be in real danger had not sunk in yet, but I was shocked by the devastation. Buildings riddled with bullet holes bore witness to the ferocity of the battles that continued to rage here. Ghassan pointed out the wrecked sports stadium and the entrances to the Palestinian refugee camps, Bourj el-Barajneh and Sabra-Shatila. In

September 1982 invading Israeli troops had surrounded them while their Christian militia allies massacred as many as two thousand inhabitants. I'd seen pictures and read accounts of the cold-blooded killing of men, women and children, but nothing could have prepared me for being so close to a place that had witnessed such horror. Less than a year before my arrival, violence had erupted here once more between the Palestine Liberation Organization and the Lebanese Shia militias. The so-called War of the Camps had left much of the area flattened.

Given the intensity of the conflict it surprised me that Ghassan could enjoy such a warm relationship with his Shia Muslim colleagues. Their job was to cover such clashes; did this not cause tension between them?

'No, we are friends. We do not want the fighting. Most of us are holding on for better times. Of course we don't want our kids to grow up with this.' Ghassan waved towards a small parade of shops: broken neon signs hung across empty windows, and tattered political posters fluttered between paint-daubed logos of rival militias. He shook his head and sighed. 'This is not a way, John.'

That phrase echoed in my mind in times of personally experienced or observed trauma and injustice over the following years. 'This is not a way . . .'

Eventually we arrived in the Hamra district, the main shopping and business centre of the capital's western and predominantly Muslim sector. The old city had been blown apart in the early years of the war, and no longer even hinted at the legendary sparkle of its heyday. The streets around the office were narrow and dingy. Ghassan showed me the edit suites and introduced me to the WTN team. He offered me coffee. I'd sampled this stuff before, of course, on holiday in Greece and in London restaurants, but watching him boil up the thick black sweet mixture in a stainless-steel pot, then decant it into small, handleless cups, was my first experience of this timeless ritual of Arab hospitality.

As dusk approached, my new colleagues headed home to the volatile southern suburbs, keen to get back to their families before nightfall. My commute was less fraught: I was staying just across the road in the Commodore Hotel. I decided to take a short walk around the block, mindful of my colleagues' warnings that I should not go far, and not after dark.

I watched a taxi driver clearing out his boot, casually adding to the piles of refuse on the ground around him. But although the side-streets were dirty and hemmed in by five- or six-storey apartment and office blocks, there was plenty of life in them. Cafés, mini-supermarkets and *bureaux de change* jostled for space alongside an antiques shop and one or two clothing boutiques. Peering in, I could see temples of elegance and chic, quite at odds with their dowdy, forlorn exteriors. Over time I came to realize that the old maxim 'Never judge a book by its cover' was never truer than in Lebanon and across the Middle East.

At the corner, the reinforced concrete frame of a building rose five storeys from the street. It was graced with walls and windows only at ground level – I assumed because the owners had decided that further investment was pointless for the time being – but a couple had set up home, with tables, chairs and beds, in the shell of the third floor. On this warm evening it looked like the best spot on the street.

As I crossed the road a boy offered to sell me some red carnations, then a man beckoned me to a cart piled high with cartons of cigarettes, so cheap that Duty Free suddenly seemed extortionate. I understood why chain smoking was the national sport.

As I walked up the steps to the hotel foyer I spotted a street sign on the corner of the building: Baalbek Street. Baalbek, the ancient Roman town in the Bekaa Valley, across the mountains to the east, was now a centre for the radical Hezbollah. As with Beirut's southern suburbs, Westerners were advised to go there only with great caution, if at all.

As the taxi driver closed his now immaculate boot, his shirt rode up to reveal a shiny automatic pistol in his belt. I hurried inside.

The faded décor of the Commodore, famous as a stopover and watering hole for the journalistic fraternity, was a throwback to Beirut's jet-set period in the mid-seventies. I liked it immediately and, despite the sense of vulnerability that now gnawed at my spirit, I donned my romantic war-correspondent guise once again. On that first night, though, I was the only one there. The circular bar was deserted, except for Coco the parrot, famous for mimicking the sound of shell fire. He looked at me forlornly from his cage, and didn't indulge me with so much as a whistle.

I woke early next morning, my sleep disturbed by some sort of warbled tannoy announcement. Looking around the luxurious but slightly tatty suite that was to be my home for the next month, I remembered where I was and that this was the muezzin's call to dawn prayers. Too excited to get back to sleep, I headed up to the hotel roof. From this vantage-point I looked east towards the mountains, beyond which lay Syria, then north-east, towards the Christian strongholds. Somewhere in between lay the Green Line, a strip of no man's land that marked the front line between the Muslim and Christian sectors of the city.

It had been cold and wet in London yesterday. Here the sky was azure blue and the air was already getting hot. A burst of gunfire reminded me that I was there to work.

Ghassan greeted me with coffee and told me that no major incidents had been reported overnight and no meetings or press conferences announced for the day. I sent a telex to the WTN newsroom in London to advise that so far, on my first full day in Beirut, all was quiet.

Then two loud bangs had me turning nervously to the window.

'It's okay, John,' Ghassan said, with a gentle smile, 'it's not a bomb, just Israeli jets breaking the sound barrier to say, "Good morning, Lebanon!"'

My mission to run a TV news-agency bureau

without looking too green wasn't going entirely to plan.

I wanted to appear cool in my new surroundings. I'd watched hours of video coverage from Lebanon's battle-grounds in the London newsroom and spoken to colleagues who'd worked in Beirut. Everything had sounded very matter-of-fact, a bit unusual, certainly, but manageable. I now saw that I still had an awful lot to learn. I hadn't thought much about Lebanon as a real place, only as 'the story'. On the ground, day to day, the picture was much richer and more complex.

When the political situation was particularly tense, or there were actual clashes in the suburbs, the streets would be deserted. After a lull, some mysterious, telepathic all-clear siren sounded, shop shutters rolled up and stalls appeared on their familiar pitches; the Lebanese passion for doing business was quick to reassert itself. One small barrow selling freshly hatched chicks caught my attention. It seemed to vanish and then materialize by magic; a dusty kerbside one minute, a teeming yellow mass the next.

The traffic would soon be snarled again, drivers honking their horns as they tried to inch past each other, determined never to stop or give way. The Lebanese Highway Code seemed to amount to one basic rule: *Watch out for yourself and keep going*. As far as I was aware, only one working traffic light remained in the western half of the city, blinking dutifully red, amber and green as cars roared past in whatever direction and on whichever side of the street the driver found most useful. Traffic police leaned against their vintage Moto Guzzi motorcycles, happy to do nothing, even to endure derision, just to keep the job.

When I came across Ghassan filling in a form and counting out a small wad of Lebanese lira to pay a parking fine, I expressed my surprise that such a ticket had ever been issued in this city of lawlessness, and that anyone would bother to pay. In a town where even the cabbies were armed, it seemed unlikely that an unpaid fine would be chased up by the local council.

'You have to stay within the laws. Not to do this is not a way,' he told me.

There was something both touching and profound about my new friend's reverence for red tape. It reflected not just his law-abiding nature, but a desire to maintain a semblance of order in his world. He wanted to be a citizen in a civilized place. Having railed against trivial bureaucracy for my entire life, I now understood its value in a chaotic landscape.

I'd led a pretty sheltered life in the Home Counties. People might be rude or aggressive, particularly at the wheel of a car, but I'd had no first-hand experience of physical violence. In Lebanon violence always threatened. While I was fortunate enough not to be close to any bombings or exchanges of gunfire during that first month, a large car bomb devastated a street in East Beirut. Our camera crew sent over their coverage of the aftermath. It was much like what I'd seen so often in the London newsroom, but viewing these images just a couple of miles from the scene of the blast made it different. As I did a simple edit in the office studio, I found myself shaking. The bomb crater, the twisted wreckage of vehicles, the blown-out shop fronts and bloodstained ground affected me in a way that I hadn't experienced before. People's faces, their eyes in particular, commanded attention. Some seemed to have put on masks, some were fractured by grief, and others just stared ahead, their expressions a mixture of shock, fear and fury.

As I walked the streets around the Commodore I tried to set the appearance of normality against the extreme brutality that was often just a breath away. Behind the smiles of greeting I began to detect darker intentions.

There was much else that I struggled to understand. The Arabic language when spoken was harsh and guttural at times, then soft and mellifluous; the script was a series of exotic but impenetrable hieroglyphs.

Mostly I relished the differences and enjoyed the atmosphere. Many of the women were covered with shawls and headscarves, and men, especially the older ones, sported the *keffiyeh*. I was fascinated to see them sitting outside cafés, drinking coffee, smoking *nargile*, hubble-bubbles, playing cards or backgammon with prayer beads dangling from their wrists. Going to restaurants and eating Arab food, which I soon came to love, or walking along the gracious promenade beside the Corniche, the road sweeping along the city's Mediterranean seafront, I could imagine how attractive it must have been before the war. Families and couples took the air, and fishermen with long poles cast their bait for dinner.

And then you'd turn a corner and come face to face

once again with the awful reality of the conflict. The Holiday Inn had been used by the militia as a high-rise gun emplacement in the early days of the war and was now utterly lifeless, its façade riddled with shell holes. And as day turned to night, the darkening sky would sometimes be lit with tracer bullets as gunmen traded fire across the Green Line. Driving me back from dinner at a beachfront hotel, my taxi driver stopped to admire a particularly elaborate and multi-coloured exchange. 'Ah, Beirut fireworks are the best!' He laughed, before going on to the Commodore.

My colleagues remained wary of taking me into Beirut's southern suburbs, home to the radical Hezbollah. Set up to resist Israel's occupation of a swathe of southern Lebanon in 1982, it was still a relatively small outfit, but believed to be linked with, or the umbrella group for, even smaller factions of highly organized and shadowy militant Islamists, probably inspired and sponsored by Iran. These groups were held responsible for a number of terrorist bombings and kidnappings and went under names like the Revolutionary Justice Organization, Organization of the Oppressed on Earth and, most notoriously, Islamic Jihad.

Given their reluctance to go to the suburbs, I jumped at the chance to join cameraman Muhammad and soundman Sami filming the funeral of two Muslim fighters, who had died in an overnight exchange of fire across the Green Line. Before the ceremony we checked out some of the militia positions on the western side of the line. We drove through the densely populated suburbs where high-rise apartment blocks flanked narrow streets, teeming with traffic and shoppers. We turned a corner and the road before us was suddenly deserted. A rutted track ran between buildings with bricked-up windows. Turning another corner, we pulled up in the shade of a derelict store front.

We walked in silence towards a low doorway guarded by sandbags and a burly middle-aged man in army fatigues. Sami greeted him and explained who I was. He looked me up and down, then nodded and stood aside.

A dank and gloomy flight of stairs led to a huge gun mounted on a tripod. Muhammad pumped the hand of the man perched on a stool behind it. Everyone else in Lebanon seemed to talk at full volume, but these two spoke in whispers. The militiaman beckoned me over and pointed down the barrel of his cannon. A few feet away, a wall of sandbags opened into a bullet-scarred shell that I realized must once have been the living room of a family apartment. Its outside wall was now barely in evidence, and beyond it, across a few hundred yards of scrubland, reared a similar rank of twisted tenements that must have harboured similar weaponry pointing right back at us.

The militiaman started whispering again and Muhammad nudged me. 'He's saying you can have a go, if you like.'

The three of them were now grinning from ear to ear. I could only manage a wan smile. 'No, thanks.'

This was my first experience of a front line. My father had not talked much about this side of his Middle East service, and never spoke of guns or bombs or military positions. Now I was wondering if he had experienced this curious mixture of calm normality and breathless tension.

The funeral cortège consisted of jeeps and pick-ups mounted with heavy-calibre machine-guns. Few of the militiamen riding these vehicles were in uniform but most sported Rambo-style headbands and looked much younger than those we had encountered at the front line. When they saw our TV camera they adopted tougher, more resolute expressions and squared their shoulders. More followed, jogging along with their two dead comrades at shoulder height in basic wooden coffins. There was much chanting and waving of guns, but despite the fierce expressions and my conspicuousness (as the only Westerner at the scene), I didn't sense any animosity directed at me.

I did sense it, though, in every fibre of my being, when Muhammad, Sami and I went south to the Palestinian refugee camp of Ain al-Hilweh. Near the port city of Sidon, which has been inhabited for more than four thousand years, the camp had been in existence since the exodus of Palestinian Arabs from what became Israel in 1948 and is still the largest in Lebanon, home to around 50,000 stateless individuals. Like their compatriots across Lebanon, Syria and Jordan, they were effectively citizens of nowhere – refugees from modern Israel, but neither accepted nor wanting to be accepted by the host country.

Ghassan was one of the few who had a Lebanese passport so could live and work outside the camps.

I became more nervous as we drove further and further into the camp, along narrow lanes between lines of simple two-storey houses. Sami kept chatting but I could tell that Muhammad was not happy. It was a year since Alec Collett, a British journalist working for the United Nations Relief and Works Agency for Palestinian refugees, had disappeared. It was believed that he had been kidnapped by the Palestinian militant group Abu Nidal. There was supposed to be a spokesman for the group at Ain al-Hilweh.

As Muhammad kept the car moving through the throng, his hand constantly on the horn, I looked out at the people we passed. A couple of kids smiled, but most stared back at me blankly. I was shocked by both the scale of the place and its poverty. Tangled electric cables ran between bare breeze-block buildings without a hint of decoration.

The stalls and stores carried little choice of goods. Over forty years the camp's population had grown steadily, so every inch of space was used. It had grown vertically to accommodate the numbers, even though there were no proper foundations. The side-streets were alleys, often just a yard wide, floored with concrete. Ain al-Hilweh means 'Sweet Spring'. I saw little children playing in pools of stagnant water. The winter rains must have flooded the place regularly.

I wanted to find out what we could about Alec Collett, and to learn more about these people still struggling so desperately to regain a homeland. The headlines branded them as PLO terrorists; those dismal back alleys told a different story. I wondered what their real homes, their old villages, now beyond reach in Israel, would have been like. What had happened to those places in the last four decades?

Eventually we arrived at the camp's central office, the *majlis*, beside a tiny courtyard. After a hurried conversation through the car window, Muhammad announced, 'I knew it. There is no one who will speak. *Yallah*, let's go!'

He started shunting the Mercedes round in a thirty-point turn while the *majlis* guard, a balding man with a grubby uniform stretched over his belly and a Kalashnikov across his chest, stared at me, his protruding eyes pulsing with hatred. Trying to return his gaze neutrally, I thought, How can you hate me? You know nothing about me . . .

Even though Alec Collett had been working for an organization that provided services to Palestinian refugees, the Abu Nidal group were to murder him later in 1986 in reprisal for the British government's support of a US bombing raid against Libya, which was itself a reprisal for a Libyan-sponsored bombing that had killed US servicemen in Germany.

The first I heard of the US raid was when the news wire machines started clattering in our Beirut office on 15 April. The story was soon on the TV news too. Though there was no vociferous Lebanese response, it added to the tension that seemed to be growing in the city. The world around me had been shrinking, the atmosphere becoming still more threatening. At the end of March two British teachers, Leigh Douglas and Philip Padfield, had been abducted as they left a Beirut nightclub. Less than a fortnight later, Irishman Brian Keenan was kidnapped as he set off for work one morning.

Muhammad, Sami and I headed off to the American University of Beirut where Keenan had been teaching English. We arrived on the tree-lined campus before any students were about. A secretary let us in and shuffled obligingly through the files. After a few minutes he grunted and handed over a passport-sized picture of a man with curly hair, a beard and very bright eyes. Sami laughed when I made some joke about crazy Irishmen, but he and Muhammad looked worried. They were probably wondering how long it would be before I became a target.

As I walked back to the Commodore that evening, just as dusk was settling, I passed two young men heading in the opposite direction. One was playing with a yo-yo. As he came abreast he flicked it at me, close to my face. Whether it was a taunt or a threat I couldn't be sure, but his blank stare felt hostile.

Nobody had claimed responsibility for the kidnappings and no demands had been made; all three men seemed just to have disappeared. Looking out across the city from the roof of the hotel, I realized they could be anywhere in the sprawling southern suburbs or, indeed, in the land beyond.

Although I wanted to stay and carry on working, I knew that getting out of the country, as many other

Western journalists were doing, was probably a very sensible idea. Early in the morning, two days after the US raid on Libya, I headed for the airport.

3

Back to Basics

WITH THE AIRPORT JUST FIVE OR SO MINUTES AWAY, my mind was already safely back in London. I was thinking about phoning my parents, meeting up with friends, having a beer.

Then a green Volvo raced past, slammed on its brakes and screeched to a halt, blocking the road ahead. For a moment nothing happened. I could almost hear the dust and gravel settling. I sat in the front passenger seat, barely breathing.

The Volvo's back door swung open and a tall, bearded young man jumped out. He stood cradling his Kalashnikov for a second or two, then started shouting. He yanked my door open, grabbed me by the scruff of the neck and pulled me out. Suddenly I was on the floor in the back of the Volvo with the gunman more or less sitting on me. '*Yallah!*' he shouted, and the car lurched off.

Gradually my mind began to function again. Before fear,

it registered discomfort. I tried to heave myself up. The gunman rapped the top of my head with his knuckles. The pain was intense. I crouched down again. A moment later the same hand was stroking my hair, as if to say, 'No harm meant, just stay down.'

After a few minutes we stopped. The gunman pulled me out and around to the back of the car. The driver, an older man with a white beard, stood there with a pistol in his hand. I thought I was going to die, there and then. But instead of shooting me he opened the boot and shoved me inside. I looked up at the two bearded faces as they closed the lid – the last faces, apart from those of my five fellow hostages, that I was to be able to see for more than five years.

The first two months or so of captivity were in many ways the worst. I was alone, and I didn't know who had taken me prisoner, or why. I tried to remain positive, but in the filthy confines of the tiny underground cell where I spent those seemingly endless days, I often found myself reduced from the young man who'd been finding his feet in a war zone to a frightened child, desperate for the comfort of his mother's arms.

My only way of escape was provided by the books I'd had in my suitcase, which, miraculously, the guards had seen fit to give me – most particularly Freya Stark's *Beyond Euphrates,* a Christmas gift from my mother. Dame Freya had spent much of the period between 1928 and 1933 exploring the region, setting out from Beirut and heading east through the Lebanese mountains into Syria and on to Baghdad. The world she portrayed, in a series of exquisite vignettes – a tiny hidden valley, an orchard, someone's house – had long since changed, of course, but it conjured up some of the Levantine spell that I had fallen under.

Although my experience of the region was limited to my brief time in the tragic, shell-shocked landscape of Lebanon, I could still feel the atmosphere, the warm days and places she had travelled through, and appreciate the hospitality she had encountered. Eating the day's meagre allowance of pitta bread and hummus or cheese, I'd close my eyes, forget that it had been doled out by unseen guards, and join her, in a tiled courtyard with a pool, perhaps, where courteous hosts in flowing robes would offer me choice fruits, delicacies and sweet tea.

Although this world was riven now with violence and political intrigue, there was much that remained beguiling. Maybe it had something to do with scale. Though so often dominating the world's headlines, Lebanon is tiny, smaller than Northumberland and Cumbria together, and neighbouring Israel and the Palestinian territories combined are only slightly larger than Wales.

There is something at once intimate and mysterious about the area. *Beyond Euphrates* was a powerful reminder of this fascinating paradox, and encouraged me to think of returning one day to see and understand more. Though I desperately wanted to escape my current confines, and knew it would be a while before I would venture to Beirut again, I was determined to come back to the Middle East and especially to Israel and Palestine.

If anywhere seemed at once familiar and strange, it was the Holy Land. Nazareth, Bethlehem and Jerusalem had featured in the New Testament stories I'd learned at school, along with the tales of Abraham, Moses and David, the triumphs and disasters of the Children of Israel fighting to take from the Canaanites and others the land God had given them.

Now I was caught up in this endless conflict. And I found myself yearning, as the Palestinians languishing in those Lebanese refugee camps did, as the Jews exiled for two thousand years did, for the sanctuary of home.

I soon realized that there were other prisoners, perhaps half a dozen of them, on the same corridor. Every day they were taken, one by one, to the derelict bathroom at the far end. I pictured these men shuffling blindfolded, like me, the barrel of a gun resting at the nape of their necks. There was never any conversation between prisoner and captor, just the clang of padlocks and the screech of metal doors. As I sat back on my filthy mattress I would look up at the grille across the top of my cell door and watch the play of twisted shadows as they passed.

The next twenty-four hours' food would have been dumped on their mattress by the time they returned. Once the guards were gone there was mostly silence. I imagined the others to be staring blankly at their metal doors, as I did when I wasn't reading. When the electric power was cut and the rudimentary air-conditioning and strip lights went off, the temperature rose rapidly and the mosquitoes swarmed in to feast on us captives. Voices would ring out in the darkness and metal doors were banged in protest. The angry, alien Arabic reminded me of how little I understood, and how far I was from home. I'd often retreat beneath my foul blanket, preferring to swelter there and feel some sense of separation from the inferno around me.

There was no escape from the cries of one young man as he was kicked and punched by the guards; they became the dreaded soundtrack to the daily routine. There was nothing to see, so my eyes couldn't help me make sense of my situation. Instead I had to use my ears to build pictures of the environment, to frame my predicament. A distant clatter would herald the entry of guards through a series of gates, perhaps on another floor. Then they would be close by and the movement of their bodies seemed curiously intimate, even beyond the cell door, because the atmosphere was so dense in that airless space. So I almost felt the blows on the young man's body, and his screams poured into my cell in a blast of hot agony.

This grim ritual lasted for some days before a whole group of guards descended into the prison. Another beating began. The young man's screams grew louder and louder, until they were silenced by the deafening shock of a gunshot. As the ringing echoes died away I knew that he was dead. My heart emptied to him. How frightened and utterly alone he must have felt.

Though I was anxious and scared for much of the time, the optimistic ostrich in me somehow managed to bury his head in the warm sand of denial. Assuming that

I was different from the prisoners around me, I kept telling myself that any day now my kidnappers would see that they had made a mistake and release me. That murder just a few feet away was a sharp reminder of my vulnerability. I didn't know why I'd been taken so had no idea what value, if any, my life held.

I decided that if I could make some connection with the guards I would be a little safer; a vain hope, perhaps, but I needed reassurance of any kind. When a couple of them squatted in my doorway I tried to speak to them. I'm sure that my tone betrayed my fear, and that I spoke too much and too quickly for them to understand.

They were faceless beyond my blindfold, the first obstacle to communication, but their manner was not aggressive. One had a little English and asked, 'You okay?'

I began a litany that was to be repeated endlessly over the next five years: 'Why am I here? When will I go home? Is there any news of negotiation for me?'

And the faceless other would always respond, 'I don't know exactly, hope to go home soon.'

In those early days I assumed that the people holding me must be Palestinians; I didn't know enough to understand why a Lebanese group might want me. In the pathetic hope of learning something, I started talking to the two guards about Palestine and Israel, and Britain's role in their recent history.

The English-speaking guard translated for his colleague, who responded – in Arabic – at some length. A couple of times I thought I heard the word 'Balfour'.

This proved correct. His speech came across more briefly in translation: 'Balfour gave Palestine to the Jews. Britain no good.'

It wasn't the most detailed historical analysis, but there wasn't much to argue with, especially from a Palestinian viewpoint. In 1917 the British foreign secretary, Arthur Balfour, increasingly sympathetic to the Zionist cause, had declared that 'His Majesty's Government views with favour the establishment in Palestine of a national home for the Jewish people, and will use their best endeavours to facilitate the achievement of this object, it being clearly understood that nothing shall be done which may prejudice the civil and religious rights of existing non-Jewish communities in Palestine . . .'

Zionism had developed as a nationalist movement in nineteenth-century Europe. Argentina and Uganda, among other places, had initially been considered as a possible safe haven, but early in the twentieth century the Zionist goal became clearly defined: a return of the Chosen People to the Promised Land of the Bible.

Under the League of Nations' Mandate immediately after the First World War, France and Britain took on the responsibility of guiding the former Ottoman Turkish territories of Lebanon, Iraq, Jordan, Syria and Palestine (which comprised what is now Israel and the Palestinian territories of West Bank and Gaza) towards independent statehood – but Britain failed to protect the rights of the indigenous population of Palestine in the process. The creation of modern Israel in 1948 forced hundreds of thousands of Arab inhabitants of the newly partitioned land into exile. Many ended up in Lebanon, some as the first residents of the Ain al-Hilweh camp, whose desolate memory had stayed with me.

As spring turned to summer and our living conditions became still more uncomfortable, I often found myself deep in despair. But my consequent introspection opened passages into the remotest of my cranial catacombs. People, places, incidents and things that had long since disappeared from conscious memory would suddenly present themselves in startlingly clear focus. In the face of possible death, my life wasn't flashing before me but presenting itself in random flashbacks. Although much of this mental activity seemed pointless, at times I recognized that my subconscious was still searching, even as I slept, for anything that might help make sense of my predicament.

Since almost half of my twenty-nine years had been spent there, school was a major feature of this slide-show. One day I woke with a portrait I'd last seen in Haileybury's dining hall looming large in my mind. Viscount Allenby, one of its most revered old boys, appeared a grand figure, with receding hair and neatly trimmed moustache, holding a field marshal's baton, his greatcoat open to reveal a dazzling array of medals, badges and stars. The face was thoughtful, the head rather delicate – the demeanour far softer than most photographs of the major general, who had earned the nickname 'Bloody Bull'.

The last great British cavalry leader had captured my schoolboy imagination. He had defeated the Ottoman

Turks at Gaza in the winter of 1917 and gone on to liberate Jerusalem, taking care to dismount at the Jaffa Gate and enter the city on foot, out of respect for the city's holy status. He had moved north to win a decisive victory at Megiddo in September 1918, then taken Damascus.

At school in the late sixties and seventies we were taught that British colonial enterprise had been carried out for the greater good of the world, and in the honourable pursuit of trade and profit. The nobility of empire was exemplified by champions of Allenby's stature, and though one learned subsequently about the less laudable aspects of our annexation of huge swathes of the planet, the reputation of these legendary figures and, of course, the courage and heroism of the men they led into battle, remained to be celebrated.

I continued to enjoy the fact that he'd styled himself 'Viscount Allenby of Megiddo and of Felixstowe'. Setting the scene of his military triumph – and that of *The Book of Revelation*'s Judgment Day – alongside a minor English seaside resort has to be one of the most extraordinary and endearing of geographical twinnings. But I did begin to think that if he had stayed in Felixstowe, I might not be sitting in that hole in the ground . . .

In the mid-1940s, thirty years on from Allenby and after another world war, the British were still in Palestine; its Arab and Jewish subjects had proved equally difficult to administer. Given the Balfour Declaration, it wasn't surprising that the Arab contingent believed the British were interested only in supporting the Jewish community. They would not recognize the terms of the Mandate: it would have meant acceptance of Palestine as a Jewish homeland – in other words, national suicide.

Hitler's rise in Germany swelled European Jewish migration. By 1936 the number of Jewish inhabitants had more than doubled to 370,000 – 27 per cent of the population. The indigenous Arabs responded with a series of strikes that spiralled into armed insurrection; the Arab Revolt ran, on and off, between 1936 and 1939, until the British beefed up their military presence and crushed it, brutally and effectively.

Allenby's glorious Palestinian high-noon sun was sinking into the dust by the time my father visited the Holy Land. He spoke of those volatile days very much from the perspective of the British soldier: both factions, but especially the Jews, were impossibly demanding. He recalled with exasperation Jewish community leaders complaining that vital supplies could not get through the British checkpoints – checkpoints installed to combat the sabotage of road and railway bridges by Jewish militant groups.

These attacks were aimed at breaking restrictions on the immigration of the quarter of a million Jewish refugees then in European camps, desperate to put the horrors of the Holocaust behind them. Groups like Irgun, some of whose members had trained and fought in the British Army, would stop at nothing to achieve their dream.

After the thorough suppression of their revolt in the late thirties, the Arab population posed a less potent threat. There were very few Arab militants then, and they lacked coordination – but in the sweltering heat of the Holy Land, risking their lives on behalf of an ungrateful or indifferent local population, the ordinary Tommy could be forgiven for thinking, 'A plague on both your houses.'

My father was demobbed in the spring of 1946. In late July of that year, Irgun bombed the British headquarters in Jerusalem, the King David Hotel. Ninety-two people – including a number of his comrades – died in the blast, and many more were hurt. A close friend commanded the squad of Royal Engineers that undertook the rescue work.

It was the last straw. In February 1947 Whitehall handed the problem to the United Nations. The partition of Palestine into an Arab and Jewish state was passed as UN Resolution 181 at the end of November. The Jewish leadership accepted the plan; the Arabs did not. Violence erupted as 1947 drew to a close, and rapidly escalated.

The British finally withdrew on 15 May 1948, and Jewish leaders declared the independence of the new state of Israel. They were careful not to limit their borders to the area assigned by the UN Partition Plan: Jewish forces were already in control of much of the territory assigned to the 'new' Arab state. Thousands of Palestinian Arabs were already exiled from their homes.

* * *

Sitting in my cell, I reflected on the two Arabic phrases that had echoed across our Hertfordshire garden, for no obvious reason, during my boyhood. *Alhamdulillah* – 'Thanks be to God' – was my father's favourite, though I discovered later that his pronunciation left something to be desired. When I first used it in Lebanon, Ghassan shook his head politely but firmly and coached me to a more faithful rendition. *Ahlan wa Sahlan* – 'Welcome!' – was the other. My father told me that it reflected the great tradition of Middle Eastern hospitality – not that he and his fellow soldiers would have been on the receiving end of it much more than I came to be forty years later.

Thankfully, my solitary confinement lasted only a few months. Thereafter I had four years' companionship with Brian Keenan, a fierce, funny and remarkable Irishman, and shorter spells with fellow Briton Terry Waite and Americans Terry Anderson, Tom Sutherland and Frank Reed. Between them, these men gave me the will to live. Their love and kindness gave me purpose: to support and encourage them in return.

Brian taught me most about myself. He prompted me to look beyond my immediate fear and discomfort to see the world from a broader perspective. Suffering fear and separation from home for five and a quarter years made me wonder how anyone could endure it for a lifetime. As I coped with my own displacement I came to see more clearly how the Israeli–Palestinian conflict was not primarily a religious or cultural confrontation but a more elemental battle for a place to belong.

I was sustained by thoughts of my parents' home. I pictured its warm, red-brick walls, the sweep of garden, the peaceful village around it and the verdant country-side beyond. It was a tangible place I could retreat to in my imagination; it was the symbolic core of the emotional security I carried with me – provided by the people I loved and who, I knew, loved me.

Brian and I invigorated ourselves by daily condem-nation of our captors. We ridiculed them as fools and barbarians. But we also thought more deeply about their predicament and, I hope, rarely lost sight of their humanity. Our initial assumption that they were Palestinians encouraged us to consider the complexity of their political and emotional limbo. Our captivity and vulnerability made us more sympathetic to and more interested in their suffering. My home was a place of refuge. Theirs had been destroyed by a conquering people.

The conflict that had dominated my father's visit to the region had led, though indirectly, to my being chained and blindfolded in Beirut. The Palestine Liberation Organization had based itself in Lebanon to take on Israel. Its heavy-handed presence had angered the Lebanese factions. That anger, and a great deal of meddling from external powers, had resulted in the out-break of the Lebanese civil war in 1975. Subsequent PLO attacks across the border to the south had precipitated Israel's invasion and occupation of a huge section of southern Lebanon.

Our captors were not Palestinians but Lebanese

Islamic Jihad, from the Shia Muslim community. They, too, were underdogs, fighting for a place in the governance of their nation and to drive out the Israeli invader. They were a mixed bunch. According to those who have researched the Lebanese hostage story far more deeply than I, most of the kidnap gangs came from one or two clans – yet they seemed to have very different backgrounds, as far as we could judge on the inside. Some were well educated, others not. Some had fluent English, some could barely speak a word; others could chat in French.

They were young men, full of bravado. They loved war movies and they loved their guns. Sometimes we'd ask them what they wanted from life. The macho ones would declare a desire to become a *shaheed*, a martyr, fighting for their cause. This generally meant taking part in a raid against the Israeli forces occupying southern Lebanon. On occasion they'd come up with grander strategies – like hijacking a jumbo jet and flying it into the Knesset, the Israeli parliament building in Jerusalem.

They rarely talked about themselves or their ambitions, so I remained confused by the political spider's web in which I was trapped. Fighting a *jihad*, a holy war, was the only motivation they would admit to. They wanted to push the Israelis out of Lebanon, of course, but also to liberate Jerusalem, not so much for the Palestinian cause but for Islam.

To have more than five years of my life stolen by thieves who claimed they were working for a higher power was as insulting as it was nonsensical. And the idea that this motley crew could muster the military clout to oust the highly professional and well-equipped Israeli Army seemed far-fetched at best – although eventually, in 2000, that was exactly what they did achieve.

Fortunately, nearly a decade before that ousting, help came to me from an unlikely source. Saddam Hussein is not a universally popular figure but, thanks to his invasion of Kuwait in August 1990, a number of Islamic Jihad prisoners escaped from gaol there. The liberation of those prisoners had been one of the group's key demands for the release of the American hostages in Beirut.

Relations between Syria, Iran and the West thawed as the US-led Coalition forces prepared to drive Saddam back into Iraq, and the final months of the year saw the last battles of the Lebanese civil war. Giandomenico Picco, special adviser to UN Secretary General Pérez de Cuéllar and a man of remarkable courage and mental stamina, finessed a deal that saw the release of some Lebanese prisoners held by Israel, the identification and return of the bodies of some Israeli servicemen who had died fighting in Lebanon, and the remaining Western hostages in Lebanon being released in stages – starting with me, in August 1991.

4

Facts in the Ground?

HIGH SUMMER 1991, AND I WAS A FREE MAN ONCE more. I knew that it would take time to find my feet again and feel truly at home with myself, but I could live with that. To be able to get out of bed and walk wherever I wished was utterly fabulous. It didn't matter if there was sunshine or rain. I was free.

I spent the first few days after my return at RAF Lyneham in Wiltshire with my father and brother Terence, while I was debriefed by a team of RAF psychiatrists. For the most part we concerned ourselves with looking forward, to me picking up my life and getting back to work. I felt I'd come to terms with most of the trauma of captivity during the five years as a hostage so saw no purpose in immediately re-immersing myself in that murky Middle Eastern landscape.

It was slightly ironic, therefore, that on our first outing from RAF Lyneham I found myself listening, fascinated, to stories of the region and the conflict there. My father and his old friend John Cowtan cast their minds back to their Palestine tour as we sat in John's pretty garden sipping Buck's fizz. I kept looking round, still stunned to be back in England at last, as he described the rescue operation he had led at the King David Hotel. For all their talk of comrades who hadn't survived, the way the two friends spoke about the place reminded me of my own first impressions. I knew that one day I would return. Lebanon held little immediate appeal, unsurprisingly, but I wanted to see Palestine and Israel.

John Cowtan was a complete tonic. He had been taken prisoner in North Africa in the Second World War and held in a PoW camp in Italy, then escaped and joined the partisans. Eventually he returned to the British lines and was given a medical check-up. 'They asked me if I wanted anything. I said that as I hadn't got the pox and wasn't barmy I didn't need any messing around with by quacks or trick-cyclists!' The much decorated major general paused and looked at me intently with his piercing blue eyes. Then he smiled. 'More fizz?'

Deep friendships were rapidly rekindled and developed. My mother had always been the family linchpin – apparently right up until her death in 1989 – but the warm atmosphere of the family home was just as I had remembered it. What had sometimes been a formal father–son relationship was now much more relaxed. I had learned in captivity that youth is no barrier to wisdom, age no barrier to folly, and that fun and caring belong to all generations.

Then, three years after my return, my father was ambushed by cancer. When I'd heard of my mother's death while in captivity, something – perhaps an instinct for survival – prevented me risking an exploration of so tragic a loss. Now that I was free, and with my feet fairly firmly on solid ground, I was able to understand what I'd miss and, later, grieve for it. His spirit was remarkable. He continued to be loving, funny and excited by life right up to the moment he left it. He refused to be self-centred, was almost careless about the disease that he knew was bringing him down. A month or so before his death I gave him a hug and sobbed a little.

'There's no need for that, Johnny,' he said. 'I've had a great life, and you and Terence are both safe and well. That's all that matters. When the cancer gets too bad, I'll just tell them to fill me up with morphine and away I'll go!' Which was just what he did, in late August 1994.

It will always sadden me that neither of my parents met Anna. Our marriage in the spring of 1999 saw me properly grounded again – for the first time in years. Together, we bought the first house that I had ever owned. Setting up home in a small town was far more exciting and profound an experience than I'd imagined. The sense of security and of independence, resulting from the possession of official documents that formally confirmed our right of belonging in that little building, wasn't just wonderful, it was visceral.

Settled on the home front at last, I immediately deserted my wife and headed back to the Middle East. Although the offer had always been there, I hadn't gone back to the WTN newsroom. I'd taken up a freelance life, combining the desire to travel with writing and broad-casting. I had been asked to return to Lebanon on a number of occasions, to report on the reconstruction after the years of civil war and to reflect on my own experiences there. But I had always felt uncomfortable with the idea, too apprehensive of going back into the den of lions. The chance of visiting Israel and the West Bank to make a radio series on Bible history, the history of the book as well as the history it told, however, was irresistible.

As devout Muslims, our Lebanese captors had assumed we must be devout Christians and had therefore nearly always provided us with a Bible. At first I'd felt I'd rather have something else to read: a volume of history, perhaps, or a novel. But in the absence of anything else I read the Bible through and through and was amazed to find that there was so much more in the Old Testament than I had ever appreciated.

Apart from its theological and historical richness, what struck me most was the vividness of its testimony to humanity. Countless characters, from crowds to kings, are doing well one minute, striving to fulfil God's plan, and back on the slippery slope the next, copping all manner of unpleasant punishments. It made me feel less of a fool about the wasted opportunities in my life. If King David wasn't above getting plastered and dancing around like a madman in front of his courtiers, then maybe I shouldn't be so worried about my own moments of folly.

There is also much to encourage the benighted, with promises of deliverance through the Lord. Who was I to argue with the Prophet Isaiah when he said that captives' chains would be loosed?

The impression left by my RE lessons at school – beyond the stories of Abraham and Isaac, Cain and Abel, Moses and Joshua – was that most of the Good Book was pretty dry stuff. Hunkered down in Beirut, I soon saw that I was caught up in an ancient struggle that went back to biblical times. The Israelis were now going head to head with the Palestinians and Lebanese; in ancient times the Israelites had been locking horns with the Philistines and Canaanites.

My discovery was hardly original – people often say that the roots of the modern Middle East conflict lie within the Bible's pages – but in the circumstances of my captivity the revelation was both startling and strangely comforting. It rendered my plight somehow less personal, and gave me another perspective.

Jerusalem cast an immediate spell over me. Its spirituality, miracle, mystery and profound historical importance as the site and source of deep human conflict provoked extraordinary and complex resonances. Walking through the narrow streets of the Old City, I discovered grand stone buildings hidden up narrow, cobbled alleyways. Dark, forbidding corners lay just beyond heavy wooden doorways illuminated by shafts of blinding sunshine. So dramatic was the contrast of light and shade, it was as if I was moving through a photographic negative. As I wandered up empty pathways, meeting nothing but a skittering cat, I breathed air that was at one moment dry as dust, the next damp and mildewed.

I'd emerge suddenly in a throng of market stalls and be seduced by the rich fragrances of herbs and the warm, enticing aromas of cooking that drifted from little cafés hidden beneath stone arches: charcoal-grilled lamb, falafel, hummus, sweet pastries filled with figs or topped with pistachio nuts and dripping with syrup. I felt myself back in touch with the world that I had enjoyed in Lebanon before my capture.

Tension was a tangible ingredient of the heady mix – of Lebanon in 1986 and now, around the millennium, in Jerusalem. In Lebanon the warring factions had had their own neighbourhoods but could assume anonymity in neutral districts, faith and politics unreadable beneath international uniforms: formal business suits or informal jeans and shirts. But here there was no camouflage. As the busy lanes narrowed, Arabs in swirling robes and Jews in black hats and ringlets squeezed past each other. Bodies touched, and the odours of men, women and children mingled. There was no eye contact, though. It was as if mortal enemies were sharing a packed lift.

Sauntering along and taking a bite from my pitta-wrap laden with falafel, hummus and salad, I caught sight of a street sign: Via Dolorosa. I nearly choked in amazement. 'Jesus walked here! He carried the cross down this lane.' After a moment or two my mind started off on its own rather elementary theological debate. How could they be sure this was the street? Did the crucifixion really happen? Was there even a man called Jesus?

In a place that holds profound spiritual and historical certainty for many, I was beset by doubts. Then the present, real world swirled around me once more. A gaggle of Jewish children, escorted by teachers in jeans and T-shirts, bumped past me. I smiled at the last of them, only to encounter a blank stare from the teacher bringing up the rear of the crocodile. He had a small but potent rifle slung over his shoulder.

Staring at the weapon, I felt a hollowness in my stomach. I looked around for a bin; no longer hungry, I wanted to get rid of my sandwich. It was too much to take in this jumble of beauty and menace, of youthful innocence among ancient stones.

Within an hour I could visit some of the world's holiest sites. In the great Plaza at the foot of the Western Wall, believed by Jews to be part of Solomon's Temple, Jews, draped in prayer shawls, rocked back and forth as they recited verses of the Torah. Above them, at the top of the Holy Mount, Muslims prayed at the al-Aqsa mosque and the stunning shrine, the Dome of the Rock, which marks the spot from which, according to Islamic tradition, the Prophet Muhammad ascended to heaven. And pilgrims prostrated themselves at the Church of the Holy Sepulchre, the site where they believe Christ was crucified and buried.

The faithful, in all manner of costumes and from all over the world, thronged the Old City. Many believed they understood their place in it because they believed in a God and understood His purpose. Despite the city's chiaroscuro, I was far from certain: I could not see things in black and white. Though most of these people would insist they followed the path of peace, they seemed to me to generate an unsettling combination of divine wonder and human aggression. It was this paradox that I wanted to probe.

Accompanied by a variety of colleagues and friends, some, like me, novices in the Holy Land, others more experienced, I became more familiar with Jerusalem over the years. I met archaeologists and theologians, politicians and historians, from whom I learned a great deal about the facts and myths that made the place so remarkable. But to learn what life was like in the city I would turn to the ordinary local people, especially the translators, drivers and fixers we worked with along the way.

Abu Ali was a great bear of a man. He moved with casual confidence, dealing with every conceivable challenge thrown up by the demands of his inquisitive British colleagues. A Palestinian, born and bred in the Old City, he'd been a young man in 1967 when the Old City and the rest of the West Bank were occupied by Israeli troops as they defeated the Jordanian Army. His Arab world had suddenly been taken over by a Jewish one.

One day, having watched him switch between Arabic with friends and Hebrew while negotiating with soldiers and police, I asked him how he maintained such a relaxed façade.

He shrugged, raised his palms and gave a toothpick-waggling grimace that Clint Eastwood would have been proud of. 'I learned to live what I call "squeezy squeezy".'

He moved his hands sinuously together. 'I come from one world that is controlled by another. I have to look for the little gaps in between where I can move, where I can squeeze!'

Away from Jerusalem, I found myself travelling across a landscape that, thanks to my father and Dame Freya Stark, already lived in my imagination. I even knew where I was – or thought I did – as the road signs carried place names familiar from childhood: Jericho, Ashkelon, Hebron, Bethlehem, Nazareth and, of course, the legendary Megiddo.

It was easy to assume that, because there were places with those names here and now, the Bible stories that played out against their backdrop must be true. Certainly that had been the attitude of early archaeologists working here. They had wandered around 'with a spade in one hand and a Bible in the other', trying to connect what they found on and in the ground with what they had read. The same attitude fired archaeologists in the first years of modern Israel. Though they might have carried a gun as well, they also sought to prove the Bible true, and thus verify Jewish claims to the land.

As I made my way around Israel and the West Bank, visiting tels (the hills created by different civilizations building in the same place) and talking to leading archaeologists from Israel, Palestine, Europe and the United States, I discovered two things: that Bible history is anything but reliable, and that archaeologists are serious about their hats. Okay, the second point isn't very significant but it was quite fun anticipating what head-gear the next teller of tels might be sporting. The younger of them favoured baseball caps; those in mid-career went for the more sensible all-round brim. My prize went to David Ussishkin, who led the excavation of the massive site at Megiddo, resplendent in a straw Stetson with a magnificent feather.

The cool brains beneath this variety of brims told me that most of the Bible's history prior to the ninth century BCE was unverifiable; there were no other sources, texts or monuments to back it up, and developments in archaeo-logical science were betraying many of the great stories as myths. Joshua, for instance, had not stormed across the River Jordan and caused the walls of Jericho to come tumbling down; they had fallen long before Joshua's day. Neither had the Israelites invaded Canaan after exile in Egypt. They had never been to Egypt. There had been no Exodus. Throughout that time Canaan was a small province of the mighty Egyptian empire. No one was searching for milk and honey. And rather than coming in from elsewhere to defeat the Canaanites and take their land, the Israelites were already in Canaan. They *were* Canaanites.

It was hard not to slip into Indiana Jones mode when driving at dawn across the Jordan Valley towards the great mound of Tel Rehov. At such sites I encountered leading archaeologists beneath huge black awnings, com-plete with hats, groups of students and volunteers, all sifting through millennia of dust and rubbish, uncover-ing the history of the place.

The lives of the ancient Canaanites and Israelites unfolded in front of me – though not quite as I'd hitherto imagined them. My understanding of the ancient history of this area was deconstructed piece by piece at digs on desert tels, among ruins, in caves beneath Jerusalem. No exodus, no conquest, and precious little evidence of the mighty kings David and Solomon. They might well have been there, but probably as little more than local chieftains, not empire builders.

Even the central theme of the Israelites turning to worship the one true God who had chosen them from all other peoples suddenly didn't look so straightforward. Up until the eighth and seventh centuries BCE, there was a huge amount of evidence that the Israelites were polytheists, worshipping gods plural, male and female.

Most scholars believe the Bible was written, or compiled, in the late eighth, seventh and sixth centuries BCE, perhaps six hundred years after Joshua's supposed conquest, and two or three hundred after the time of David and Solomon. It appears to have been assembled at a time when the Israelites faced destruction by the Assyrian and then Babylonian empires. They brought together old stories, oral traditions and a sense of what should be their relationship with God to make sense of their situation.

This interpretation struck a real chord with me. That a beleaguered people would stand, backs to the wall, and make their big statement – 'This is who we are and what we believe' – seemed entirely reasonable. It underscored the essential humanity of the Bible stories that had so moved and encouraged me in captivity.

All these findings had stayed within the confines of academic papers and journals until October 1999, when Professor Ze'ev Herzog of the University of Tel Aviv's Institute of Archaeology highlighted them in a *Haaretz* newspaper article.

Secular Israelis reacted most angrily to this challenge to the Bible's historical accuracy. Herzog's views, which were shared by the majority of Israeli and international archaeologists, were seen to strike at the very essence of Israel's claim to the land. Ze'ev Herzog is very mild-mannered for a man who had set off such a firestorm. When I met him in 2000 he told me that he believed the new findings were actually helpful to his country, contributing to its development as a modern state and a more enlightened community, liberated from 'messianic beliefs'.

I was very impressed with this argument. If you took the Bible out of the equation then you might be able to look at the conflict between Palestinians and Israelis as a political dispute that could be settled through compromise, rather than confused by claims of God-given rights. Israel had been there a long time now; it wasn't going away and should be ready to deal with its neighbours on a normal footing.

Many in Israel may share Herzog's views, but the state's attitude seems unlikely to change. More than a decade has passed since his article was published, and Israel's existence is still rooted in myth.

* * *

Those first visits to Israel and the West Bank sharpened my abiding fascination with the area and its history. Subsequent trips brought me closer to the modern, human realities of life in the Holy Land.

In 2003 I interviewed Azmi Bishara, the then golden boy of Palestinian politics within Israel and a Member of the Knesset. We spoke in the garden of the American Colony Hotel in East Jerusalem. Beneath its rippling palm trees, Bishara told me how it felt to be a Palestinian citizen of Israel. 'You have here a nation-building process which excludes you in every step since it began. This includes nationalization of the land. This includes nationalization of the history of this place. This includes nationalization of the religious myth. Every single thing that is done in the process of nation-building in this country excludes the indigenous people.'

Bishara looked every inch the sleek, worldly political operator, yet as we talked his eyes filled with fire and he chopped the air with his hand. 'How do we get in? We get in through citizenship, not through a national identity. By the fact that we are citizens of the state of Israel, we were granted, we were given, the right to participate. But democracy from the beginning is not meant for us. So from the beginning it's very conditional. You have to behave as a guest in this democracy . . . and to respect the fact that you are given rights. And if you don't respect it you are reminded, "Go to Syria, go to Jordan, go to Egypt. They don't have democracy there. You have here democracy, you have to be grateful for that." '

Looking out across the hotel gardens Bishara ran a

hand through his mane of hair and laughed harshly. 'Sometimes I tell them, "Give me back Palestine and take your democracy."'

Though I was intrigued by his views, the Palestinian community within Israel still seemed a rather remote, rarefied group. At that point I think I had only half a mind on Middle Eastern issues. I was grieving the loss of my brother Terence. His death from cancer a few months earlier had broken my heart. He was the last member of my immediate family, and I think it was only as I mourned him that I truly grieved for my parents. I was rocked by distress, not just from their immediate disappearance from my world but also, I think, from recognizing the terrible pain we had all been through during the hostage years.

Then in 2005 Anna gave birth to Lydia. Having my own flesh and blood to hug and hold again brought me properly back to life. My broken heart was repaired. In the captive environment I'd learned to empathize with people living in harsh and trying circumstances. Now I found being a father took that empathy into a much more profound space – which was perhaps why meeting the Azbarga family in Lod as Lydia approached her first birthday meant so much to me. Visiting them with Suha Arraf in the summer of 2006 moved me deeply. My connection with them as a family sharpened my interest in their wider community. I wanted to find out more about the Palestinian citizens of Israel, about their life today, and also about the community's experience from the foundation of Israel in 1948.

5

Ha'atzmaut and Nakba:
Independence and Catastrophe

DRIVING UP THE COASTAL HIGHWAY FROM BEN-GURION Airport north towards Haifa, the late-afternoon sun bounces off the surf as the waves crash in on the Mediterranean shore. A year after meeting the Azbarga family at Lod, I am back in Israel. A surge of excitement runs through me; in the days ahead I'll be hearing more about the lives of Palestinians in Israel. I feel as though I'm about to become immersed in a world that until now has been hidden from me.

The highway takes me past the town of Netanya set up by Jewish settlers in 1928, then past Hadera, with its vast power station, and on past signs to the rich community of modern Caesarea and the ancient site of the same name, built by Herod the Great some years before the birth of Christ. My little car seems to fill with the muddle of history and mystery that is such a part of the atmosphere of the Holy Land. Soon I'm picking out villages dotted along the sides of Mount Carmel, which rises steadily from the coastal plain before reaching its peak above the Bay of Haifa.

Reaching the outskirts of Haifa, I follow the coast road round to Carmel's northern face and head towards the old port area of the city. After the day's travelling it's great to reach Fattoush, a café on Ben-Gurion Boulevard. I sit out on the wide pavement in the warm evening air, order a beer and watch the world go by.

An Arab couple at the next table are talking in Arabic and laughing, heads close together. The young woman and man are dressed to the nines and appear to be very much in love. Behind me are a mother and two small boys, chattering away in Hebrew. Further off two young Jewish women, both soldiers in uniform, are enjoying the Arab food and laughing with the waiters, who are Palestinian.

After reading about the Arab–Jewish conflict leading up to and after the declaration of Israel's independence in 1948, I am surprised to be witnessing this happy scene with Jews and Arabs sharing a café terrace so naturally. Although it was long ago, Haifa saw massacres committed by both sides, and the bitter fighting ultimately led to the eviction of most of the city's Arab population.

Under the UN Partition Plan of 1947 Haifa was to be in the new Jewish state. The Jewish leadership accepted the plan as 'the indispensable minimum'; the Arabs rejected it. The intended Arab state of Palestine was granted 42 per cent of the land, with a population of more than 800,000 Arabs and around 10,000 Jews. The

Jewish state would get 56 per cent of the territory, with 499,000 Jews and 438,000 Arabs. Jerusalem, because of its religious importance, would be administered separately by the UN.

Civil war was inevitable and developed rapidly from small attacks by militants on both sides. As the British troops pulled out through Haifa's port in May 1948, the conflict became vicious.

Tonight, though, there seem to be no echoes of that deep hostility. And my thoughts on it are happily broken by the arrival of Suha Arraf. She has agreed to help me discover the story of the Palestinian citizens of Israel, and once we have caught up on each other's news, she gets down to business with an outline of the places we'll be visiting and the people she's arranged for us to meet. Suha has a phenomenal network of contacts. She started out as a journalist on the *Haaretz* newspaper some twenty years ago, then worked in television. Now she is first and foremost a screenwriter of films, such as *The Syrian Bride* and *Lemon Tree*.

As we talk she is constantly looking around, watching people come and go, keeping an eye open for friends or an 'interesting character'. Sometimes I think she's not listening, but suddenly she'll look straight at me with a smile and ask a question that shows she hasn't missed a word. There is an urgency and intensity about her: she is often tossing her thick dark hair and tucking it behind her ears, where it stays for at least two seconds.

Once the agenda for the next few days is fixed, we relax. We order some food – hummus, and the Arabic

75

dish for which this café is named. I'd first tried it in Lebanon and loved the way pieces of deep-fried pitta bread were tossed into a salad, heavily drenched in oil and vinegar – a very refreshing meal.

We chat on, but as soon as we have finished eating, Suha abruptly announces, '*Yallah*, we must go to the nuns!'

For all Suha's intelligence and eye for detail, directions are not her strong point. The St Charles Guesthouse is, she says, just two minutes away. A quarter of an hour later we are driving slowly down a darkened street. It doesn't look promising. A large man clambers out of a car festooned with Israeli flags. Suha winds down her window and asks for directions in Hebrew. Does he know where No. 105 Jaffa Street is?

He stares at her blankly for a moment and, my neurotic antennae going haywire, I wonder if he knows she's a Palestinian and is getting angry. His response is abrupt, apparently dismissive, but then he pauses and his face creases into a broad grin as Suha throws back her head with a great shout of laughter. 'Ha-ha-ha! Let's go, John!'

'What did he say? Did he know?' I ask.

'Good Jewish humour,' Suha explains. 'He said, "No, I don't know number 105 and I'm afraid I don't know number 106 either!"'

Fortunately the next man we stop does know and we are soon standing at the gate, ringing the bell. The guesthouse is a well-proportioned stone building, 120 years old, run by the Rosary Sisters of Jerusalem – the 'nuns'.

A buzzer sounds and we go through the gate and up a steep flight of steps to an imposing double front door. One door swings open to reveal a small person in black. The nun looks at us quizzically from behind her spectacles. Her round face remains impassive for a moment or two before she nods, as if deciding we're not bad sorts, and says, with a sweet smile, 'You are very welcome.'

In the serene presence of Sister Reeta, even Suha's natural vibrancy calms a little. The nun's manner is a warm blend of humility and instruction. The instruction focuses on the remote control for the air-conditioning. I may switch it on and off but must not, under any circumstances, make any adjustment. Once I've taken this on board we all smile and Suha, glad to have found me this pleasant and economical base, goes out to hail a cab, saying she'll be back first thing in the morning.

Sister Reeta takes down my passport details, gives me a room key and wishes me a good night. I climb the stairs to my room, feeling my way in the gloom for a light switch. The place is very quiet indeed; there is no restaurant or bar and, as far as I can judge, no other guests. But that's fine: peace and quiet and a cool room after the summer heat outside are all that I want. As I unpack my bags I find a printed notice fixed inside the wardrobe. It contains some house rules. One should be in by 10.00 p.m., one should not hang wet clothes in the room, guests are not allowed and, of course, one must not adjust the air-con settings. These brief commandments are followed by the words 'Signed, The

Administration'. The Administration is, I assume, Sister Reeta. In another place this title might sound rather ominous, rather Orwellian Big Brother, but I think that here it will be more Benign Sister.

Half an hour later, having switched on the air-con and resisted making any adjustments, I am in bed.

Opening the curtains at seven the next morning, I see that it is going to be a hot day in sunny Israel. Starving, I head to the dining room, which is at the far end of a long, stone-flagged passageway. A buffet table is laden with bread and hard-boiled eggs, tomatoes, olives, cucumber, small cakes, water, juice and urns of hot water for tea and coffee. But there is no evidence of other humans – no guests, no staff, no nuns. The whole building feels as deserted as it did last night. I look up and down the passageway. I wait and listen. Nothing. It seems odd that some mysterious person should have prepared this spread if I am the only guest. Perhaps it's not for me at all. Uncertain of breakfast protocol, I wait a little longer. Then hunger gets the better of me.

Looking down from my first-floor vantage-point I see little children being taken through the guesthouse garden to nursery school. Looking up, I get a feel for Haifa's geography. The city tumbles down Mount Carmel's steep northern face from the broad ridge at the top, which is home to the exclusive and mainly exclusively Jewish suburbs of the town. Halfway down is the older residential and business district of Hadar, which used to have a very mixed Jewish and Arab population. Below this, on the lowest slopes, the oldest part of town emanates from the port and industrial areas. It is home to local-government offices as well as modern business centres.

As I finish my solitary meal my mobile phone starts buzzing frantically and playing a horrible tune, shattering the peace of the St Charles dining room. It is Suha to say she is on her way.

I gather my guidebooks and maps, then go downstairs to greet Sister Reeta and dutifully hand in the air-con remote. I ask if it was right just to help myself to the breakfast buffet. She tilts her head slowly to one side and down a little, in a rather regal way, and says, 'Yes, John.' Her half-smile has me worrying that she thinks I'm a simpleton. I beam back, stupidly, I fear, and say, 'Marvellous, thank you!'

Suha arrives sharp at eight, immaculately turned out in a summer frock of red flowers on a white background and wearing sunglasses that cover half of her face. We drive out of town, towards a town called Acre. Looking at the map, I reckon we need to follow Ha'atzmaut Street to leave Haifa. Suha confirms this. 'Yes, Ha'atzmaut is right. It's Hebrew for "independence". Every town in Israel has a Ha'atzmaut Street, to celebrate Israel announcing its independence in 'forty-eight.'

'Not much for the Palestinians to celebrate, though,' I say.

'No, of course not. We call that time the Nakba – that's "catastrophe" in English.'

The two peoples, Jewish Israelis and Palestinians, have

such an utterly different experience of the founding of the state, yet they live here together. Haifa is regarded as the most mixed and tolerant town in the country – I'd seen evidence of that last night at the café.

We drive past what were once fine stone mansions, reminders that this had been a thriving Arab business and residential district in the nineteenth and early twentieth centuries. But these buildings have not been restored like those around Fattoush on Ben-Gurion Boulevard. Although this area is home to local-government offices, businesses and the local headquarters of national and international organiz-ations, it seems run-down. Some churches and mosques are still just standing, but many of the old houses have been demolished or are derelict and boarded up, their ground floors now home to car body workshops, their decaying pillars and architraves breathing but a whisper of past grandeur. Alongside this decay sit ultra-modern 'statements' like the twenty-nine-storey Sail Tower, which is a government building, and nondescript office and apartment blocks. This architectural mish-mash at the working heart of Haifa suggests a place with an identity crisis, a place that doesn't know how to deal with its past and is unclear how to present itself now. I wonder whether the physical appearance of this part of town says more about the underlying nature of co-existence in Israel.

Our route takes us away from the port to skirt the oil refinery and pass through a string of rather uniform Haifa satellite towns, known as the Krayot, which lie along the coast. It's probably down to my driving but it soon becomes clear that Suha is not a happy passenger. Although the route to Acre is simple enough, there are series of roadworks with bumpy stretches and odd lane shifts to cope with. No doubt I'm a bit nervous on my first day driving here and probably overreact to aggressive driving by the locals, but I am concerned that Suha keeps clutching at the door with one hand while her face is turned towards the back seat. I don't remember her being like this when we worked together before, but maybe I wasn't driving then.

'Sorry,' I say. 'I'll take it a bit more slowly.'

'Yes, please do that!'

Soon her phone rings, mercifully distracting her from the dangers of the road. Though she is ten years my junior, I had found Suha rather forbidding when we first met. I felt that often she was frustrated with those around her. Soon, though, I realized that this derived from nervous energy, and that often she was having to think in three languages at once, Arabic, Hebrew and English.

Arriving at Acre in one piece, we gratefully abandon the hot, sticky car and walk through an ancient gateway into the Old City. Passing a jumble of small restaurants and gift shops, we come to a square that overlooks a harbour filled with fishing boats. The minarets rise into the blue sky beside the roofs and colonnades of the old khans, traders' inns and storehouses that marked the western end of the Silk Road.

Acre's souk is big and lively. We weave our way

through gaggles of people, chatting, haggling, local Palestinian customers joined by tourists and local Jewish families. As well as fruit, vegetables and household goods, the stalls sell all manner of clothes. There are fantastic displays of herbs and flowers, and even a booth selling specialist jewellery for belly-dancers.

Beyond the wide, covered arcades of the souk we meander along old streets, stepping aside as elderly ladies bustle past in long dresses and headscarves, flickering in and out of the sunshine and shadow. Pushing a barrow, a tradesman is jostled by passing children. Some alleys are so narrow that you feel as if you're in a tunnel, the old buildings rising out of sight above the cobbled pathway. There are surprising vignettes when an even smaller passage leads off at a tangent to an elaborate front door or to a gloomy yard where a man grooms his horse.

After the lanes the light is dazzling when we emerge into a small square where some boys are kicking a football. Tall stone buildings line this open space, but there are no shops or cafés here. Suha leads me across to a corner where another alley disappears.

The smell of warm bread and herbs fills the air, and I realize that this is a bakery, a dark, windowless place at the foot of a tall stone edifice. Inside there are tables laden with bowls of dough or with *manakeesh* fresh from the ovens. From my first mouthful of *manakeesh*, on a Beirut street in 1986, I had been a fan. At first glance they look like small pizzas, but they are much better: soft, light and chewy, most often topped with *zatar*, a mix of ground sesame seeds, oregano, thyme and olive oil.

Sometimes they come with cheese or minced meat. Whenever I eat them I think I could make my fortune if I opened a stall selling them in London.

A man, who barely comes up to my shoulder, appears from the gloom of the bakery. He is plump, with a well-rounded belly that speaks of regular tastings of his wares. A pair of thick spectacles, behind which his black eyes sparkle, is perched on a pudgy nose.

Suha introduces him as Fakhry Beshtawe. Dusting off his floury hands, he says, 'Welcome, and please call me Abu Adnan.'

I am surprised by his voice, which is low and rasping, somehow at odds with his gently rounded exterior. Once we are settled on the plastic stools in the shade outside the shop, I ask him what he remembers of the events of 1947–8.

'A tragedy,' says Abu Adnan, lighting a cigarette. 'We lived in the old downtown area of Haifa. That's where I was born. My father was a baker and we were rich. All the aunts and uncles lived around us. I was eleven years old and up to then I just remember it as a beautiful life. The Arabs lived in the downtown and the Jews lived up in the Hadar area. All the time we were hearing about the Second World War and that the Jews were coming here. My father tried to build good relations with Jewish neighbours, but he simply had no real idea of what the Zionists wanted. In those days we didn't understand them.'

He breaks off to serve a customer, the serious expression on his face changing rapidly to a smile of greeting as he shakes the man's hand. Abu Adnan, who looks younger than his seventy-one years, hands over a paper bag loaded with *manakeesh* and waves his friend off. Then we plunge back into the dark days of 1947.

'There was a lot of shooting between the Jews and Arabs, and a lot of people were killed in the clashes,' Abu Adnan tells me. 'Every week there was a funeral for someone shot by snipers. I remember one of our neighbours was sitting in the balcony at the back of her house drinking coffee and she was shot dead by a Jewish sniper from up the hill.'

The violence became more intense in the closing days of 1947. Members of the Irgun, the Jewish terrorist group that blew up the King David Hotel, threw bombs into a crowd of Arabs waiting outside the Haifa refinery, leaving six dead and forty-two injured. Arab workers retaliated by killing thirty-nine Jewish colleagues. Then the Haganah, the main Jewish paramilitary force, left as many as sixty dead after a raid on a nearby village where many Arab refinery workers lived.

Although we are in the shade, the morning is very hot and the heat combines with the story Abu Adnan is telling to make me feel hemmed in and almost anxious. I ask him what the mood was, if people had any idea of what would happen next.

Abu Adnan explains that his father thought that Hawassa, a very poor district on Haifa's outskirts, would be attacked as refinery people lived there too. He went there to bring an aunt to stay at the family home in Haifa. Abu Adnan's hoarse voice becomes little more than a whisper: 'Hawassa *was* attacked,' he says, 'and I remember the horrible sight of people running into downtown Haifa, escaping from the massacre. Those that couldn't run died. All my life those images have been in my head. I have never felt safe.'

Even before this escalation in violence, wealthy Palestinians had begun leaving Haifa and other cities to wait in Beirut, Amman or Cairo for the return of peace. As the fighting intensified through the early months of 1948 it was not just the rich élite that took flight. By mid-March more than a third of Haifa's 65,000 Arab inhabitants had departed.

While Arab radio stations were full of bombast, saying that the Jewish forces posed no real threat, men like Abu Adnan's father were far less confident. In every neighbourhood the youths were filling sandbags to make barricades and protect windows, but actual military organization was minimal. The military capability of the Palestinian community had never recovered from the British crushing of the Arab Revolt in the thirties.

'The radio had said, "One bullet and the Jews will run." They were very wrong,' says Abu Adnan, with a shrug. 'We had no army, no fighters.' A thin smile crosses his lips. 'Some individuals might buy a gun but that was about it. We were very scared. The Jews were well armed and organized.'

There were some Arab fighters in Haifa and elsewhere but they had no central command and were usually fighting to defend their village or district. In some places the local groups were supported by members of the Arab

Liberation Army (ALA) made up of volunteers from Arab countries.

The Jewish forces, on the other hand, were able to call up an army in excess of 50,000 well-armed men and women. They were highly trained, many having served with the British Army in the Second World War. Even though the Arabs outnumbered them by more than two to one, they would prove to be no match for the Jewish military as the civil war escalated in the first months of 1948. The British, responsible for keeping the peace, lost control of the situation. They became preoccupied with ensuring that their withdrawal from Palestine would be as smooth as possible.

The remnant of Arab resistance in Haifa, a few hundred fighters, was defeated by a five-thousand-strong Haganah brigade towards the end of April 1948. The fall of Haifa demoralized the Arab population right across Palestine. The Arabs still in Haifa were isolated and terrified, a community living on tattered nerves and prey to the wildest rumours: 'Every night some man would be out on the streets shouting, "Run to the port! The Jews are coming!" Maybe it was a collaborator. Many people were so scared that they left. The man would keep it up for two hours and then stop. Every night.'

Abu Adnan shakes his head at the memory. Then, sighing, he squints up at the bright blue sky, lights another cigarette and continues, 'One night the man came down the street, shouting that there were ships in the port waiting for us. A neighbour went and found that there were ships there. Then everyone was shouting, "To the port, to the port!" It was chaos. Family members got separated from one another. I saw a woman running along holding a pillow to her. She thought she'd picked up her baby. Then she stopped and started running back.'

In the spring and summer of 1948 such scenes of civilian flight occurred in many Palestinian towns and villages. In fear of imminent attack from Jewish forces, people raced from their homes, abandoning all their belongings. Crowds trampled over fallen neighbours, the old or sick were left or forgotten and mothers lost their children.

Abandoned by the educated and political élite, finding the British unwilling or unable to protect them, unable to protect themselves, the Palestinians had fallen prey to the insidious, creeping terror of voices like the mysterious nocturnal town-crier announcing imminent doom, as well as the real bombs and snipers of the Jewish forces. By mid-May fewer than four thousand out of 65,000 Palestinians remained in Haifa.

His eyes half closed as he looks back to that terrifying time, Abu Adnan carries on with the story of the night he left his childhood home. Yet he still raises a hand in greeting and says a word or two as neighbours pass the bakery. 'I don't really remember getting on the boat but the next morning I woke up in Acre and nobody knew what was happening. My father didn't want to leave Haifa so my mother took my brothers and me. We didn't know where the rest of the family was.'

For those Arabs who, like Abu Adnan's father,

remained, Haifa was a ghost town. Visiting neighbours' houses to see if anyone was left behind, they'd find food on tables and washtubs still full of clothes. People had just run from their homes with nothing.

Under the UN Partition Plan, Acre was meant to be in the new Palestinian state, but less than a month after the fall of Haifa it, too, was conquered by the Jewish forces. Most of the Arab population fled, as they had from Haifa. But Abu Adnan and his family had taken sanctuary in a monastery.

'The Jewish forces came into this area and lined up seven children from one family and shot them all. I saw the bodies. They killed a lot of people here. But we stayed with the nuns and then, after a few months, moved into a house that had been left by people who'd gone to escape the fighting. We were refugees and every day we would be given food by the nuns. It hurts so much to remember how we were. One moment we had a big house in Haifa and owned a bakery, the next we had to beg for bread.

'I lost my childhood. We had nothing, no money, no home, no friends and no family. It took me years to understand what had happened – and start coming to terms with it.'

Driving back from Acre, Suha and I are silent. My mind keeps going back to Abu Adnan saying that he'd never felt safe. On the surface he appeared a confident man, a respected figure in his community with a successful business. Although his family had lost their home, they now lived in a beautiful old city. But vulnerability had been etched deep in his young heart and was still there beneath the worldly exterior of a man in his seventies.

As we drive through the outskirts of Haifa, I ask Suha if she'd like me to run her home.

'No. First I want to show you a little of the old city, what's left of it. The Wadi Nisnas district is probably still much as it was when Abu Adnan was a boy.'

Parking is hot work: the kerbs are packed and I have to move fast to get in ahead of other drivers hunting for the elusive spaces. Much backing and shunting ensues, watched by a group of unsmiling Palestinian youth, or *shabab*.

Once free of vehicle and audience, I begin to cool down as Suha leads me through streets of stone buildings that are a mix of shops, small businesses and homes. On a smaller scale than Acre's souk, the busy Wadi Nisnas market has stalls selling fruit, vegetables and household goods. Birds cheep from small cages at one stall, their cries mixing with Arab pop and traditional music. The sounds of children playing echo down the narrow lanes leading off from the wider avenues of the main market. Old men and women, many in traditional Arab dress, stop and greet one another beneath black awnings stretched between palm trees.

'I like this place,' I tell Suha. 'It feels relaxed and welcoming.'

'Yes,' says Suha, 'but it's also tough. There are problems with drugs and poverty. You know, in 'forty-eight the last three thousand Palestinians in Haifa were pushed here. Then others came from all over the north.

The government of the new Israel wouldn't let them go back to their own villages so they ended up here as what we call "internal refugees".'

We walk on for a while and come to a café. Through the window we can see grey-haired men sitting at tables. 'Maybe they'll know what it was like in 'forty-eight,' says Suha, going up the steps to the entrance.

Although it's called Café Suhail, this is clearly more of a social club than a regular café. A counter takes up one corner of the large, plain room. A number of tables and chairs are neatly laid out, some with backgammon sets sitting ready on them. Only one table is occupied, where five old men are playing cards.

The man behind the counter nods as we sit down and ask if we can have coffee. Suha offers a general greeting to the card players and says we're interested in the life of Haifa in the old days. Going on past experience of asking Arab men such a question, I expect a barrage of information, with everyone eager to share their thoughts and memories. But here the reaction is very muted.

Suha looks uncertain. She gives me a little shrug, then turns back to the men and asks if anyone would like to talk to us, explaining that I'm visiting from Britain and am very interested in the history. Eventually one of the men agrees to talk and joins us at our table.

Speaking very quietly, he introduces himself as Ibrahim Anis. He tells us about life before the Nakba, describing a happy and comfortable life and speaking of friendly relations with Palestine's Jewish community. His family fled to Syria in 1948 and returned to Haifa three years later when he was fifteen. Ibrahim is unusually still, barely moving as he talks. But his deep-set eyes shine brightly.

'I got work as a truck driver when we came back from Syria. But I felt like a stranger in my own town. Relations with the Jews were obviously much worse after the Nakba.' He pauses, and runs a hand over his neatly trimmed moustache. 'The foreign Jews, from Russia, from Iraq, brought a lot of racism. Before, we were brothers. It was the foreigners who made us separate – made us strangers.'

One of the card players interrupts his friend to ask Suha where I am from and what I want. She tells him again that I'm British and am interested in the Palestinian story in Israel. The man looks me over, grunts and turns back to his cards. Suha looks at me, clearly puzzled still, shakes her head a little, then asks Ibrahim to carry on.

'I got married in 'fifty-eight, and my wife was also from Haifa. I have nine kids, eight boys and one girl. I have forty grandchildren!'

Suha and I congratulate him: '*Mabrouk*!'

'Yes, we are okay. My boys are in business, two work for the municipality – they all have houses. We are all neighbours, in fact. I have a big house at the centre of the family so everyone comes there. It's an old Arab house and very beautiful.'

Another card player starts talking and Suha smiles across at him. '*Yallah*!' she says. 'Come and join us.'

He stays put. Ibrahim, now speaking even lower, turns

to Suha. I pick out the words *Yahood* (Jews) and Iraq.

'Ah!' says Suha, with a smile of understanding. She looks at me, eyes wide with interest and excitement.

Ibrahim points across at the card players. 'That man over there is a Jew. Every day he comes here but he is very racist.'

I look at the man, then back at Ibrahim and Suha. Even with Haifa's reputation as a city where Jewish and Palestinian citizens live side by side, and the evidence of the bars and cafés on Ben-Gurion Boulevard, I am totally surprised by this revelation. I would never have imagined that a solitary old Jew would choose to spend his time in such a completely Arab environment, especially when he is openly denounced as a racist.

Voices are raised now among the card players. Suha explains that the Jew is shouting for them to stop talking about the Nakba and to play the game. He doesn't like to hear them talking about such things.

It is fascinating. The more the Jewish man complains, the more determined the other men are to have their say. Ibrahim sits quietly, as poised as ever, watchful. The other men are talking loudly now and chairs are shunted around. There's a kind of strange tension in the air. Were they younger men, the tension would be so much more intense, I am sure. Although powerful feelings are at play, they are held in check.

Suha tells me that the Jewish man came to Israel from Iraq in 1951. She says he is making sarcastic jokes about the men and their stories. 'Everyone here was a millionaire, if you believe them!' he says. 'They had thousands of dunams [a quarter of an acre] of land and they ran away! In the Mandate they sold their land for five shekels!'

Ibrahim's eyes go very steady, very hard indeed, when his Jewish card-playing companion pours scorn on the suffering of the Palestinians, but he doesn't say anything.

The old Jew suddenly stands up and stalks out of the café. Moments later he is back, standing tall and thin beside our table, which is now surrounded by angry old Palestinians. He starts speaking to Suha in Hebrew and gestures towards one of the men.

The man slumps slightly in his chair and shrugs. 'Ah, well, yes, in 'fifty-six I joined the Israeli Army.'

'Why?' Suha and I ask together, amazed.

'I was a kid – I didn't understand anything.' He carries on quietly, 'I was a soldier for three years.'

Clearly he is deeply uncomfortable talking about this. It must have been seen as an act of betrayal, or at least of collaboration. After a few seconds of embarrassed silence, the men ask Suha where she is from and start swapping names of people and families they know from her village.

I can tell that Suha is astonished by this encounter. Her eyes, always dancing anyway, are positively flying now as she takes in the immediate faces around her, listening and translating snatches of the conversation for me.

'But why do you come here?' I ask the Jewish man, who stands beside us, looking forlorn. 'Why not go to the Jewish areas of the town, like Carmel and so on?'

'I live in Kiryat Bialik,' he says. That's one of the

Krayot satellite towns that we passed on the road to Acre. Suha and I look at him, bemused, but he says no more.

Then, almost as if taking pity on him, one of the Palestinian men explains, 'He feels more welcome here and he speaks Arabic. He feels more Arab than Israeli.' Then, to everyone's amusement, he adds, 'Every day he comes and plays with us. And every day he wins!'

The Jew starts speaking again: 'We were thrown out of Iraq – that's why we came. The government fired all the Jewish workers and if you were caught listening to Israeli radio you would be thrown in gaol for three years.'

One of the Palestinians butts in, but without real venom, 'You're lying.'

'No, I am not lying.' The anger seems to have drained from all the old men and everyone listens quietly. 'For the rich people it was okay but we had no work and nowhere to live so we came here by aeroplane in 'fifty-one. Then we lived in tents for seven years.'

The old Palestinian men nod, acknowledging that Israel's treatment of Jewish immigrants from the Middle East had not been good. They all start talking about the hardships they faced in the early 'fifties: queuing for a few grams of rice, very rarely eating meat – never having enough food.

Watching them, and thinking back to the conversation with Abu Adnan outside his bakery this morning, it strikes me that these are ordinary men who lived through extraordinary times. The Palestinians have seen their homeland taken over by the mass immigration of people like the man from Iraq. Yet despite that enormous divide, they are united by their humanity. They may have done things they regret, some things they may be ashamed of, but in the end they have done the best they can to provide for their families and build a home for them.

With Café Suhail more or less as calm as it was when we arrived less than an hour ago, Suha and I take our leave. Out on the pavement we look at each other, still bewildered by the scene we've just witnessed.

My head is spinning. I've heard many stories of violence and dispossession today, of people denied their homelands. The old Jewish man's tale of his own suffering and his sense of belonging more with the Palestinians than with the Jewish community has made me think about how complicated people's notions of home and belonging are. What is amazing is that, despite all the bitterness, all the history, these old men still meet every day and play cards.

When I get back to the St Charles Guesthouse, Jaffa Street is deserted. Lined with old stone buildings, most now converted to apartments, with small shops or offices at street level, the neighbourhood is a little run-down, but it feels peaceful. After getting some bottles of water from a small general store across the road, I ring the bell and wait at the gate. I'm beginning to think that even though it's not yet ten o'clock I may have missed curfew and a night in the car beckons. Then the quiet of the street is disturbed by the buzz of the security lock and I'm in. Sister Reeta stands serene, small and sweetly smiling at the top of the steps.

'Good night,' she says, as she locks the door, and I take my key from the counter.

'Good night, Sister.'

Abu Adnan's story of finding sanctuary with the nuns in the terrifying days of 1948 somehow reinforces my sense of security as I go upstairs to my simple little room. I am shattered. The heat is exhausting, but I'm over-whelmed by the stories I've heard and the scenes I have seen. Given the late hour, I don't intend to call home. But Abu Adnan's description of the mother running with a pillow, imagining it was her baby, takes me back to a moment when I'd thought my own child, my little girl Lydia, had been lost. On a beach busy with holiday-makers, she had disappeared for a few moments. Staring desperately this way and that, I'd felt my life draining into the sand beneath my feet. All the bodies and parasols seemed to spin in front of me and the shouts of happy children deafened me. Then suddenly, through the din, I heard, 'Daddy!' and my eyes focused on the little smiling figure just twenty feet away, waving her yellow spade. I sprinted over, picked her up and squeezed her tight. Unreasonably anxious now, I phone home, and Anna reassures me that all is fine: my little one is tucked up fast asleep and safe.

6

The Conquest of
the Galilee

IT'S ONLY JUST AFTER NINE IN THE MORNING BUT THE day is already hot so I have the windows wound down as I drive up the steep road to the top of Mount Carmel. For once I'm a little ahead of schedule, so I pull the car over and stop to admire the view across the Bay of Haifa. A fresh breeze blows, cooling me after the heat of the car. Behind me is the spiritual home of the Carmelite Order, the Stella Maris Monastery. Though it is called 'Star of the Sea' out of devotion to the Virgin Mary (from her title 'Our Lady, Star of the Sea'), the name suits Haifa itself and its location beside the Mediterranean. Way below me I can see the port laid out, with ships tied up at wharves and lighters working their way around the docks. Looking up and north I can see almost to Acre across the rich blue of a sea that glitters with reflected sunlight.

Directly beneath me, at the foot of a tree-covered hill and at least half a mile from the sea, I'm surprised to see, parked next to each other, a green submarine and a small warship. On the landward side of the coastal highway, these craft look sadly stranded, or maybe their skippers were just sailing too fast and they ended up beached here. When I consult my *AA Explorer Guide to Israel* I discover that I am, in fact, enjoying a bird's-eye view of the National Maritime Museum. Next door to it is the Clandestine Immigration Museum, which tells the story of the Jews who were smuggled in during the British Mandate. Mount Carmel, rising serenely above Haifa port, must have been a truly uplifting sight for those refugees escaping the horrors of Nazi Europe. But the guide makes no reference to the violence of 1948, which saw much of the Arab half of the city's population fleeing from this same port, or to the fact that after the civil war very few of those Arabs were allowed to return.

Suha's apartment, in one of many blocks built on the wide ridge that forms the top of Mount Carmel, is just a few minutes' drive from here. From her balcony she shows me the stunning view looking west straight out over the Med.

'What an amazing place!' I say. '*Mabrouk!*'

No sooner has the Arab word passed my lips than a woman appears on the next balcony. Suha chats in Hebrew for a minute or two before her neighbour disappears inside again.

'You're obviously on good terms,' I say. 'Is it as comfortable as it looks, a Palestinian living side by side with a Jew?'

'Many people of my generation are like me,' she

explains. 'We know what happened in the past but aren't frightened by that. We are determined to live our lives the way we want to. You can fight for your rights as an equal citizen, but also enjoy the life you can have here.'

We stand a little longer, enjoying the view, then Suha asks, 'Did you have breakfast at the nuns'?'

'Not much.'

'Good. We will go to my parents' house and eat there. If you liked Abu Adnan's *manakeesh*, you will love my mother's. They are the best.'

We follow our route of yesterday up to Acre, then carry on further north before heading inland. The road rises steadily from the coastal plain and is soon sweeping through the Galilean hillsides, covered with woods and olive groves.

'My driving isn't too bad today, I hope?'

'Ha, no, it's fine!' The beautiful scenery clearly relaxes Suha. 'I love this countryside. Wherever I am I think of this as my home. I like to have my own place in the city and to travel and work, but this landscape is deep inside me always.'

The Arraf family home is in Mi'ilya, a village right in the heart of Upper Galilee. It is a small place with houses and apartment blocks packed tightly together, just off the main road. When I comment that the village looks rather cramped, Suha explains, 'In 'forty-eight Mi'ilya owned something like thirty thousand dunams, most of it private land. Today that figure is down to just thirteen hundred and sixty-five. The land has shrunk but the population has grown. In 1948 there were seven hundred and twenty-five people; now there are nearly three thousand.'

Mrs Arraf greets us warmly and immediately lays out a small banquet: bread, olives, tomato and cucumber, cold drinks, tea – and *manakeesh*. Suha was not wrong: her mother's *manakeesh* are delicious. She offers us the *zatar*, cheese and minced-meat varieties I've tasted before, but also a new variety with a sauce of strained yogurt and mint. While Suha and her mother catch up on family news I try to eat with decorum and not go wild.

The front door flies open and a little boy appears. He screams with delight, throwing himself at Auntie Suha. A few moments later the door opens again, but more slowly, and Suha's father appears, a quiet, diffident man. Suha has told me how hard he and his wife have worked to ensure that she and her siblings had a good education. Although neither parent speaks English, they make me very welcome.

While so many of their children's generation seem confident to proclaim their Palestinian identity, Suha's parents grew up in the aftermath of the Nakba, when even the word 'Palestine' dared not be whispered. Suha had told me a year earlier that she had only discovered her nationality, begun exploring her people's history and understanding her country at the age of twelve, when a chance reading had given her a new word to ask about.

I remembered her telling me that when Hezbollah rockets were landing all over this area, in 2006, she had urged her father to leave the village and stay with friends in Jerusalem. But he had refused.

'Why didn't you leave, even just for a while?' I ask.

'I wasn't going,' Mr Arraf explains. 'I was worried that if I went, the Israelis wouldn't let me back. That's what happened to so many Palestinian families in 'forty-eight.'

At first Mr Arraf's argument strikes me as an over-reaction, to say the least – but, of course, hundreds of thousands of Palestinians were driven out in 1948. And recent scholarship has made clear that, from the Zionist movement's earliest days, back at the end of the nine-teenth century, its adherents were dreaming of an Arab-free Jewish homeland in Palestine.

Theodore Herzl, the founding father of Zionism, wrote about the ideal of removing the Arabs: 'to spirit the penniless population across the border' by denying them work at home and paying neighbouring countries to give them employment.

Once the idea of a Jewish homeland had been endorsed by the Balfour Declaration it was no longer politic to talk publicly of removing the indigenous Palestinians, whose rights Balfour and subsequently the League of Nations, then the UN, insisted should be pro-tected. Even so, by the late 1930s the leader of the Jewish community in Palestine, David Ben-Gurion, was supporting the idea of the compulsory transfer of Arabs from what was to be Israel. He argued, as people still do, that there were plenty of other places for them to live.

By 1948 most Zionists saw the removal of the Palestinians not only as desirable but as necessary. For them this wasn't just about having an exclusively Jewish state, but about ensuring its security. Under the UN

101

Partition Plan, nearly half of the population of the new Jewish state would be Arab and most of those people lived in the towns and villages of the narrow coastal plain stretching from Haifa to the south of Jaffa, bordered by the Mediterranean on one side and on the other by what was to be the new Palestine.

As the violence escalated in early 1948, clearing this mass of probably hostile people was an attractive option to the Jewish military. Plans that were initially intended only to safeguard Jewish settlements and defeat small but sometimes effective pockets of Palestinian resistance saw Arab villagers expelled and their homes destroyed. Though the clearance operation was never announced as a deliberate policy, such was its scale that, by the time the Mandate ended and the new state of Israel was declared on 15 May 1948, around 300,000 Palestinians had become refugees. The towns and villages of the coastal plain stood empty; the agricultural, economic and social heart of Arab Palestine had stopped beating. Jewish forces were already occupying land and villages that had been assigned to the proposed Arab state and evicting their inhabitants.

After breakfast we drive to the nearby Palestinian town of Tarshiha. Compared with Mi'ilya, it looks massive, with industrial units sited beside the main road, which runs along the valley floor. White apartment blocks with red roofs are set among stands of trees, spread out across the hillsides. This is a surprisingly large, modern town. But Suha explains that Tarshiha is only a small part of what we can see, the old Arab village having been over-whelmed by the modern Jewish development town of Ma'alot.

In 1948 Tarshiha was a large, thriving, self-supporting place of around five thousand people – the majority Muslim with about a fifth Christian. The village was predominantly a farming community but there were also artisans: blacksmiths, shoe-makers, carpenters and traders. There were two elementary schools, one for boys and one for girls. In an area where no Jews had yet settled, Tarshiha continued more or less unaffected by the war until very near its end, late in October 1948. The inhabitants, like those of Mi'ilya and all of the surrounding area, were expecting to become part of the new Arab state of Palestine under the UN Partition Plan.

In the last week of the war Tarshiha was bombed by the warplanes of what was now the state of Israel. The local resistance – made up of perhaps a hundred men who had been in the Palestine Police Force, the Jordanian military, or been trained by the British Army – withstood the invading Israeli ground troops to the last.

Turning off the main road and away from the new buildings of Ma'alot, we climb uphill into the centre of old Tarshiha, to meet a woman who had lived through that turbulent time.

While Abu Adnan, the baker, seemed to have rounded and filled out with age, eighty-year-old Wafia Abu Hassan has gone in the opposite direction. She seems barely more than a wisp, with thin legs, deep-set brown eyes and a slightly stooped back. Her long hair is grey and sparse, her skin grooved with deep, sad wrinkles. A sob frequently comes into her voice as she looks back to the dark days and darker nights of 1948. It is an old voice, gentle but with a parchment-like creak, at times little more than a whisper. Her eyes often fill with tears.

We sit in her living room – an unusual space, circular at one end, with windows shuttered against the midday heat. From the balcony outside you can look down on the busy souk and out across the town. I feel almost as though I am on the prow of a ship overlooking a port. Wafia sits with her husband, Mahmoud. Children and grandchildren are gathered around them. Welcome ice-cold drinks are served.

Wafia speaks of the conflict: 'First there were clashes on the roads and then came the air raids. We were so frightened we ran from the houses and hid among the olive trees. My family and my aunts, uncles and cousins all stayed out there.'

Rumours spread between the families hiding among the olive groves that many had died during the bombing. After three days people began to creep back into the village. Wafia's family found that their elegant, new house had been demolished along with the whole neighbourhood.

Listening to the old lady talking, I recognize a few Arabic words, 'here', 'later', 'smoke', 'village', 'army', 'go' and 'we', but am unable to decipher the details of her story. But, as she speaks, I suddenly glimpse a twenty-year-old just beneath her skin. Looking into her misty eyes, I can imagine her frail body when she was a slim girl, flitting through the olive groves, heart pounding with fear and confusion. Her safe, civilized world, with a forthcoming marriage and new house, had been over-whelmed suddenly by the terror of diving war planes.

'There were dead bodies on the street and an eerie quiet about the place. Many people, including my fiancé, had fled to Lebanon. I never saw him again.'

A fan turns the air but I still find it stifling. The room is silent, apart from the low sound of Suha murmuring, '*Haraam* [for shame],' over and over. Wafia's voice becomes thinner and thinner and breaks into a sob. She speaks through her tears. 'My father said that we shouldn't go to Lebanon but to Yirka, a Druze village where he knew the *mukthar*, the village leader, Sheikh Marzuk, a highly respected man who might help us. So we walked all the way across the hills south-east to Yirka.'

The Druze, a small and tight-knit Muslim sect that developed around a thousand years ago, has communities in Lebanon and Syria. In Israel they are centred in the Galilee and around Mount Carmel. Many Druze villages had developed good relations with the Jewish community and most were left alone by Jewish forces during the civil war.

Sheikh Marzuk lived up to his reputation and helped Wafia's family and friends from Tarshiha and, indeed, people from other villages who came seeking refuge. Eventually so many people had gathered there that the Red Cross came to offer assistance. They gave out basic supplies, such as rice and sugar. Just a few miles from their prosperous village, these families were refugees, thanks to Israel's conquest of what should have been Palestine. Wafia's family stayed in the rooms provided by the sheikh for four years. Not everyone was so lucky, as Wafia explains: 'One man we knew was unable to find anywhere to stay, so he went back to Tarshiha and was shot dead by the Israelis. People had left with absolutely nothing, no clothes, no food, nothing, and many were killed going back to the village to get things.'

Unable to return to their businesses or tend their fields, the refugees in Yirka initially had only the Red Cross handouts to live on. Wafia's father had been one of Tarshiha's many tobacco farmers and, after a while, was able to lease some Druze land and start cultivating a crop once more to earn a living.

As Wafia tells of her community's life being overrun by the new state of Israel, I reflect that I grew up with accounts of this period that portrayed the Jewish people as desperate and ill-prepared, facing a monolithic force of well-armed, modern Arab armies attacking from every direction. Although forces from five Arab states (Lebanon, Syria, Iraq, Transjordan and Egypt), with small units from Saudi Arabia and Yemen, did support the Palestinian cause, these disparate and disorganized groups were never a real challenge to Israel's military superiority. The Arab forces made very few incursions into the territory assigned to Israel by the UN Partition Plan. In contrast, within weeks of declaring independence, the Israel Defence Forces, as the Haganah was now known, had occupied most of Palestine, leaving only the West Bank and Gaza under Arab control.

The landscape of Upper Galilee that we had driven through earlier is so serene that it's hard to envisage it as a place of terror. Yet I remember looking out over the very similar landscape of southern Lebanon twenty years before. In early March 1987, almost exactly a year after my kidnap and in the company of fellow hostage Brian Keenan, I had been moved south from Beirut by our captors. The journey had started with a real feeling that we would be free within a few hours. During the first leg of the journey, in the back of a van, wearing blindfolds but no bindings, I had felt as though my heart would burst with excitement, so sure was I that our ordeal was about to end. That vaulting optimism had been torn down and replaced with terror and despair when we were taped up like Egyptian mummies, gagged and then stuffed into a metal box bolted beneath a truck. Claustrophobia and freezing cold, coupled with the skin-tight tape, made the journey torturous. I was frightened of being helplessly trapped, should we crash, of being overwhelmed by diesel fumes or of choking on my own vomit, and couldn't stop thinking that, as they were treating us so badly, they must have given up on us as human beings and were about to kill us.

Hours later the truck stopped, the box was unbolted and we were pulled, limp and shattered, into what seemed to be a small farmhouse. It was just a stop-over before we were moved on to a more permanent prison. But it was during that interlude that I had my 'Galilean' view. A guard took me to the bathroom and I noticed a crack round the frosted-glass window. The view revealed a small plateau, ringed by low hills. A number of small houses, little farmsteads, I assumed, were scattered around this green and fertile bowl of land. In the distance a cock crowed. Everything seemed so peaceful and welcoming, totally at odds with the violent world that held us. I feasted my eyes on this vision of freedom until the guard banged on the door with his pistol.

I wanted so much to be out there, walking towards those hills. Yet even as I thought that, I realized that, were Brian and I able to escape, we would not be walking but running, scared and barefoot, with angry and violent men hunting us down.

This memory of natural beauty contrasting with human aggression chimes with the story Wafia has just told me. Not allowed to travel and unable to work, her family and neighbours had to risk their lives to sneak over their hills and through their valleys under cover of darkness to take fruit from their own trees.

After leaving Wafia and her family we drive through Me'ona Moshav, a collective farm. Established by Jewish immigrants from Romania just down the hill from Tarshiha, it was built on land that had belonged to the village, and the neat houses there were made with stone taken from destroyed Palestinian homes.

Exactly when the Jewish leadership under Ben-Gurion had decided to force Arabs from their homes, expropriate their land for use by Jewish immigrants and then deny the Arabs any right to return is not clear, but the policy was certainly in place soon after independence was declared in May 1948. Ministers insisted that Arab areas would be cleared, or 'cleaned', as some put it, and that the evicted people would not be returning.

Although the 'cleaning' of the Galilee was not, ultimately, as thorough as it had been across the coastal plain and further south, the population of the north was devastated nevertheless. By early November 1948 around 100,000 urban residents and some 220,000 rural inhabitants were driven into exile. Just 28,000 Arabs were left in the towns and only 65,000 remained in the countryside after the emptying of 200 of the 250 villages.

7

The Military Period

By what law do the defeated claim their rights from the conqueror?

Emile Habiby

ROTHSCHILD BOULEVARD IS A GRAND, TREE-LINED thoroughfare in Tel Aviv. A large pedestrian area with seats and gardens runs between the traffic lanes. Driving along I feel as though I could be in suburban Paris near the Rive Gauche rather than in Israel not far from the West Bank.

'That's it over there, I think,' says Suha, pointing across to a large building, a mix of old and new architecture, set back a little from the pavement.

We enter through a modern office block where we are checked in by a uniformed security team of Israel Defence Forces personnel, then directed down a corridor, which takes us into the older building, a 1930s mansion. This is the home of the Haganah archive; indeed, it was the home of Eliahu Golomb, one of the founding members of the paramilitary organization set up in the early 1920s.

The archive room is high-ceilinged and narrow, its walls lined with glass-fronted shelves crammed with books. With tiled floors and shuttered sash windows, it feels very old-fashioned. Wooden desks face each other in the centre of the room where two elderly men sit poring over documents. Cautioned by their somewhat frosty stares, Suha and I speak only in whispers. Ollé, the librarian, is far from frosty: she is helpful and jolly. We request documents relating to Suha's family village of Mi'ilya, then wait quietly. For someone who is usually so animated, Suha sits very still in her elegant white and red summer dress, her tanned face in repose.

Put together by Haganah intelligence agents in the years up to 1948, the archive contains reports on up to a thousand Arab villages in Palestine. Started in the late 1930s, the village files were part of a project to understand the physical and social layout of Palestine. The agents, working under cover, listed everything: the number of families, their relationships with each other, the British and the Jews, political affiliations, the amount of land owned by individuals and by the village, livestock, cars, weapons, everything. They also looked for evidence of any connection the places might have with ancient Israel.

The intelligence was seen as vital to securing the upper hand in any fight over the land. The files were used extensively by the Jewish forces in the 1947–8 war; consulting them alongside their detailed maps, the military

111

could confidently go into any area knowing the exact layout. They could also gauge likely resistance and likely
collaboration.

After a while the papers appear. All the records are being
copied on to computer files and Mi'ilya's is already done.
Suha sits and reads the page and a half of Hebrew script.
She whispers, 'All the families are named, what animals
they have, their land.' She carries on reading. 'It says some
people have guns.' Then she gasps and grips my arm. 'My
dear, it's here, the car! Maybe it is the one given to the spy!'
She translates an entry stating that there was one car in the
village and that it was used as a taxi.

Suha tells me a story that has passed down through the
village families. In the 1930s, a village man had
collaborated with the British and been rewarded with the
gift of a car. Most of his neighbours despised him for his
treachery. One individual, who was particularly
vociferous in his condemnation, owned a fine camel.
Desperate to win back his community's affection, the spy
decided to share his ill-gotten grandeur by taking the
village children for a ride in the motor. Sadly – driving
faster and faster to impress the children – he lost control
of the vehicle and crashed straight into the camel. The
children were catapulted, some into the ditch, some into
a tree. Most were slightly injured, but one suffered a
broken leg. The camel died. Apparently the collaborator
emerged from the wreckage physically unscathed, but,
seeing that he had now compounded the initial perfidy,
he realized there could be no way back. He started
walking and was never heard of again.

Suha reads through to the end of the document, then looks up, her expression a mix of admiration and shock. 'It is *all* here!' she says simply.

She makes some notes and we hand the papers back to Ollé. As we walk out through the lobby, furnished as it would have been in 1948, Suha observes, 'This furniture was probably taken from the home of a Palestinian family who'd been forced to leave.'

A few minutes later, sitting down outside a café, I feel ill at ease. There was something so calculating and ruthless about the archive, the way all that information had been collected. That the material is there for anyone to inspect is good – it's important that historical documents are publicly available in a democracy – but there is a real menace in the fact that the material was gathered and then used with the aim of dispossessing the people being surveyed.

'The Palestinians didn't have a chance against that level of organization,' I say. 'The Jewish forces had *such* an advantage.'

'And it didn't stop in 'forty-eight,' Suha tells me. 'All that information was used after the war to keep the Palestinians under control – and to take the land of the refugees.'

We sit in silence for a few moments before Suha announces, '*Yallah*, John, let's go. This place is trying to be Europe and it's not. It's fake!'

After years of conflict with the Jewish immigrant community and the British Mandate authorities, Israel's

113

Declaration of Independence in May 1948 signalled that dreams of a sovereign Arab state across historic Palestine had finally evaporated. The greater portion of what had been Palestine was now Israel and some 700,000 Arabs, who should have been inhabitants of the new state, were in exile in Lebanon, Syria and the two remnants of what the UN had planned would be the Arab Palestinian state, the West Bank and Gaza. Those who remained, just 170,000 of them, had witnessed violence, known fear and were now in a state of communal depression.

During the spring of 1949 a set of Armistice Agreements was signed between Israel, Egypt, Lebanon, Jordan and Syria. Though the agreements ended the official hostilities between the Arab states and Israel, the boundaries agreed in the documents were seen by all sides as ceasefire lines, not permanent borders. Israel has since settled its borders with Egypt and Jordan, but still has territorial disputes with Lebanon and Syria. And the boundaries between Israel and the Palestinian areas of the West Bank and Gaza are, of course, still not agreed. In 1949 the West Bank was under Jordanian, and Gaza under Egyptian, control. King Abdullah of Jordan, who had been in secret negotiations with the Jewish leadership before 1948, annexed the West Bank. Gaza was administered by an Egyptian military governor. In September 1948 the formation of an All-Palestine Government was announced in Gaza. A month later this government, which had no power whatsoever, announced Palestinian independence; an announcement that is still to be matched with a Palestinian state.

Despite the impotence of the Palestinians, the Zionist leaders of Israel wanted to consolidate their hold on the territory and people they had conquered. At the top of their agenda were the issues of security and the need to ensure a Jewish majority within the population of Israel. The Palestinians were deemed a threat on both counts. The Israeli leadership was determined that those now in exile would stay there, despite UN Resolution 194 of December 1948, which called for the return of all refugees. The Palestinians still within Israel would be kept on a very tight rein, isolated from the Palestinian community outside.

As well as controlling the people, Israel's leaders had an urgent ambition to use the legal apparatus of the state to assume ownership of as much of the Palestinians' land as possible and to repopulate it with Jewish immigrants. Those policies of population control and land appropriation were helped enormously by the bank of information now collected in the Haganah archive.

After the war the Palestinians in Israel seem to have entered a kind of half-life. Most of their neighbours and many members of their families had been dispersed and their world order destroyed. They were now in a new state, run by people building a homeland for Jews, not Arabs. What was life like for them after the war?

I ask Suha if we could make another visit to Abu Adnan Beshtawe – I'd taken to thinking of him as 'the baker from Acre'. We find him moulding *manakeesh* in the sweltering gloom of his bakery. Looking at Abu Adnan, his T-shirt and trousers streaked with flour in this very ordinary, humble environment, I feel as though I'm intruding. It seems a little voyeuristic, encouraging him to delve into his dark memories again, but I ask him what the atmosphere was like in the newly formed Israel.

'They wanted to keep us frightened,' he says. 'One man was taken up on to the sea wall and made to stand there for hours. Then they shot him and his body fell to the shore below. We could hear his wife crying through the night.'

Abu Adnan says this in such a matter-of-fact way that it takes a while for the horror of this statement to reach me. He pauses, disappears into the darkness, loads the oven with another batch of bread and re-emerges. The heat emanating from the cavernous little bakery fuses with that of the midday sun above us. The narrow, cobbled street is hot and airless; a trickle of sweat runs down my back.

Abu Adnan describes how Israeli forces took all the men who could work, aged from seventeen to the very old, gathered them in the square and then carted them away to prison for two years, saying they were prisoners of war, even though the war was now over. Red Cross inspectors revealed that 'prisoners of war', like those taken from Acre, were put to forced labour. It was described as 'essential' to the new state and might involve quarrying or even moving stones from destroyed Palestinian villages.

Though Israel's Declaration of Independence had

appealed to Arab inhabitants 'to preserve peace and participate in the upbuilding of the State on the basis of full and equal citizenship and due representation in all its provisional and permanent institutions', the new government's real attitude to its Palestinian citizens was made transparent through the resurrection of the Defence Laws (State of Emergency) Regulations. They had been introduced by the British in 1945 and used against Arab and Jew alike. Now they would be used by the Israeli government to form the backbone of a system that discriminated between Jew and Arab.

When the British had introduced the Regulations to Palestine in 1945, leading Jewish figures angrily condemned them as uncivilized and compared them to the laws that had been deployed against the Jewish population in Nazi Germany. But this comparison was forgotten when it came to using the laws against the Palestinians in Israel.

Consisting of 170 articles divided into fifteen sections, the Defence Laws were indeed draconian. They controlled more or less every aspect of the lives of Palestinian citizens, from what they could say to where they could go. And military, not civilian, governors enforced them. They could impose their authority in any way they saw fit. For nearly twenty years the Arab citizens of the new state would live under the Regulations during what became known as the Military Period.

One of the most notorious of the regulations was found in Article 125. This allowed military governors to declare an area 'closed' for security purposes. Access in and out of that area, for non-Jewish citizens, was then restricted. Abu Adnan explains how another regulation, Article III, affected people's lives: 'In the military time, there was no way to appeal. The military governors could lock up anyone, for anything, for as long as they liked. They didn't even have to make a charge or have a trial.'

A trial of a Palestinian citizen might be conducted by just one officer, at whose whim the civilian could be sentenced to two years in prison. In the senior military courts a triumvirate of one senior and two junior officers could impose life imprisonment and even the death penalty. No wonder the women of Acre had wanted to keep the young boys out of the hands of Israeli soldiers.

'I remember Acre without young men, just kids, women and grandfathers,' says Abu Adnan, waving to two youths pushing a trolley loaded with a battered old washing-machine. 'My mother was so worried that they'd take my sixteen-year-old brother that she kept him in shorts to look like a kid. Many mothers dressed their sons as girls, and even some men did it, sitting among the women when the Jewish force came to check the houses.'

When the Israeli searches became less frequent and men were not at such risk of being rounded up and imprisoned, Palestinian society still faced enormous difficulties. Employment opportunities were very limited and, like everything else, dominated by the military. Abu Adnan explains that there was very little work. A lot of people from villages like Kafr Yasif and Judeida, inland from Acre, had left their oranges and olives on the trees when they had fled. The Israelis hired Arabs, on very little money, to harvest these orchards, then took the fruit for themselves. Abu Adnan's father had worked in this way for a while.

Even if you were lucky and managed to start a small business, life was still extremely fraught. Abu Adnan's father eventually decided to open a new bakery in Acre. 'Every night my father and I came here to work.' Abu Adnan points behind him to the dark, cave-like interior of his workplace. 'For a long time a curfew was imposed by the military, so we had to creep along the alleyways and work quietly through the night by candlelight. One time my father asked me to go and wake Abu Khalil, an old man who worked for us. I got very frightened when I heard voices on the street, but Abu Khalil said he'd look after me. But then some Jewish soldiers arrested him. I was so scared that I ran away. I ran into more soldiers. I ran up and down the narrow lanes, terrified. Some soldiers caught me and searched me but I got away again and went back to my father. I was so frightened. I couldn't speak for half an hour and just sat crying and crying. My dad said he'd never send me on such an errand again.'

Looking up and down the narrow street and then up at the blue sky above, it is hard to think of this city, once a jewel of the Arab world, turned into a ghetto of fear. Acre had become a distorted space, whose population scuttled through the maze of old city streets, like creatures cowering from a monstrous bird of prey that might swoop at any moment.

I ask how Abu Adnan and his family had kept going.

'We always hoped that we would return to our first home in Haifa. Even though we went there and found that all the houses had been destroyed we would go and sit in the ruins of our neighbourhood. Every year we'd go, even when I was married and we had small kids. We stopped going when they built new houses there and we had to accept that they wouldn't let anyone return.'

We thank Abu Adnan and leave him preparing another batch of loaves for the oven. His simple, painful descriptions have set my mind whirling with outrage and sorrow. Yet even though the baker had gradually lost hope that he would regain his old family home, at least he could visit the area still. For those Palestinians who were refugees outside Israel, there was no chance even of seeing the ruins of their homes.

Despite demands from the refugees and the UN that they should be allowed to return, the Israeli government refused to let them back in. Palestinian refugees trying to re-enter the country would be taken back to the border or shot. By 1956, eight years after independence, Israeli forces had killed some five thousand people who had tried to return to their homes.

8

Military Control Turns to Massacre

Open your gates, O our village
Open them to the four winds
And let fifty wounds glow with fire.
Kafr Qasim,
A village dreaming of grain, violet flowers,
And flocks of pigeons:
'Mow them all down in one full sweep,
Mow them down.'
They mowed them down.

Mahmoud Darwish

RATHER THAN TAKE THE MAIN COASTAL HIGHWAY south from Haifa I decide to use an older road that runs inland from the coast. It will be slower, but I want the chance to see more than the towns lying beside the Mediterranean and go deeper into the landscape of central Israel. The route takes me along the foot of the western slopes of Mount Carmel, then down along

121

the coastal plain, through or around a whole range of towns and villages. Once through the sprawl of Hadera, there are countless smaller towns, with buildings and roads under construction everywhere. I begin to regret not taking the coast road. Heavy traffic, roadworks and traffic lights sometimes reduce the pace to a crawl. It's hot and I'm anxious I'm going to be late. I'm on my way to a town called Kafr Qassem to meet Haya Sarsour, whom Suha recommended highly: 'She is a very strong woman, very intelligent and a serious activist.'

Kafr Qassem sits above the coastal plain just a couple of miles from the West Bank border. It is one of only a couple of Palestinian towns left in the whole of central Israel. When I eventually reach it and turn off the highway, I stop for a minute to cool down and look at the view. Central Israel is spread before me to the north, south and west. It looks as though the land is so full of humanity that it is about to burst its seams. The town of Petah Tikva is in the near distance, and beyond that Tel Aviv and the Mediterranean, just ten miles away. It is hard to imagine how empty it must have been at the end of 1948 when the Palestinian exodus left areas of central and southern Israel deserted. Approximately 330,000 people from 180 villages and four towns from this region were suddenly gone.

I drive uphill, past a parade of shops and garages to a roundabout and then on up, winding through a small residential area where shrubs and palm trees line the road. Passing a large mosque on my left, I come to another roundabout. A large black and white marble column sits in the centre of the junction, '1956' inscribed on it in large numbers.

I pull in and phone Haya. She lives in the town and says she'll drive down to meet me. I wait by my car until another draws up beside me. The window rolls down and the smiling face of a young woman appears. 'Hi! Welcome to Kafr Qassem! Wait there. I'll park my car and we'll go in yours.' She pulls over towards the side of the road, stops and gets out.

'Erm,' I say hesitantly, 'you're about a metre from the kerb. Is that okay?'

'It's fine, I think,' Haya says, blushing slightly. 'I only passed my driving test this week, so it's all a bit new still.'

Armed with Suha's brief description of a serious and intellectual activist, I'd been expecting someone rather more austere. Haya comes across as a warm and friendly person, with a quick sense of humour. Though she seems a little shy, she tells me she has been involved in Palestinian activism since she was fourteen. After university she spent four years with a local government committee, and now works on women's and children's issues and with Wellcome Foundation programmes in high schools.

'Our focus is "What positive things do kids lack?"' explains Haya, 'rather than, "How bad has life been?"' She pauses. 'My work is very important to me.'

As we wait to make a turn a carful of youths races past us. The tough-looking driver laughs maniacally as he executes a handbrake turn and screeches to a halt ten feet from us. Heart pounding, I concentrate on the road just in front of my bonnet but Haya opens her window and starts shouting at them.

After they've driven off, she explains, 'I was telling him to go slowly.'

The man makes a scything motion with his right arm, jumps to his feet and starts pacing the room. This is Ismael Bdeir, a small fellow with a grey brush of hair standing up straight on his head. He is never still. He roams the room – part family living room, part business office – in sudden, jerky movements, his voice often rising to a shout as if he is declaiming in court or on some grand stage, raging against the injustices he has faced. His nervous intensity makes it very hard to follow what he is saying and puts me off interrupting him.

He makes the scything motion again. '"Mow them!" That's what the soldier said.' He slumps into his chair, motionless. I look at Haya, who is watching Ismael intently, her head on one side, waiting for him to continue.

'The next thing I remember was hearing the commander speaking on his radio, "Thirteen killed," and the answer coming back, "Go on!"' Ismael runs a hand through his hair, almost tearing at it. 'A couple of times I tried to get up and run away. But the bullets had wrecked my leg and I just fell down.'

Ismael explains that he and the other villagers returning home from work that afternoon had had no idea that a curfew had suddenly been imposed by the Israeli military authorities. 'My cousin and I were walking home with our cart.' He is on his feet again. Haya and I watch him as he paces round the room. 'We'd been taking onions to Petah Tikva. I was fifteen years old. Three soldiers stopped us. There was a Bren gun on the ground. Other neighbours were coming back, on trucks or on bicycles. The soldier in charge said to us all, "Come and stand over here." There were thirteen men at that point. Then he asked, "Are you from Kafr Qassem?" We replied, "Yes." The soldier looked at the other two, who immediately got ready by the Bren gun. That's when they started shooting.'

The date was 29 October 1956. That day, on the other side of the country, Israeli forces invaded the Sinai desert in Egypt. Eager to weaken this dangerous neighbour, Israel was acting with Britain and France, who wanted to regain control of the Suez Canal, which the Egyptian President Nasser had nationalized. Israeli intelligence believed that Jordan, which then occupied the West Bank, might enter the war in support of Egypt, so soldiers were stationed along the country's border with Jordan, just a couple of miles from Kafr Qassem.

In all, forty-nine villagers, including seven children and nine women, were 'mown' between five and six p.m. The massacre was carried out by members of the Israel Border Police, who had been ordered to shoot anyone breaking the curfew.

Abruptly Ismael sits down again, rolls up his trousers and unstraps an artificial leg. 'For more than fifty years I have been walking with this, thanks be to God.'

I stare at it, appalled. I can't think straight. Ismael's whirlwind of action and emotion has set my mind spinning. Most of the time he talks in Arabic but when he's very upset I notice he switches to Hebrew, which seems odd to me. Surely he knows that Haya, who is translating, speaks Arabic and is Palestinian. He wanders from his central story once or twice to talk about land he once owned that has been confiscated, rifling through drawers in this chaotic room for papers and legal documents to show us. I wonder if he sees me as someone who can do more than listen to his story and maybe tell others about it. Does he think I can help him practically, help him get his land back?

Gently Haya manages to interrupt him so that she can translate what he's saying and bring him back to the main track of his story. He calms down a little and carries on. 'In those days it was normal for people to go and work in the Jewish Israeli cities, like Tel Aviv, or on the land around places like Petah Tikva.' Ismael is sitting with his 'leg' lying across his lap. 'On that particular day the Israeli officer came to the village chief, the *mukthar*, and said that there was a curfew at five o'clock. But it was already four thirty, so how could people on their way home from work get to know about it? The officer said the *mukthar* should tell the people inside the town and he'd take care of the people coming back in.'

The *mukthar* arranged for people to go round shouting that a curfew was in force. Two families sent their children to call in the people who were working in the fields close to the town. Those two children were killed. Most of the victims died at a junction on the edge of town. Now it is a roundabout – the one with the black and white marble column I saw earlier.

The call to prayer echoes into the room over the roar of the traffic on the street. I ask if there was ever talk of revenge.

Ismael turns his glittering gaze on me. 'But who would do that?' he replies, with explosive energy. 'You knew if you did that they'd come and kill your whole family. People were very scared. Even sitting in the café drinking coffee you wouldn't dare say anything because at that time if you said anything you would not be able to get permits to travel, you'd be fired. Teachers were very scared in those times because if anyone said something political or nationalistic they would lose their job.

'This country is very proud of its democracy but where is this democracy?' Ismael is on his feet, his voice loud once more as he turns from Haya to me and back again. 'Our existence here is very important. We should never leave.' Having made this statement, he straps his leg back on and we chat a little before taking our leave.

Stepping out into the buzzing street, I feel drained by the story of this atrocity and the ongoing injustice, but also by the frantic, painful energy that poured from this deeply scarred man. I hope that somehow he will find peace – but I doubt it.

'This is it,' says Haya.

'It's a petrol station,' I say rather doubtfully, while parking the car.

Haya smiles, pointing at the petrol pumps. 'That is a

petrol station, yes, but that,' she indicates a bland one-storey structure, 'is the Filfilla restaurant.'

I can't say it looks inviting, but beyond the institutional double glass doors lies an airy space laid out with wooden tables and chairs and huge tropical fish tanks. It is busy. Haya explains that the restaurant is very popular with Palestinians, and also with Jewish people from the next town. After a brief look at the menu we order food, Haya chatting to the young waiter, who is a family friend. As he goes off to the kitchen she exclaims, 'Hebrew music!' She shakes her head and points at the loudspeaker on the wall, which gives out some tinny pop music. 'They shouldn't play it. If people want to eat Arab food, they should listen to Arab music!'

Her comment reminds me that Ismael had spoken in Hebrew some of the time, and I ask Haya why he'd do this when he knows that Haya is Palestinian and speaks Arabic.

'He wasn't talking to me. He was talking to you,' she says. 'He was telling his story to a stranger, trying to get you to understand what he'd been through. Whenever he's done that before, in court, say, he's had to make his case in Hebrew. I've read that when people speak about being oppressed, they will use the language of their oppressor even when they know their audience doesn't speak that language.'

Haya asks about my experience as a hostage in Lebanon and how I'd come to terms with it. I tell her about the support I'd had when I'd come home from Beirut, and the elation of being free. Each day had started with a huge sigh and a smile as I remembered, 'I'm safe at home.' My father, brother and friends had helped me settle back in, and even strangers on the street wished me well. Writing about the experience was important too. Putting it all down, making it into a coherent story rather than a jumble of memories, had been cathartic. And what was really important was that my story was believed: no one doubted it, and people listened to me.

Haya has another question for me. 'If Arabs did you so much harm, why are you here, interested in our problems?' She laughs. 'Haven't you had enough of us?'

'You're right!' I say, sitting upright and adopting a shocked expression. 'What on earth *am* I doing here?'

But it's very likely I wouldn't be sitting in this restaurant, talking with Haya about the story of Palestinians in Israel, had I not been kidnapped in Beirut. Through that experience I began to appreciate how much conflict is born out of fear, and a desire to preserve or gain a safe home. I developed an empathy with people who don't have a voice, who are dispossessed, who are denied freedom.

A group of Jewish diners pass the table, laughing and calling farewell to the waiter.

'I suppose it's important to be able to speak their language,' I say, 'to be able to argue and just to live together.'

'Yes, that is right, of course,' she says, then goes on, her eyes flashing, 'but I will not be told where and when I can speak my language.' She tells me of a time when she was in Tel Aviv and there was a suicide bombing. 'I was walking on the street, talking on my mobile phone with my uncle Zachariah. "Where are you, Haya?" he asked. I explained I was on such-and-such a street, that I was far from the bomb site, and safe. "No, you are not safe. You are walking along talking loudly in Arabic! Stop it!" It was very funny,' she says. 'I started lecturing my uncle. "I refuse to deny my identity and speak another's language." And he began shouting down the phone in Hebrew – "Get off the street! Stop speaking Arabic – you'll be shot!"'

We laugh. But talk of being shot on the street brings us back abruptly to the event we've been hearing about today. Haya has arranged for us to meet another survivor of the 1956 massacre. 'The gentleman we're going to see now is older and, I think, less troubled than Ismael. His experience was terrible, though.'

I tell Haya I'm amazed that people are ready to meet me, a stranger, and talk so freely about this tragedy in their lives.

'Yes,' she says, nodding and smiling gently. 'But you have done that and you feel it was worthwhile. They want to explain what it was like and to make sure people remember those times.'

The massacre of innocent men, women and children at Kafr Qassem was an atrocity such that one would assume, if not the action of extremists taking the law into their own hands, it must have been a freak accident of communications. Civilized states do not gun down children on their way home for tea. But the Palestinian citizens of Israel, eight years after the Nakba, were already conditioned to living in a state of intense vulnerability, with the military government controlling every aspect of their lives.

In the summer of 1950, the remaining two-thousand-odd inhabitants of a southern Arab town named al-Majdal were shipped to the border of the Gaza Strip to make way for the new Jewish city of Ashkelon. And more than 15,000 Bedouin Arabs were expelled from the Negev desert region between 1949 and 1953.

Yitzhak Rabin, then commanding officer of the Northern Command and subsequently prime minister, revealed in his memoirs that, on the day after the massacre at Kafr Qassem, up to five thousand inhabitants of two northern villages were forced over the border into Syria. No wonder, then, that fears of expulsion from Israel were still very much alive.

After lunch, Haya and I head to meet another survivor of the massacre. I am slightly nervous that this might also be a fraught encounter, but the atmosphere at the home of Mahmoud Freij is very much calmer than we encountered in Ismael Bdeir's chaotic front room. On a quiet side-street, a bush covered with white and yellow flowers marks the front door of Mahmoud's ground-floor apartment. He and his wife welcome us into a large, high-ceilinged room with a tiled floor, a couple of ornate landscape paintings and a large television. Sofas and chairs line the white walls and small tables are dotted around the room. Mrs Freij comes in with figs and grapes grown in their yard. Mahmoud clears his throat and begins to tell me about what happened to him in 1956. Unlike Ismael, he speaks slowly, choosing his words with care and pausing every few sentences to allow Haya to translate for me.

'I was twenty-four years old, with three children,' explains Mahmoud. 'My brother, Ahmed, was two years older. We both worked in a quarry five kilometres south of here. We weren't fighting Israel. We were serving the country, if you like, by working in the building industry and on the land. It was very hard work – they wanted us to build the Israeli state. We were providing food and homes.'

It had been just like any other day as Mahmoud, his brother and two companions made their way home. There was no television in the village and precious few radios so they knew nothing of the imminent conflict between Israel and Egypt. When they arrived at the entrance to the village, where the monument is, they saw an army jeep. When the soldiers spotted the men they got into the jeep and drove towards them. Without asking any questions, they opened fire. Mahmoud was on one side of the road, his brother and the other two men opposite. 'They shot at my friends first, then just turned the gun at me. On other occasions they had shot in the air to get the people to go back to the village so I thought that's what was happening. Of course, after a second I knew they were shooting at us for real. Bullets hit me in the leg and I went down. I heard the officer say, in Hebrew, "Stop shooting randomly like that. Use one bullet in each one's head. It will be cheaper!"

'There were three shots and the soldiers walked over to me. But they were distracted by a herd of sheep coming round the corner with the village shepherd and his boy. "They are all finished here," a soldier said, and that's when I realized my big brother was dead.'

Mahmoud sits across from me, still and straight-backed. He sighs deeply and pauses, staring ahead. I watch the second hand of a clock on the wall work soundlessly around its dial. He clears his throat again. 'They killed the shepherd and his boy. It was after five on an October afternoon and the light was going fast. The soldiers assumed I was dead so I lay there beside a pile of stones where they sat, waiting for the next group of villagers to come. If people were straggling they'd stop the first ones and ask them questions until the others caught up. Then they'd shoot them.'

A strange stillness has come over the room as Mahmoud speaks, as if the rest of the world is somehow very far away. Haya is motionless, just her lips moving as she tells me what is being said. He describes how a truck came up to the group of soldiers with a crowd of workers in the back. The soldiers pulled their jeep out in front of it and told the driver to follow them. But, thinking that they might be deported across the nearby Jordanian–West Bank border, the driver swerved off the road, raced away and got into the village another way. All twenty-five people on board and the driver were saved. When another truck, carrying women who'd been

133

harvesting vegetables, came along, the soldiers immediately told them to get down and killed them all.

'From five o'clock to nine in the evening I was lying there in the same position by the stones,' says Mahmoud. 'All that time they would be killing, one by one or in groups, as the people came in.'

Eventually the soldiers left and he managed to crawl into an olive grove to hide. As the soldiers had been killing anyone coming back to the village he assumed that everyone in the village must already be dead or have been taken away. But around four in the morning, having lain all night freezing under the olive trees, Mahmoud heard a man calling from the village, 'Curfew, curfew!' If the man was warning that the curfew was still on, it must mean there were still people in the village.

'I crawled to the nearest house, which by chance was a relative's place. Apparently my parents thought both of their boys must be dead and had started going mad with grief. One of my relatives crept round to their house to tell them that I, at least, was still alive.'

Shot at five o'clock on Monday afternoon, Mahmoud did not receive any proper medical care until the curfew was lifted at eleven o'clock on Wednesday morning. He was put on a truck and taken to hospital.

'At the hospital entrance there were some army guards. "Are you from Egypt?" they asked me. "No," I said. "I am from Kafr Qassem," and they said, "Ah, you're from the village where they were throwing stones." You see, already the authorities and the press were saying that we had started something.'

For two months the government tried to sit on the story but eventually it had to acknowledge what had happened. With an eye on broader public and international opinion, as well as on calming Palestinian feelings in the country, it decided to show contrition by making *sulha*. *Sulha*, or settlement, is an Arabic tradition of bringing two parties together after a killing by one side, a family, for example. They make *sulha* to prevent one killing becoming a feud.

'Why on earth would we want to do *sulha*?' Clearly Mahmoud is still affronted by the idea, yet he also remembers the reality of the times. 'But who was going to stand up and say we wouldn't do it? Everyone was too frightened. Yes, we were broken, spiritually. We were unable to resist, or to say no.'

Arrangements were made by the mayor of the Jewish town of Petah Tikva, who knew the traditions of *sulha*. The Jewish authorities brought sheep and killed them; and Arab people were brought in from other towns and villages to generate the *sulha*. The 'settlement' decided on by the government was £1,000 to those who were wounded and £5,000 to the families of those who were killed.

'You lost a brother and witnessed the murder of so many neighbours,' I say. 'Have you ever been able to feel comfortable with the Israelis? Can you accept them?'

Mahmoud shrugs. 'We have to live together. We have no other choice. Our children work with the Jewish people so we have to live with them.' With ten children and forty-five grandchildren, the old man says he is determined to look to the future and not always be harking back to what happened in 1956. Mahmoud says he would rather sacrifice all that had happened to his generation in order that the next can live normally.

I ask Mahmoud if he really thinks future generations of Palestinians will be able to have a more normal life, as equal citizens.

'God knows,' he replies. 'We cannot judge how this state will act but it must be obvious to the whole world what the Israelis have been trying to do. Time makes a difference.'

The trial of the eleven Israeli soldiers involved in the killings lasted until October 1958, two years after the incident. Although much of the evidence was heard in secret, the verdict was made public. Convicting the men, Judge Binyamin Halevy dismissed the plea that they had only been following orders; during the trial he even asked one of the defendants if he would have condoned a Nazi soldier making the same plea after murdering innocents. The judge, setting a legal precedent in Israel, said that a 'black flag' flew over 'manifestly' illegal orders – orders that even a simple person could see were illegal without talking to a lawyer.

Three soldiers were acquitted; the remaining eight were found guilty of killing civilians and sentenced to terms of imprisonment ranging from seven to seventeen years. Yet for all that the judge had sentenced the men, showing that the Israeli legal system did work, the sentences were still light for the crimes committed. Not only that, but they were reduced in stages, by a court of appeal, the chief of staff and the Israeli president. Then the Committee for the Release of Prisoners ordered a final remission so that all the men were released from prison within three years of the massacre and were able to pick up their careers successfully.

The colonel, who had ordered that anyone breaking the curfew should be shot, was only found guilty of 'exceeding his authority'. The court fined him just one piastre, maybe a penny in today's money.

Leaving Mahmoud Freij and his wife with their memories and hopes, I drive Haya to collect her car at the roundabout. The early-evening sun is catching the black and white marble of the monument, illuminating the names of the dead that are etched on it, as I thank her and we say goodbye. She stalls the car once, then heads off steadily up the hill towards her home.

I turn my car downhill and drive back towards Haifa. It is right and proper that the Jews of Israel should tell their story and remember their hardships and triumphs. So should the Palestinian people of the state. Yet there are none of the brown signs that denote places of historic interest, guiding visitors to the labour camps where Palestinian men were kept after 1948, and there is no brown sign leading to the roundabout on the road into Kafr Qassem. There is no effusive entry about the place and its people in the *AA Explorer Guide*. Even the monument wasn't erected for a long time, and the military government banned gatherings to mark the anniversary. Printing or distributing posters for such gatherings was illegal.

Stopping the car before joining the highway, I look out over the coastal plain. Until 1948 the people of Kafr Qassem would have looked out here and seen their homeland. After that time the plain had become alien territory, where the rights of Palestinians were always uncertain and their presence unwanted. With the sun about to set over the Mediterranean, the sky is darkening and thousands of lights are beginning to twinkle in the towns and cities below. Despite what I have learned today, I find the view to be utterly uplifting and am surprised to feel a terrific sense of freedom, of possibility.

9

For a People Without Land

M Y PARENTS AND BROTHER ARE BURIED IN A
churchyard deep in the Essex countryside.
Whenever I go there, I am flooded with the usual
confusing mix of happy memories and profound sadness.
We once lived in an old and pretty house next door,
which has now been extended into a hotel. As I walk
around the churchyard and then the hotel gardens, my
thoughts go back to our time here.

A timber-framed Elizabethan farmhouse, it had a
sweeping gravel drive at the front, which served also as a
car park for the church. I loved going through the front
door into the hall and looking through the mullioned
windows at the back to the garden beyond. This was a
special place, full of roses, intriguing paths between yew
hedges and a paddock where a neighbour kept some
cows. There were even a couple of walnut trees. We all
felt very lucky to be able to call it home, and even though
it is now a hotel, when I walk around it I still think of it

as our home, a place where we felt we belonged. We moved there just after I'd left school and I remember us decorating rooms and working in the garden. This was a place where we enjoyed each other's company and spent, it seems, endless sunny days talking, wandering along shady walks and sitting on the terrace.

It was a time, too, when we were all in good health and enjoying life. My father worked from home and saw much more of my mother than when he'd commuted to his office every day, and although Terence and I were both at university we spent most of the holidays there. We liked to come home to this quiet rural retreat after the busyness of life on campus.

Although the tranquillity was often shattered by passing planes bound for Stansted Airport, and my parents eventually decided to move on because of this, our attachment to the place remained. And that attachment made the pretty churchyard the natural final resting place for my family. All three of my immediate family, parents and brother, died too young.

I haven't yet brought Lydia here but it will be important for her to have this place to come to and think about, and hear stories of the grandparents and uncle she never knew. We will always be able to go to that church and stand by those graves to grieve and celebrate.

There is a myth that the Palestinians were a shiftless people who, long before the foundation of modern Israel in 1948, were happy to sell their lands to Jewish immigrants and move on. The *AA Explorer Guide* states that almost all of Israel had been legitimately purchased by Jewish settlers before the setting up of the state. In fact, by 1948 Jews owned only 1,800 out of a total of more than 26,000 square kilometres.

Although the 1947 UN Partition Plan pledged more than half of the land for a Jewish state, the land was meant to come with the Palestinians who owned it, farmed it and lived on it. Yet by the time the war ended Israel had taken just under 80 per cent of old Palestine and was denying a similar percentage of Palestinians the right to return to their land. This whirlwind of dislocation had taken little more than six months. More than four hundred villages left empty by those refugees would be destroyed by the Israelis.

The new state desperately needed the land and buildings of the Palestinians to house and start feeding the hundreds of thousands of Jewish immigrants. Without the expropriated Palestinian property, the project of absorbing the influx would likely have ground to a halt. The vast majority of new Jewish settlements built in Israel's first decade were established on absentee-owned land. Likewise, a quarter of a million Jewish immigrants were housed in urban areas formerly inhabited by Arabs.

Israel's leadership wanted to legitimize what had been achieved by force, and was determined to have 'legal proof of ownership' of the land it had taken. This would put them in a stronger position, they believed, to resist demands by Palestinians and the UN that refugees should be allowed to return to their land. If the land was now legally in the hands of others, Israel would argue, then there was no reason for the refugees to return. And, on a more profound level, perhaps, to fulfil the Zionist dream of creating a Jewish homeland, it was imperative that as much of the land as possible was 'officially' brought under the ownership of the Jewish people for ever. However tenuous the thinking, all the government believed it had to do to make this happen was to create laws that rubber-stamped the taking of Palestinian land.

I have my usual breakfast at the St Charles Guesthouse. Some days I eat in solitary splendour; on others there are more guests eating eggs and hummus and drinking juice and tea. Some are Christian students, and there are often parties of followers of the Baha'i faith, of which Haifa is a main centre. These groups tend to be multinational, very quiet and polite. Sister Reeta is preoccupied with such a party when I drop off my key and head out towards the Galilee again. Although I am beginning to find my way around, I am still relying heavily on the map that came with my hire car. Its layout of roads and locations hasn't let me down yet. As I travel around I have taken to putting the Europcar map beside a copy of a 1946 vintage British Survey of Palestine map to see what has changed. At first glance it is the similarities that leap out – the main towns and the general lines of main roads. But, on closer inspection, you begin to notice that many smaller places on the old map have either moved slightly and changed their name or simply disappeared.

This morning my destination, the village of Sheikh Danun, is clearly visible on both maps. It is home to

Daoud Badr, a campaigner for the land rights of Palestinians dispossessed by Israel. Suha has arranged for me to meet him. Once out of Haifa I go north a little way, then turn east through the Krayot town of Kiryat Ata to pick up a highway that runs north along the foot of the Galilean hills. It's a fabulously crisp, clear morning and I have the road more or less to myself. On my left there are fields full of crops, and on my right, low hills are dotted with orchards of fruit and olive trees.

Once in Sheikh Danun, my progress is more tentative. Street signs are in a mix of Hebrew and Arabic script, both Greek to me. On my second run up what I think is the right street, I notice a figure waving from a first-floor balcony. I stop the car and wind down the window. 'Daoud Badr?'

'*Ahlan*, welcome!' comes the reply.

As we settle down on Daoud's balcony, which looks out over the village and the rolling Galilee land to the south, I tell him of my visit with Suha to the Haganah archives, commenting on the incredible attention to detail within the records.

'Yes. Their organization was incredible!' says Daoud, with a wry smile. 'In June 1948, within one month of declaring the state, Prime Minister Ben-Gurion had a ministerial committee for all the "abandoned" property and they were setting up emergency laws and regulations.'

Formal legislation, lots of it, with clauses making its tenets retroactive, followed. Most important was the Absentee Property Law of 1950, which allowed the state

143

to confiscate the land and other property of anyone who had abandoned it for whatever reason during the war. It was then taken over by the Custodian of Absentee Property. So the refugees in Lebanon, the West Bank and so on automatically lost their lands, even though most of them had fled simply to escape fighting.

Daoud sweeps back his silver hair from his broad, tanned brow. 'Not only did the Israelis make laws that said the refugees had abandoned their land, the 1952 Law of Nationality said non-Jews could only be citizens if they could prove they had been living *continuously* in Israel since 1948. So the refugees lost their land *and* their right to citizenship – by law. And all the laws were made to work backwards, retrospectively.'

While there was no chance that Palestinians would be allowed to come back to their historic homes and lands in what was now Israel, the Law of Return, passed in July 1950, offered any Jew, anywhere in the world, immediate full Israeli citizenship.

I sit across the table from Daoud, shaking my head. It all sounds so matter-of-fact, so simple and utterly ruthless. The eviction of the native Arab population from the Jewish homeland had been on the Zionist agenda for a long time. But with the recent horrors of genocide during the Holocaust, leaving hundreds of thousands of European Jews displaced and desperate for a new and safe home, the need to secure a homeland became ever more pressing. Although I can understand why such actions might have seemed necessary, it is so sad to me that a dispossessed and persecuted people would act in this way towards the indigenous population.

Making laws to take land and citizenship rights away from refugees on the other side of the border was one thing, but what about the Palestinians within the new state, people like Abu Adnan, 'the baker from Acre'? How did the state 'legally' discriminate against people who were – technically – equal citizens?

'Israel is a good democracy, of course,' intones Daoud, with a very serious face, 'so the laws apply to everyone! Those people who left their homes had abandoned their property. That's the Law of Absentees!' Then his tanned, leonine face cracks as he bursts out laughing. 'But they are present, not absent!'

I can't quite get my head around what he's saying. How can someone be present and absent at the same time?

'Exactly,' says Daoud, still smiling. 'We call it "The Law of the Present Absent" and it makes no sense.'

As well as the restrictions imposed on their movements, the Palestinian citizens of Israel were faced with a surreal manipulation of property law to take away their land. The meaning of 'absentee' in these laws and regulations was very broad. Effectively an 'absentee' was defined as anyone who had vacated their home during the war, regardless of whether they returned. So, even though families like that of Abu Adnan had stayed in Israel, they were deemed to have forfeited their property because they had fled the fighting to another town. They had become refugees within the new state. These 'internally displaced' people, as many as 30,000 in all, were not allowed to return to their homes or use their land.

But Daoud explains that the Israelis were so eager, and still are today, to get legal hold of Palestinian land that they can be flexible over 'presence' and 'absence'. 'If I want to sell my land or give it to the Jewish Israelis, then I am deemed "present" and able legally to make such a decision. Maybe they'll give me a little compensation. But if I want to have my land back, to return to my land, to claim my rights, suddenly the law says I am "absent".'

'But what about Jewish people?' I ask. 'Surely some of them must have run away from their homes during the fighting.'

'Ah, yes, you are right.' Daoud nods again. His soft, fluting voice sounds tired. 'The Israelis needed another rule to cover that one, so they wrote a clause to exempt absentees who left their home because of fear of Israel's enemies. And, of course, those enemies were all Arabs.'

Daoud tells me that the military government, which was running the lives of Israel's Palestinian citizens, was enormously useful in this programme of land confiscation. Once an area had been declared 'closed', the military governor could then transfer land in the security zone that was lying fallow to kibbutzim or other Jewish settlements. 'Of course the land was lying fallow because, although Jewish citizens could move about freely, the Arab owners were not allowed to enter the zone,' says Daoud, the smile finally fading from his face. 'It creates terrible pain, this stupid Law of the Strong. Because they are strong they can make their laws and they take our land.' He swallows hard and shakes his head, 'They take our land from us and give it to the Jews. It is ethnic discrimination.'

We sit in silence for a few moments, and then the peace is shattered as a truck comes up the street with a tannoy wailing from its roof, hawking the mattresses piled high in the back.

'Who was Sheikh Danun?' I ask. 'Does anyone know?'

'Sheikh Danun was an Egyptian who fought with Saladin,' Daoud tells me. 'He died here with his two sons in a battle against the Crusaders. There has been a village on this site for hundreds of years.'

The history of the place goes even deeper. The Israel Antiquities Authority has discovered human burial sites on this hillside dating back more than four thousand years, and there was probably a Canaanite town here in ancient times. No wonder, then, that Daoud looks so at home here. But then he explains that this was not his original village and that, like Abu Adnan, he, too, is one of the 'present absent'.

'Most of today's population of Sheikh Danun are "internal refugees",' he says, looking out into the distance. 'They came here from other villages in the area that were destroyed by the Israelis. Most of the houses were empty because the owners left Danun in 'forty-eight, forced to go to Lebanon. My father was from Sheikh Danun originally, so when we left my home village he said we'd come to his family house here. Of course, the soldiers said we couldn't use it.'

I try to imagine how the situation Daoud describes might have played out in my own country. An enemy force would have taken my house, flattened it and given my land to an immigrant from Sweden (for example). Then I would have managed to rent a house two miles away that belonged to someone else, who was now in a refugee camp in France (for example). I shake my head. It seems utter madness.

Invading armies always take land by force and colonizers always usurp the land of the indigenous population. As this area was meant to be in the new state of Palestine, according to the UN Partition Plan, the Jewish forces had undoubtedly invaded it. And they had used that force, as colonizers, to displace the indigenous Palestinian Arabs and settle Jewish immigrants in their place.

'Where was your first home, Daoud?'

'It is the village of al-Ghabisiyya. Would you like to see it?'

'Yes, indeed – if that's possible.'

I get out my maps to locate the village. On the 1946 British map it is easy to spot – and is extremely close to Sheikh Danun. It doesn't feature on the Europcar map.

The drive to al-Ghabisiyya takes no more than five minutes. Just down the hill to the main road, turn right, half a mile along and then right again. As we go along the main road, Daoud points out the little valley that lies between Sheikh Danun and al-Ghabisiyya. 'That's the River Majnoon.'

'Majnoon?' I repeat, laughing. 'Doesn't that mean crazy?'

'Yes, it does.'

'It sounds like the politics of your life are what's crazy, not the river.'

'The river can become crazy with the winter rain,' replies Daoud, smiling, 'but, yes, the politics are always crazy.'

Off the main road again, a track winds up through a wood to the site of al-Ghabisiyya. The heart of the village sits on a wide flat area of land on the crest of the hill. Daoud shows me around the streets he played in as a boy. Except there are no streets: the whole place was demolished by the Israeli Army. The village centre has been planted over with well-spaced cypress trees that soften the bright sunlight. The atmosphere would be serene but for the mosque. It is the only building still standing but is in an advanced state of decay. An iron fence, eight feet high, erected by the Israeli police, prevents any access to it. There is no other sign of former habitation.

'My house was just over there behind that big tree,' Daoud says, 'and my father was building us a new house on a plot of land just over there. He started the work in early 'forty-eight. It was never finished.' He waves his hand to the other side of the area. 'That's where the olive press was. When I half close my eyes I can remember it. There were three shops, two butchers, and there was a large oven for baking bread ... We were self-sufficient. We had all the food we needed. There were many trees, olives, apples, grapes, and we had plenty of animals and a lot of land – around twelve thousand dunams [three thousand acres].'

Even when one allows for a little rose-tinting brought on by time and loss, the pre-'48 al-Ghabisiyya was clearly a prosperous place. The farmers would hire trucks to take their vegetables to the markets in Haifa and Acre, and the mosque in the village meant that when people from the surrounding villages came to pray they would also shop.

In May 1948 the village *mukthar* had traded information with the Jewish forces to save the village from attack. However, the Israeli Army did attack and thirteen civilians were killed.

'Very early one morning, my mother woke me up, took me outside the house and told me to sit while she gathered some clothes together. I had no idea what was going on – I was just six years old at the time. Even though I was so young, inside I knew something had changed. Now I know what it was. We had become refugees. We became refugees because we were afraid that we would be killed. This is why people ran away.'

Daoud's father wanted to get them to safety in Lebanon but his mother refused to move. The father decided to stay but sent the older boys to Lebanon. 'He thought we would all be killed if we stayed – so he sent the others away.'

In late 1948 and early 1949, as peace returned so did around half of the population of al-Ghabisiyya, eager to resume their quiet village life and get back to tending their fields and orchards. 'I still have a letter from an official, dated 6 June 1949, to my father at our address in al-Ghabisiyya,' Daoud explains. There was no immediate move by the authorities to expel them, yet fear of the new Jewish rulers was never far off. 'One day I was with my oldest brother at our vegetable garden near the village, tending our two cows. A Jewish man came by and wanted to know what we were doing. He spoke good Arabic. My brother said we were just working on our land. The man then said he'd come back in an hour. "If you are still here," he said, "I will shoot you." So we just ran away. In this period people were killed by Jews, and nothing was done about it.'

A light breeze chases through the cypress trees, taking the edge off the midday heat. It is a very peaceful spot. The villagers must have dreaded losing this home again, yet within a year they were moved.

'The soldiers came again in 1950. I remember everybody left here without any talking. Everyone was very afraid.'

While the priority of the new state's leadership was to ensure that the Palestinian refugees could not return and that Jewish immigrants could be taken in, there were Jewish voices, including leading political figures, who called for a return of Arab refugees and an end to the expropriation of Palestinian land and property. Although those voices were not loud enough then, and have never been loud enough, perhaps, it is an important part of Israel's story that there has been a consistent opposition within the Jewish Israeli community to discrimination against Palestinians within and without the state and the abuse of their civil and property rights. For one thing the courts were always there and citizens could challenge the government's laws in them.

'We went to the High Court. We had a Jewish lawyer working for us,' explains Daoud, 'and on the thirtieth of November 1951 we were given the right to return to the village. A week later we all came back. But the military police were waiting and prevented us returning – it had been declared a closed military zone.'

Though the new 'democratic' state would let them fight their case in the courts, the villagers were doomed to lose. They might win one battle and then the government would change the rules. 'They always find a solution for such things,' says Daoud, with a wry smile. 'The message is always the same, that there is no place for the return of the Palestinians. For the Falasha from Ethiopia, yes, for Jews from anywhere, yes, but for the Palestinians who have always lived here, no.'

Further legislation was brought in to ensure that Arab land could be put a step further away from its original owners, and allow the holding authority, the Custodian of Absentee Property, to sell land on to certain institutions, primarily the Israel Development Authority and the Jewish National Fund (JNF).

Under the Basic Law: Israel Lands, 1960, expropriated land is held by the state of Israel and the JNF as the inalienable property of the Jewish people. Eventually 93 per cent of Israel would be state-owned, with as much as 70 per cent of that land having been confiscated from Arab owners.

Within a few months of the villagers' second expulsion

from al-Ghabisiyya, Jewish immigrants from Iraq and Iran were brought in to settle on all the village land. Each immigrant family was given twenty dunams (five acres). Daoud pauses and looks away from me, out into the light woodland around us. Standing erect, his sports jacket buttoned over a checked shirt, he is an elegant man, not just in his physical bearing but also in his manner of speech. 'The Jews take our land and then we have to pay them to rent other fields. If I am from al-Ghabisiyya they will rent me land from another village but not from my own.'

The land, not just owning it and belonging to it, was vital to the Palestinian community in the 1950s and 1960s. Arab society was still predominantly agricultural, even though so much of the best land had been expropriated. Not only did they have to make do with poorer land, they also faced routine discrimination in all areas of farming life.

Grants to buy machinery or improve land were almost impossible for Palestinian citizens to secure, and they were paid far less for their crops than their Jewish neighbours. Daoud manages to smile at the outrage of this. I find his sense of humour quite remarkable. To be able to look at something and appreciate the humour in the grotesque is very moving. It makes his story all the more potent to me.

'Life in the fifties was very hard. It was like a siege. People worked very long and hard for very small salaries. When we wanted to go out of the village we had to get written permission from the military commander.' Just trying for that permission could find you contravening the regulations. The precise frontiers of the military government areas and the closed areas were known to no one in the country except the staff of the military government. To find out where they could and couldn't go the Palestinians had to visit either a police station, which wasn't likely to have the correct information, or an office of the military government. These offices were few and far between. So you might cross entirely innocently into a prohibited area – even while you were trying to find out where such areas were. Basically, no rural Palestinian citizen could move far: 93 out of 104 Palestinian villages in Israel were constituted as closed areas out of which no one could move without a military permit.

The psychological strain of being denied the freedom to move around your own land must have been appalling. Any loss of freedom is, of course, anathema to the human spirit. Being confined in small, often subterranean cells in Lebanon took me, at times, to the brink of breakdown. Yet for all the dehumanizing effects of the conditions we were held in, and though some of the hostage-takers abused us brutally, for the most part they did not want to break us; they just wanted us to be passive and patient. And while there was no physical escape, there was always 'home' to run to mentally. For the Palestinians under military rule there was no hiding place: their home had been taken over by forces determined to destroy them. It was a life in an eerie world where you were constantly being played for

a fool by a power at once meticulous and casual.
You asked the officer, 'Can I go across the road?'
'Yes.'
You walked across the road and were arrested. 'But
you said I could cross the road!'
'You can cross the road – on Mondays, Wednesdays
and Fridays. Today is Tuesday.'

For all that Daoud's sense of humour survived, the
Military Period was a time of general depression for the
Palestinians in Israel. 'There was a lot of silence in our
house,' Daoud explains, gazing intently at me. 'As a kid I
hated that atmosphere. I wanted to be happy. My father
was fifty-nine years old when Israel came into being. He
was a very quiet and serious man. He never expressed
himself; the pain was inside. And my mother was very
depressed. She was always talking of her other children,
my brothers and sisters, who fled to Lebanon. In the
fifties and sixties she used to cry a lot.'

For many Arabs, survival was the best that could be
hoped for during that time. In order to survive they had
to be subservient to the Jewish population, so the idea
that the new rulers must be superior became widely held.
'My older brother and sister felt that our family was
broken and that our world had been destroyed.
Inevitably I began to share these feelings and, like many
others, I started to see the Jewish people as they saw
themselves, that they were better than us. To survive, to
eat, we needed to work the land and now it belonged
to the Jews.'

Public holidays were based on the Jewish calendar and on Israel's anniversaries. On state holidays there was, of course, music and celebration, but for Palestinian children like Daoud this was another distressing experience: 'For me it was often painful. These were Jewish celebrations, and I felt a stranger in the land because such things were not part of me.'

Then, in 1956, all the houses in al-Ghabisiyya were destroyed, blown up and bulldozed, replaced with the cypress trees that now bend in the light breeze. 'To lose your land, your house, your country – it's more painful even than losing a relative because you feel like you've lost yourself. They are killing your hope, that is what they are doing, and trying to kill your memory.' Daoud pauses for a moment and turns, as if trying to hear something. There is nothing, apart from the sound of the wind in the trees. Then he smiles at me. 'That's funny – suddenly I was remembering waking early in our house to the sound of the cocks crowing.'

The Israeli aim to destroy memories has failed, but it seems the establishment still wants to obliterate any lingering connection with the village site. 'The old people used to come here all the time to remember what it was like and to attend the mosque.' Now even the mosque is inaccessible, gradually decaying behind the metal fence, and the old village lands are farmed by the inhabitants of the Jewish settlement of Netiv ha-Shayyara. On a flat strip of land near the main road, and just two hundred yards from the old village cemetery, billboards in Hebrew declare that a new cemetery, for the Jewish population, will be built here. The ancient Jewish cemetery at the coastal city of Nahariya is overflowing and, regardless of the protests of the Arabs who claim ownership, al-Ghabisiyya land has been designated as the city's new burial place. In what has to be one of the maddest pieces of local politics on the planet, the site of the old village, in peaceful farmland in the middle of the country, is still decreed a military zone. Because of this the former inhabitants are not allowed to maintain the graves of their forebears and al-Ghabisiyya's cemetery has long gone to rack and ruin. The villagers cannot come here and think quietly of generations and times past.

Daoud's generation had to cope with being separated from their living relatives too. One of his sisters and two brothers went to Lebanon in 1948 and were not allowed to come back. Throughout the Military Period there was no communication between the siblings. They didn't speak or meet for decades. 'I've only seen them twice in sixty years. In the early nineties I managed to get special permission for one brother and one sister to come here for a visit. The second time I saw them was on the twenty-fifth of May 2000, when Israel withdrew from southern Lebanon.

'For just one day we could all get to the fence on the border. There were thousands of people on both sides. I was pressed right up to the wire and was able to kiss my brother through the fence. I was very confused, very happy to see them, my brother and sister – my family! But at the same time there was a lot of pain. We couldn't

157

talk – the soldiers were around us, pushing us. It was a very weird meeting, touching each other, seeing each other through a fence. Human beings must be free. We must sit with each other and talk. That was the last time I saw them.'

The track winds down from the old mosque at the top of the hill, through the derelict cemetery and then across the flat land to the main road. Just as it hits the level ground there is a huge old tree to the right. 'That is a *sidr* tree,' Daoud explains. 'They used to hold weddings there. Girls would dance under the tree, and in the open land between here and the road, men would race on their horses. For hundreds of years this tree belonged to the village. People used to tie green cloths to the branches, for good luck. It was part of the village. It had grown up with the village.'

The tree has a broader significance in Islamic tradition since the Prophet Muhammad is said to have seen a *sidr* tree in Paradise. Such trees are also believed to be inhabited by the spirits of sheikhs and imams; dressing the branches in green is said to help cure ill health and ward off other problems.

The tree has meaning in Christian folklore too: it is, or is a close relation of, *Ziziphus spina-christi*, the tree from which Christ's crown of thorns is believed to have come. The smaller shrub *Ziziphus lotus*, encountered by Odysseus and his crew when they came to the land of the lotus-eaters, is of the same genus. Homer writes that its fruit, as sweet as honey, made any man who sampled it lose the desire ever to journey home.

Daoud, and many like him, have not been tempted to eat that fruit. Their yearning to return to their homes remains undimmed and their determination to achieve it has grown, rather than withered, with time. 'We couldn't continue to live the way we were then, so gradually we started fighting back. In the beginning it was a surprise to realize that we were equal to, not less than, the Jews. Slowly we've come to understand the Israelis more and more. We know them better, so we are stronger.'

10

New Maps for the New State

THE FIRST TIME MY FATHER SPOKE TO ME ABOUT Palestine was as we sifted through a box of old, well-worn maps. Most had been produced by the Ordnance Survey of Great Britain, with their rather drab buff and orange covers. There was something so familiar, solid and decent about them, but they were still magical. Having mastered basic map-reading, you could 'read' the landscape, see the lie of the land. In those pre-Google Earth days, you created a mental image of a place. Yet for all the detail, of roads and rivers, forests and villages, you could only get so close. Place names caught your eye and started you wondering. Who lives there? What are their lives like? What stories do they have to tell of the old times?

My father had picked up other maps on business travels around Europe. Leafing through them as a boy, I was mesmerized by their foreignness. They came in all shapes and sizes: small, glossy town guides, for Basle or Cologne;

thicker, stiffer country guides for Holland, Italy and the places he visited beyond the Iron Curtain. A map of Czechoslovakia was covered with dark red card and heavy black lettering. I remember opening it, heart in mouth, fearful that the chill hand of the Cold War menace might reach out and take me into that forsaken territory.

But there was one map that was simultaneously very foreign and very familiar to me. It was of Palestine. I struggled with exotic place names such as Kharrubá, Nisf Jubeil and Meithalun, but others, like Nazareth, Jericho and Jerusalem, flowed as smoothly as Pimlico or Potters Bar. On the one hand the map read with the easy familiarity of a school Bible lesson; on the other, it showed somewhere utterly alien. I was fascinated. Sadly, it has long since disappeared. It was probably an army-issue 1946 British Survey of Palestine map – like the one I'm using now.

The importance of maps lies not just in helping us navigate unfamiliar places. They also act as the official, truthful record of a place – they show what exists and what doesn't. They represent the 'facts on the ground' of geography and political control.

'Creating facts on the ground' is a phrase often used in relation to the Israel–Palestine conflict. It refers not only to the seizing of physical control of the landscape but also to the changing of historical and social perspectives. Nowadays the phrase is most often used with regard to the illegal Israeli settlements in the occupied Palestinian territory of the West Bank. Despite international con-demnation the Israeli government continues to build these settlements. The intention is that they will come to represent such enormous 'facts on the ground' that they will be accepted by the international community, though not the Palestinians, of course, as being the logical framework for any eventual boundary agreement between the two sides.

The idea of creating facts on the ground goes right back through Zionist thinking; promoting the myth of Palestine as a people-less desert can be seen as part of that continuum. It wasn't surprising that in the early years of modern Israel, a process began whereby the physical usurpation of the Arab landscape was consolidated by cultural and semantic usurpation: evidence of Palestine was steadily erased. With their determination to create a Jewish reality where once the Arabs had predominated, the Jewish leadership of the new state was determined to establish as many 'facts on the ground' as possible.

In July 1949 a government committee, which included archaeologists and biblical scholars, those men I'd heard about, surveying 'with Bible in one hand and machine-gun in the other', was set up to oversee the Judaization of the map of the Negev (Naqab in Arabic). In early 1951, following the enactment of the Absentee Laws in 1950, another committee was established, briefed with carrying out the same process for the map of all the Holy Land.

Any sites that were, or could be seen to be, close to Jewish biblical locations were given those names. Not all names could be changed, especially those of the smaller towns or villages whose Arab people had not moved. But wherever possible Arab names would be modified to something in Hebrew that sounded similar, or the Arab name – for a hill, perhaps – would simply be translated into Hebrew. The Jewish homeland was to be owned by and for the Jewish people, and the new map would reinforce that.

Comparing my 1946 British map with the modern Europcar one, I can see that the Zionist project was a success. In 1946 the village of al-Ghabisiyya, for example, was clearly shown, as were the nearby villages of al-Nahr, al-Tall and Kuwaykat. None features on the modern map since, like al-Ghabisiyya, they were destroyed by the Israelis. Some old Arab names, like Kabri and Amqa, can be found on the Europcar map, but on inspection, these are now Jewish settlements that have taken the name as well as the lands of the Palestinian villages which were depopulated and destroyed. Careful reading of the landscape, though, as well as the map, can reveal the other side of the story. It's about looking for evidence of absence as well as of presence, about watching for signs of where those destroyed villages might have been.

The Galilean landscape has entranced me. Roads wind across hillsides and through valleys, past small villages and towns. Fields of vegetables sit beside orchards and, as the terrain becomes steeper, there are olive groves and then woodland. As I've noted before, the frequent brown tourist-board notices along the roadsides point out sites that are nearly always to do with Jewish history.

It is left to natural signs to draw attention to Arab sites of historical interest. A clump of ugly cactus, looking out of place on a hillside, is likely to indicate the location of a destroyed Arab village. In the old days, Palestinians planted cacti to create simple, low-maintenance and very effective fences. The Israelis may have destroyed and levelled villages, but the cactus is so hardy that it keeps coming back to give the lie to the landscaping.

Israel's great stretches of woodland also have a story to tell. Some is old forest but much has been planted since 1948, mainly under the guidance of the JNF, which promotes and raises money worldwide for this activity. They portray it as an important ecological project, creating a fabulous green lung for the nation. While the ecological benefits are valid, JNF fundraising literature doesn't mention that many of the new forests and attendant picnic sites are planted over Palestinian villages. I'm learning to watch out for stands of new woodland – eucalyptus on the coastal plain, European pines in the hills, cypress, too, as I've seen at al-Ghabisiyya. Very often a quick comparison between a modern road map and my old British one reveals that the green lung actually represents a suffocation of the indigenous landscape.

I uncover a similar dual story with regard to Israel's national parks. These areas reflect the nation's desire to set aside space for recreation and reflection. They also preserve areas of wilderness and natural beauty, and maintain locations and buildings of historical importance. They are one of the ways in which the nation presents itself to the world with pride. When I pull up in the car park of Bar'am National Park on a sunlit afternoon, the place is almost deserted. A sign tells me that the park contains the remains of a third-century synagogue – one of the oldest in Israel. A Jewish community lived here until some point before the thirteenth century CE. The sign makes no mention of a Christian Arab community having been here too.

Standing by the ancient columns and archways of the old synagogue, I consult my *AA Explorer Guide*. When describing the history of Bar'am (Kafr Bir'im in Arabic), it says that 'In late 1948, Israeli forces, fighting desperately against invading Arab armies, arrived at the Christian Arab village of Bar'am ... The Israelis were welcomed and, to assist the soldiers, the villagers agreed to leave for an estimated period of two weeks ...'

It is true that the Israeli forces were fighting Arab armies and that the villagers agreed to leave. What the guide doesn't mention is that it was not the Arabs who were invading but the Israelis. According to the UN Partition Plan, the village of Kafr Bir'im was in Palestine. In November 1948, the village was taken by Israeli troops and the eight hundred or so inhabitants 'agreed to leave' only at gunpoint and with the guarantee that they would be allowed to return.

The people of Kafr Bir'im were aware that Palestinians who had fled north to Lebanon or east to Syria earlier in 1948 were not allowed back into Israel. So, most of the villagers remained in what was now Israel, moving to the nearby town of Jish. Now clearly dominant, the Israeli Army had lost some of its zest for driving civilians across the border. That the villagers were Christian might also have worked in their favour: Christian communities tended to be treated less harshly than predominantly Muslim ones.

The villagers might have been allowed to remain in Israel, but the agreement to let them return to the village was never honoured. In 1949, less than a year after the villagers had been driven out, a Jewish settlement, Kibbutz Bar'am, was established and given some of the village lands. In 1953, the Israeli military blew up the empty Arab houses and expropriated more than two thousand acres of village land, dashing any hopes that the villagers might ever return. But the village church was left standing and is used by the descendants of those refugees today. The sad remains of their houses are still there too.

The church sits right on top of a hill. It's a simple stone structure with a small belfry topped with a plain cross. An external stone staircase leads up to the flat roof, from which, at almost 2,500 feet, there are views over the wooded hillsides south into the Galilee and north into Lebanon.

As soon as I walk down from the church, I am among the old village passageways. Wandering along grass-overgrown tracks, I come across crumbling stone doorways and imagine the place buzzing with human life. Now only birds flit between the old walls. Walking up one narrow lane, I turn into the shell of an old house and find myself in a room dappled with green light. The walls still rise to full height but the only roof is formed by the branches and leaves of a tree. My heart skips a beat: there is a carpet on the floor. I feel rather spooked. Then I remember that Suha told me the old villagers come here every year and camp for a while, telling stories of life before Kafr Bir'im's destruction. They must have left the carpet behind.

Returning to my car, I'm struck by the fact that the only information sign in the park is at the synagogue. These modern ruins are not explained.

'I will check, John,' Sister Reeta says, calmly and firmly.

My washing has disappeared. I sent it to the local laundry recommended by my kindly hostess a few days ago and it has not been returned. I'm running low on fresh clothes.

Sister Reeta takes up the phone and is soon talking nineteen to the dozen in Hebrew. For all that her face, neatly encased in its wimple, remains as placid as ever, I get the feeling that the person at the other end of the line is saying something like, 'Yes, Sister. Certainly, Sister. We'll be there immediately, Sister.'

Sure enough, when she puts the phone down, she nods. 'It will be here within one hour, John.'

'Thank you very much, Sister.'

Relieved, I go back upstairs to the dining room. Two groups are already eating. We nod. After a little eaves-dropping I discover that one group is a family on holiday from France, touring the holy sites, and the other group are Baha'i pilgrims from Spain.

Just as I'm finishing a cup of tea my mobile rings.

'Hi, John,' says Suha. 'You are invited to a wedding!'

'*Mabrouk!*' I reply. 'Who is the lucky man?'

'Not my wedding!' Suha roars with laughter. 'No, it's the Bedouin family from Lod. Saud just phoned. His brother's getting married and they'd like us to go. But I can't. Do you want to? Can you find your way to Lod okay?'

'Yes and yes!' I reply. 'That'll be great. When's the wedding – and can you help me get a present?'

'The wedding is this evening. Pick me up in thirty minutes and we'll go to the mall.'

Two hours later I'm back at the St Charles Guesthouse, carrying a huge bag containing a vast candle.

'It will be a very good present,' Suha had advised.

Another large bag is sitting on the reception desk. 'Your laundry, John,' says Sister Reeta, smiling broadly.

My freshly laundered shirt has wilted slightly by the time I get to Lod, but my spirits are lifted as I head away from the main road and towards the Azbarga home. It's a year since my first visit but I recognize the area of industrial parks that lies between the highway and their neighbourhood. Following a one-way street around a vast space of derelict and parched earth, I realize I'm almost there. I turn right and then left to see a mass of parked cars.

On the way down from Haifa I'd been worrying that the Azbargas' small home would no longer be there, but while there are still piles of concrete everywhere, Saud and Rania's house is still standing. This brings a wave of relief.

In the shade of a huge tent erected for the wedding, I find Saud and his brother, Moadi, who greet me warmly. They tell me the latest news about their battle with the local council and the demolition orders the community has been living under. It turns out that not only has Saud's house been left standing, but that the demolition orders have been withdrawn at present and they are going to be allowed to stay. Tentatively, I wonder if this news is as good as it sounds.

'It's not that simple,' says Moadi, with Saud translating for me. 'Although many of the people have been granted the right to live here and given a licence to build new homes, the plot size for each family is so small that they won't really work.'

'So, more battles ahead,' I say.

The brothers nod. I can see that they are weary. The news isn't exactly bad but the future remains uncertain. But at least the threat of imminent eviction is not hanging over the lively family celebration. Saud's older brother Muhammad is the one being married and looks pretty happy about it, dressed in a smart dark suit.

Annis, Saud's little boy, runs up and jumps into his dad's arms, looking at me shyly. People come and go, paying their respects, drinking tea or coffee. 'Family are coming from all over Israel,' Saud explains, as Annis pulls at his ears. 'We Bedouin have big families so they are coming from the north and from the Negev in the south as well as the centre, around here.'

169

One old gentleman, wearing the traditional black and white checked *keffiyeh*, is pushed over the earth floor of the tent in his wheelchair. He snorts when he hears I am British. 'Damn British! Many of my father's generation served in the British Army – fat lot of good that did us when you decided to leave!'

'Yes, yes, I know,' I say, shaking my head.

Saud slaps me on the back, laughing. 'Come, John, you must say hello to Rania.'

The women have a tent of their own on the far side of Saud's house – in the street where Moadi's home once stood. Dusk is falling and the street is lit with garish neon light. There is music and women are dancing with each other, occasionally breaking into ululation. The bride is wearing a billowing white dress, gold bracelets and necklaces. Heavily made-up, her hair decorated with white beads, she looks fantastic. Sitting like a queen on a raised sofa, with a richly coloured Bedouin carpet on the wall behind her, she nods regally at the well-wishers gathered around her.

Rania comes up. 'Hi!' Her two daughters, Jenna and Nowa, are with her, eyes shining as they skip up and down with excitement.

'I'm so glad your house is safe,' I say.

'We hope so,' Rania replies, a shadow crossing her face. 'Nothing is a hundred per cent.'

Back in the men's area I realize I'm still carting the monster candle and am quite relieved to hand it over to Saud. By now every square inch of car parking space is taken and the area outside the tent is filled with men and boys sitting at small tables. Youths wander around look-ing for friends. Then a truck appears. The doors open and a chain of men begins unloading hundreds of ready-cooked meals – traditional fare of lamb stew, rice and bread. Quiet descends as everyone tucks in.

After the meal I say my farewells. Saud escorts me to the car, loading me down with Arabic cakes, 'in case you get hungry on the road'.

'Thank you,' I say, 'and thanks so much for having me. It was great to be here.'

'Come again,' he replies, shaking my hand firmly. 'You are always welcome.'

11

Here We Will Stay

Here we shall stay,
sing our songs,
take to the angry streets,
fill prisons with dignity.

In Lidda, in Ramla, in the Galilee,
we shall remain,
guard the shade of the fig
and olive trees,
ferment rebellion in our children
as yeast in the dough.

Tawfik Ziad

THERE ARE SOME ARAB PHRASES THAT REALLY SEEM TO sing, that have a sound that echoes their meaning. Two favourites of mine are *mish maoul*, 'incredible', and *mish momkin*, 'impossible'. But I've learned another while exploring the history of the Palestinians in Israel: *farok tassod*, 'divide and rule'.

Farok tassod was an important element of British control in Palestine. It was used against the Arabs, the Jews and between the two communities. After 1948 the Israeli leadership acted to keep *farok tassod* alive and kicking, trying to divide the Palestinian community by encouraging collaboration with the new government.

Opportunities for employment and 'getting on' in life were extremely limited for Palestinians in the Jewish state. The temptation to win favour by passing on information or promoting government ideas would undoubtedly have been attractive to some. The presence of such collaborators eroded the Palestinian community: people became wary of speaking out against the system – even of speaking to their neighbours. Not only were they fearful of Israelis but they had to be wary of their own community too. To have promoted any idea of a Palestinian national identity would have been extremely dangerous when singing a Palestinian song at a wedding was reported to the authorities.

But the newly formed state of Israel was a complex and confusing place. It was a police state, as paranoid and ruthless as any other, but it also functioned as a genuine democracy. So, even though the Palestinians lived under martial law for nearly twenty years and any expression of their national identity was suppressed, they had the vote. Indeed, a handful of Arab representatives sat in the Knesset, the Israeli parliament, from its very first session.

With most of the former Palestinian political élite in exile, the Israeli Communist Party, comprising both Jews and Arabs, was the only organization actively working for the Arab community during Israel's first decade. The Communists, the only legal non-Zionist political party, called for the right of return for all refugees, the establishment of a Palestinian state in line with the UN Partition Plan and fought for the rights of Palestinians within Israel. It was Communist Members of the Knesset (MKs) who lobbied for the lifting of the news blackout over the Kafr Qassem massacre, for instance.

In the state's early years, there were also parties holding Knesset seats that were made up exclusively of Palestinian citizens. But these groups, with names like the Democratic List of Nazareth, Progress and Development, Agriculture and Development, Co-operation and Brotherhood, were not the vanguard of a Palestinian national movement. They were merely ciphers of David Ben-Gurion's ruling, and fervently Zionist, Mapai Party.

Perhaps in the belief that it was the best way to help their communities, or maybe just out of self-interest, some Arab politicians accepted Mapai's financial backing and help in promoting their election campaigns. But this came at a price. While Ben-Gurion claimed that he wanted Arabs to be involved in the running of the state, the reality was that these affiliated parties would act as a fig leaf to the continued erosion of the Palestinian position in Israel. Astonishingly, these parties routinely supported the imposition of military rule over their fellow Arabs, right up to 1966.

The cynicism of Ben-Gurion's and Mapai's claims that they valued the inclusion of the Arab constituency in Israel's new democracy is shown in the way they used fear of the military governors to coerce Arab voters. A few days before a general election, a meeting would be held in the village hall, attended by the heads of the local clans. A representative of the military governor would tell everyone that the government had decided who the inhabitants should vote for, usually one of the Arab parties connected with the Mapai. The voting was then observed by a supervisor appointed by the military governor to ensure that everyone did as they had been told and was 'loyal to the state'. As the military governors controlled every aspect of the villagers' lives – including essential matters like where they could live, go, what work or business they did, and the granting of loans – there was an enormous motivation to be 'loyal'.

The Zionist project has been remarkably successful in creating a homeland for the Jewish people. But the mirror of this creative urge has been a destructive one – denying and destroying the home of the Palestinians.

With their policies of land confiscation and of changing names on maps, Ben-Gurion and his followers, from the 1950s until the present day, have striven to 'disappear' the Palestinian people and the idea of Palestine.

Suha told me that she had never heard the word 'Palestine' until she was twelve years old. That was in the late 1970s and the word's disappearance from public usage was deliberate and enforced by government censors during the Military Period. In that time publications in Arabic, whether newspapers or books, were few and everything had to go through the censors' offices. In most cases content that talked about Palestine and the subject of homeland was forbidden. When Mahmoud Darwish, the best-known Palestinian poet, submitted his poem 'A Lover from Palestine' to the Israeli censor, the word 'Palestine' was crossed out and replaced with '*Eretz Israel*' (Land of Israel).

It was very important for leaders like Ben-Gurion not to let the *idea* of a Palestinian people be accepted. To recognize the concept of Palestine would undermine the Jewish people's right to be there; if there was a Palestine and Palestinians, then the Israelis were invaders. From the Declaration of Independence in May 1948, the Israeli authorities started to use terms like 'Arabs of Israel', 'Arab Israelis', 'Israeli Arabs', 'Arab population of Israel', 'Arab inhabitants' or the 'Arab sector'. The non-Jews in Palestine were thus defined with the general term 'Arabs', not recognized as an indigenous people of the land.

The state continues to use these terms but in more recent times a growing numbers of 'Arab Israelis' have felt confident enough to refer to themselves as 'Palestinian citizens of Israel'.

Given the terrible experiences that occurred during the Military Period, especially the massacre at Kafr Qassem, I am amazed that the Palestinians in Israel managed to hold on to any sense of their national identity, let alone begin rebuilding it. To find out how they began this process of fighting back, I go to meet Muhammad Mi'ari, a veteran Palestinian national leader, politician and human-rights lawyer. Suha has said he will be able to guide me through much complicated history, and has arranged for me to go to his home in the Wadi Gemil district, on the slope of Haifa's western escarpment beside the Mediterranean.

The living room where we meet is furnished with elegant, ornate wooden furniture and lined with bookshelves. Muhammad, who is nearing seventy, has seen up close most of the political developments of the Palestinian people in Israel, from witnessing his father's role as a fighter in the brave but doomed efforts to prevent the disintegration and destruction of the old Palestinian society, to the dark years of military oppression and the rebirth of a belief in a Palestinian identity and development of a political culture.

Muhammad was nine years old in June 1948 when Israeli troops drove out all the inhabitants of his village. Like so many families, the Mi'aris spent the next few months living rough in the Galilean countryside. His father was often away, fighting against the Jewish military.

After a year of wandering, the family found a permanent base at the villages of Judeida and Makr. Having left their village during the conflict but remaining in what had become Israel, they were refused permission to return to their homes, and classified as 'present absentees'. Like Abu Adnan in Acre, Daoud Badr in Sheikh Danun and tens of thousands of others, they had lost everything.

While the Mi'ari household was full of debate about

the Palestinians and the Jews, most families were discouraged from political activity. The demands of merely surviving and staying out of trouble with the military meant that most families kept their heads down. But, as Muhammad tells me, the killing of the forty-nine innocent civilians at Kafr Qassem in 1956 worked to provoke rather than contain Palestinian feelings.

'We must not underestimate the importance of the massacre at Kafr Qassem,' he says, leaning forward, elbows resting on the arms of his chair. 'Until this event, the Arabs were still in shock from what had happened to them in 1948, the loss of land and people and so on. But after the massacre and the 1956 war with Egypt, some people began to try to organize themselves, to express the feeling that we belong to another nation and that we have a case to defend.'

Muhammad pauses, chuckles and lights a cigarette as he looks out over the sea. I find myself warming to him: he doesn't have the gloss or the *froideur* that often afflicts the 'elder statesman'. He continues his story.

'When I was still at school in Kafr Yasif, where the Communist Party was very active, I began to develop an interest in politics. Then at university I got involved with the Arab Students Union. I was impressed with President Nasser of Egypt and his ideas of pan-Arab nationalism. This put me into conflict all the time with the Communists around me.'

The pan-Arab ideology of a union, or at least close co-operation and solidarity between Arabs, rejected Communism for being universal and incompatible with

Arab traditions. 'But sometimes we worked together. On May Day 1958 there was a demonstration in Nazareth. The Communists went and so did members of the Arab nationalist group. There was a clash with the police and many people were wounded. Around two hundred were arrested.'

Bruised bodies and shared cells encouraged the two groups, a month after the demonstration in Nazareth, to create an organization called the Arab Popular Front and to attempt to have it formally registered. The Israeli authorities refused, saying it was a racial organization. So the word 'Arab' was dropped and the Popular Front came into being.

Thus, a decade after the Nakba, still facing land confiscations and living under the oppression of military rule, the Palestinians in Israel began to fight for their rights as a people. Yet this solidarity of purpose didn't last. After only six months the Popular Front split into two, with the Communists going their way and the nationalists, including Muhammad, establishing al-Ard (the Land) in late 1959.

'Our challenge to Israel's legitimacy was very direct,' Muhammad explains. 'We demanded a solution for the Palestinian people based on the UN plan for division from 'forty-seven, and a right of return for refugees. Al-Ard stated that the Arabs in Israel were part of the Palestinian people and belonged to the Arab nation. We called on Israel to shun all relations with the imperialist powers and be part of the Middle East under the control of the Arab national liberation movement led by Nasser.'

'They must have loved you,' I say, laughing. 'Talk about waving a red rag at a bull.'

Muhammad rolls his eyes and spreads his hands wide. 'Sure, we became a target for Shin Bet [Israel's internal security service]. Although at university we were *taught* that Israel was a democracy, outside the lecture hall we knew we were living under military rule and that they would not allow us to organize. But then we had an idea. We could publish books and papers if we registered ourselves as a company.'

The first application was turned down, but after the leaders had taken the case to court, the company was deemed legitimate as long as it did nothing to harm state security. Shares in the al-Ard Company were issued so that, rather than joining a political organization, interested people became shareholders.

Forbidden to publish a regular newspaper, the organizers discovered a legal loophole that allowed each shareholder to issue one paper or report. One week someone published a paper titled 'The Call of the Land' and another week someone else published 'The Light of the Land' and so on. 'We managed to put out twelve or thirteen publications in this way,' Muhammad tells me, animated. 'We wrote about Palestinian issues and problems, about the Israeli police shooting people in demonstrations, about transport. We wrote about land confiscation, about education, and we supported the political movements of the Arabs and Nasserists. We issued about five thousand copies a week. People paid for it and we think it was passed from one hand to another, so its readership was quite wide.'

Smiling, Muhammad spreads his hands apart again, then clasps them together, clamping his lips tight shut.

'But then, early in 1960, the authorities said there was a conspiracy to issue a paper without permission. Some of us were taken to court. Five of us were put in prison for six months.'

While there were individuals around who had been active in politics before the end of the British Mandate, the vast majority of the Palestinian intellectual and political leadership had fled in 1948. So Muhammad and his colleagues were building an independent nationalist movement from scratch – an enormous, as well as dangerous, task. As I sit looking at him in his elegant living room, I try to imagine this dapper figure, in neat grey slacks and sports jacket, as a young man being taken from court and thrown into gaol, a political prisoner in a supposed democracy. Though young he was no naïve, impetuous activist, but someone very well aware of the hardship he was courting. Even at just twenty-one years of age Muhammad, like others in the group, was undeterred.

Through the terrace doors there are wide views over the Mediterranean, which sparkles on this bright summer's morning. I am filled with respect for Muhammad and his colleagues. Having experienced dark prison cells myself, I am not sure at all that I would sacrifice my liberty by taking on such a powerful and determined establishment. I ask him what happened after he was released.

'It was a very difficult but also very interesting time,' he says, nodding and laughing lightly. 'You know, we had to go to the military governor every month to get permission to go to the Hebrew University in Jerusalem. Sometimes students weren't allowed to go to their own home, so a university friend might have to come and stay with me at my house and then his family would visit him there.'

The students' activities were monitored, and participation in a demonstration in Jerusalem in the early sixties would often lead to a summons to the military governor's office back in Kafr Yasif. It was a game of cat and mouse in which the authorities wanted to control the activists and thwart their plans, and the young Palestinians were trying to hoodwink the system so they could continue meeting and spreading their ideas.

'We felt that we were making a revolution.' Muhammad leans forward, his urbanity slipping a little to reveal the passion that had driven him and his colleagues. 'Many people were eager to hear from the movement. We would arrange talks about Palestinian history and so on to encourage the people to think of themselves as part of the Palestinian nation and to value their own culture. We were not treated like heroes exactly, but we were respected as people who were serving the Palestinian cause.'

In 1964 the young activists decided to step up their campaign and register themselves as a political party, Harakat al-Ard, the Movement of the Land. The authorities refused to register the party, and when the activists appealed, the application was again rejected on the grounds that the group was dangerous to Israel's security.

The group responded by sending a memorandum to the United Nations, to foreign embassies in Israel and to many other organizations. This outlined the situation of the Palestinians in Israel, highlighting issues such as land confiscation, discrimination in education, the nature of the military government and the clamping down on political activities.

Two weeks later the minister of defence, Levi Eshkol, declared that everything associated with al-Ard was illegal and ordered that its papers be confiscated. Citing the Emergency Regulations, the courts decided to sentence four of Muhammad's fellow leaders to a period of internal exile, so that they had to live far from their own homes.

Listening to Muhammad I'm reminded of a poem by Mahmoud Darwish, a contemporary of his, who came from the same village and had been to the same school. A member of the Israeli Communist Party, in the mid-1960s he was also involved with al-Ard and, like many of the group, spent time in prison for his beliefs. His poem 'The Reaction' reveals how being locked up often reinforces the individual or group spirit rather than breaking it.

> Dear homeland.
> My chains breed within me
> The rigour of the eagle
> And the tenderness of the optimist.

I carved your map with my teeth
Upon the walls
And wrote the song of fleeting night.

And if I die
Upon the cross of my cause
I am a saint,
I am a struggler.

All too often my own prison chains seemed to breed not so much the rigour of the eagle but the nervousness of a sparrow. However, over time in captivity in Lebanon, I discovered a resilience within me that in my previous life I would never have imagined. Home – memories of it and the desire to regain it – was an essential spur to keeping strong and maintaining optimism. It isn't surprising that prison chains encourage a struggle for freedom and a determination to overcome the oppressor: being wronged can help you define right.

Whether Muhammad would claim to be a saint for his efforts I rather doubt, but clearly, like Mahmoud Darwish, he has been a struggler. Despite being outlawed under Israel's Emergency Regulations, he and his colleagues tried to build a 'list', a group of candidates, to take part in the Knesset elections in 1965.

'We brought in new people, names not known to the authorities, and called it Socialists for Arabs. But the election committee, who were responsible for running the elections and made up of Knesset Members, said that as the list was supported by the outlawed al-Ard movement, it was forbidden to take part in the election.'

Nevertheless, the nationalist camp continued working with student groups and local non-governmental organizations (NGOs).

Muhammad and his colleagues were not the only Arab political activists in Israel. A new pro-Palestinian party was taking part in that 1965 election. The Israeli Communist Party was split between a predominantly Jewish faction and a new, largely Arab, group over the Soviet Union's increasingly pro-Arab position. The new Arab group was recognized by the Soviet Union as the 'official' Communist Party in Israel. They won three seats in the new Knesset.

Off the national stage, people were concentrating on more local issues. Abu Adnan, the baker of Acre, was working with his neighbours to improve conditions in the city. They were trying to help families who could find no work, clearing up the streets and improving education in the face of very limited state support for their community. Daoud Badr, from al-Ghabisiyya, and other members of the internally displaced Arab community in Israel were fighting protracted legal battles to win back their confiscated villages and lands.

Outside Israel, Palestinians in the West Bank and Gaza, the refugees there and beyond, had also been politically restricted. Jordan, in the West Bank, and the other Arab states where refugees had settled since 1948 sought to direct and control Palestinian national and political aspirations. Even the founding of the Palestine

Liberation Organization (PLO) in 1964, by the Egyptian-dominated Arab League, was seen by many Palestinians as an effort to control their political factions. However, just as a generation of educated young Palestinians with new ideas and aspirations was growing up in Israel, so too were young men and women who had grown up as refugees. This generation, led by Yasser Arafat and others, would become the driving force of the PLO while it developed as a political and paramilitary organization.

Events at the end of the 1960s, nearly two decades on from the Nakba, would give the Palestinian communities within and without Israel the chance to reconnect.

12

The End of the Military Period and More Violence

IN 1966 THE MILITARY PERIOD CAME TO A SUDDEN END. Prime Minister Levi Eshkol believed that the community was well enough contained in the Israeli system and simply turned off the Defence Laws (State of Emergency) Regulations. Theoretically, discrimination against Israel's Arab population would cease and they would have exactly the same rights as Jewish citizens.

On the face of it this was a remarkable change of circumstances for the Palestinian citizens of Israel. But the move towards equality was to prove more hope than reality. While Palestinian people could now move around freely, there was no increase of funding for Arab municipalities and no change in the state's drive to take yet more of the dwindling area of Arab-owned land. However, although discrimination continued, the community was now in a stronger position to establish identity and purpose.

One year on from the ending of martial law, the Six

Day War of 1967, between Israel, Egypt, Jordan and Syria, brought an unexpected reconnection between the Palestinians in Israel and those outside. Since 1948, Gaza and the West Bank – designated as part of Palestine under the UN Partition Plan – had been occupied by Egypt and Jordan respectively. Now both areas were occupied by the victorious Israeli Army. Tens of thousands of Palestinians left the West Bank and Gaza as a result of the fighting. And, just as in 1948, the Israeli authorities allowed very few to return to their homes once the violence had ceased. They had to join the ranks of refugees in neighbouring countries.

But for those who had stayed put, the Israelis were to allow a substantial amount of free movement throughout Israel and the occupied territories. Families who had been kept apart for almost twenty years could meet once again. Palestinians who had been living in exile in the West Bank and Gaza could visit their former homes, though in most cases the Israeli state had taken over their property and often destroyed it. For the Palestinian citizens of Israel, there was the chance to reconnect with a vibrant Palestinian culture and rebuild a sense that they were part of the wider Arab world, through newspapers and literature.

For the first time since 1948 Palestinians, from within Israel, those in Gaza, the West Bank and those who were part of the wider diaspora, could communicate fairly easily. A community that had been fragmented, that had lost much of its leadership and been economically broken, could begin to develop a sense of national purpose. Alongside their struggle for equal rights as full citizens of the state, the Palestinians in Israel could now also identify with the external struggle, led by the PLO, against the occupation of the West Bank and Gaza and for the right of return for refugees.

After the Six Day War, and in contravention of the Geneva Convention's Article 49, which states, 'The Occupying Power shall not deport or transfer parts of its own civilian population into the territory it occupies', Israel began establishing settlements in Gaza and the West Bank. This meant that fewer settlers were available to move into areas *inside* Israel, particularly the Galilee in the north and the Negev in the south, both areas that had a high proportion of Arab residents.

Despite the continued policies of land expropriation and settlement of Jewish immigrants, the 'demographic nightmare' in which the Palestinian population within Israel could match, even regionally, the number of Jews continued to haunt the Zionist establishment. Plans to Judaize the Galilee are as old as the state. To break up blocks of Arab-held land, the state has steadily expropriated land in and between Arab towns and villages. The breaking of agricultural and economic connections with the land aimed to undermine the Arab population's direct link with it, as well as damaging social and political cohesion. The plight of the Palestinian farmer was dire during the Military Period and many gave up trying to sustain their old lifestyle. In 1948, 60 per cent of Palestinian Arabs worked in agriculture. By the 1970s that figure had dropped to less than 20 per cent. Most took jobs in Jewish factories or the construction industry.

To resist continuing land expropriations, a new organization, the Committee for the Defence of the Land, was set up in 1975. Muhammad Mi'ari was its secretary. 'We set up a local committee in every village across the Galilee. We organized meetings, using local mayors to help us, and in October 'seventy-five gathered two to three thousand people in Nazareth to elect a council and a secretariat.'

In early March 1976 the government announced the confiscation of some 6,000 dunams (1,500 acres) of Arab land near the villages of Arraba, Sakhnin and Deir Hanna. The land would be used for new Jewish settlements and a military training camp. The Arab community, supported by the Committee, organized a national strike against the land seizure for 30 March. As if the Military Period had never ended, the government responded by imposing a military zone around the affected villages. A curfew went into force from five p.m. on 29 March.

'One of the prime minister's advisers gathered the Arab mayors and pressurized them to delay the strike,' Muhammad explains. 'Many were from the older generation and some owed their positions to the Israelis, so they agreed. When people heard about this, a crowd gathered to attack them. The police and border police were called. Many people were injured and arrested.'

The government threatened public-sector workers, such as teachers, who participated in the strike or encouraged others to do so with the sack. But the strike went ahead.

'Yom al-Ard, the Land Day, was very important. Sometimes if they confiscated land, we would go to the place and protest. But this time it wasn't just the owners who had lost land and a few supporters taking part, it was everyone.' Muhammad pauses for a moment and looks out from his cliff-side apartment over the Mediterranean. As he thinks back more than thirty years, I wonder at the mix of excitement and fear that had mobilized the Palestinian people. Muhammad nods and tips his head to one side. 'It was a total protest. The "land" was not thought of as a personal commodity but as having a national value. This was the first nationwide strike by the Arabs, from the Negev to the Galilee.

'The Israelis cannot endure Arabs acting together. The policy is always *farok tassod*, to divide us – into sects, Muslim, Druze, Christian – and into regions: the Negev, the Galilee and so on. But this day really struck at that policy.'

From the government's point of view such a display of community spirit needed to be crushed. People would get hurt. Muhammad describes receiving a call from the mayor of Arraba, one of the other villages at the heart of the proposed land confiscation. 'He called me at four o'clock in the morning, saying, "We have victims on our streets."'

Army tanks had entered the small town of Deir Hanna during the evening to break up a meeting. Eight people were injured. Troops began arresting everyone on the streets. They went into houses, smashing furniture in some. There were also clashes between civilians and soldiers in Sakhnin and Nazareth. The uprising was spreading across all the Arab areas.

The army operation to crush the protest was led by Major General Rafael Eitan, commander of the northern zone of the army. Eitan was an Israeli hero, who had fought in every war since 1948. The depth and breadth of the Arab protest had rattled the authorities, and Eitan acted as if he were taking on an enemy army in battle.

Muhammad describes the fierce conflict: 'In Arraba, the village was surrounded and the tanks were sent in with their guns firing.' His eyes flash brightly as he recalls the unprecedented level and scale of this confrontation. I sense his emotions then: excitement, pride in his community's resistance and his part in it, and shock. For all his awareness of the ruthless nature of the Israeli state, for all his political savvy, to witness tanks taking on unarmed civilians was devastating. 'People surrounded one tank and captured three Israeli soldiers whom they took to a private house. When General Eitan heard that some of his men had been kidnapped, he said he would bomb the whole village if they were not released. The mayor responded by saying that the soldiers would be released when the army withdrew from the village.'

Israel has a proud record of retrieving military personnel who go missing in action. Anybody taking an Israeli soldier hostage knows that the full military force of Israel will be unleashed against them. It is a policy

Top left: Saud and Annis Azbarga, who set me off on my travels, at the Bedouin wedding, Lod.

Top right: Suha Arraf, my friend and guide, in trademark sunglasses.

Below: Garden of the St Charles guesthouse, Haifa.

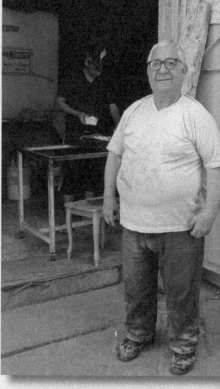

Left: Old City, Acre.

Above: Haya Sarsour, a gentle and fearless Palestinian, Kafr Qassem.

Top right: Abu Adnan Beshtawe, the baker from Acre.

Bottom right: Hassan and Wajiha Asleh, in the saddest room I've ever visited, Arraba.

Below: Khalil Alamour inspecting a demolition notice, Alsara, Negev.

Above: A boy at the unrecognized village of Amra, Negev.

Right: The author with Attia El Assam, my desert guide, at the site of a former Bedouin village, Negev.

Below: Bedouin villages, Negev.

Above: Nuri Elokbi, a poet and campaigner, Negev.

Left: Fadi Shbeita, a passionate activist with a sense of humour, Jaffa.

Below: Fishing boats in the forlorn harbour, Jisr El Zarqa.

Above: Tel Aviv seafront, looking north from Jaffa.

Below: Awni Ahmed Iryashi, bewildered by cruel bureaucracy, the Old City, Jerusalem.

Above: Damascus Gate, Old City, Jerusalem.

Below: Independence Day 2008, the world turns blue and white on Ben-Gurion Boulevard, Haifa.

Top: Hisham Naffa, Nakba Day March 2008, Saffuriyya.

Above: Nakba Day March 2008, Saffuriyya.

Right: 'Happy Nakba': Special Forces firing tear gas and chasing marchers, Nakba Day March 2008, Saffuriyya.

that has continued to this day – when Hezbollah captured soldiers on Israel's northern border in 2006, the Israelis invaded Lebanon, and the abduction of Corporal Gilad Shalit, by Hamas in the same year, led to enormous efforts to gain his release. Here, though, the threat didn't come from a paramilitary group but a formerly docile village suddenly disarming tanks and capturing the crew. It was an affront to Israeli military might that would not go unpunished.

'Once the three soldiers had been released, Eitan went against his word and attacked Arraba,' says Muhammad. 'During that attack, at nine o'clock in the evening, the first person was killed.'

A couple of days before my meeting with Muhammad, I had heard a personal account of the violence of this first Land Day. Suha had taken me to Sakhnin, another focal point of the clashes between army and civilians. As in most Arab towns in Israel, Sakhnin's main street is wide and chaotic. Petrol stations stand next to general stores and plots containing half-built apartment blocks. Car body workshops are squeezed between small supermarkets and cafés. Parades of shops include butchers, bakers, grocers, general household-goods stores and 'salons', with window displays offering old-fashioned clothes and gaudy wedding dresses. The tarmac is buckled in many places and peters out to gravel at the edges.

We went through some back-streets to the home of Suha's friend Abu Nidal Shalaata. Our arrival was greeted with much shouting and kissing, and for ten minutes or so I sat quietly on the sidelines as she and the family swapped news. One of Abu Nidal's daughters was soon to be married, so there was discussion of dresses and party plans, and a review of photographs from the engagement celebration.

Eventually we turned to the sombre subject of the events of March 1976. Abu Nidal is a thin man with short, greying hair and a smoker's cough. I found it hard to picture him as the twenty-three-year-old he had been in 1976. He described seeing the body of the victim from Arraba, just an hour or so after he'd been shot. 'We were all gathered in the town square to see what was happening,' Abu Nidal said, in his rasping voice. 'Suddenly a taxi raced up. The driver jumped out, pulled the back door open and showed us a body. "This is a martyr from Arraba!"'

The young crowd reacted angrily and decided to march to Arraba to show support to their neighbours. But they didn't get far. The roads out of town were blocked by tanks, trucks, soldiers and police. According to Abu Nidal, the soldiers opened fire, prompting the marchers to retaliate by throwing stones.

'I was shot just after one o'clock in the morning. I got separated from the other guys. I found myself in a small building surrounded by the soldiers. I thought they might crush it with a tank so I ran out.' At this moment, Abu Nidal had paused, coughing. 'They shot me in the leg. I tried to get up and they shot me again. They left me for dead.'

I turned to Abu Nidal's wife, Dina, who had been a

teenager at the time. 'Did you have any idea what was happening?' I asked.

'I was waiting at home with our three very young children,' she replied, shaking her head. 'I had no idea where he was. I heard shooting and at one point the troops came down our street firing at the houses.'

A curfew was imposed, and the next morning the troops went through the town, searching houses. All the young men who were found were taken to the town square, hands tied behind their backs. Many were beaten.

Abu Nidal lay where he'd fallen for three hours before friends could get to him and take him to a hospital in Nazareth.

Now he rolled up his trouser leg and showed me his scars. The doctors had wanted to amputate his leg, but his brother wouldn't let them. It had never recovered fully. Looking at his withered calf, I remembered Ismael Bdeir at Kafr Qassem showing me his artificial leg. It is very disturbing to meet people who have suffered such wounds as a result of being attacked by their own state's military. Abu Nidal never received any compensation for the disability he suffered from the shooting. But he was fined 5,000 shekels for taking part in a demonstration.

Muhammad Mi'ari listens as I recount my meeting in Arraba. Nodding slowly, he fixes me with a steady gaze. 'What happened that night was terrible. Six were killed, a hundred wounded and they put about three hundred people in prison. They beat them and humiliated them in many ways.

'Some of those injured sought government compensation,' he goes on, 'but the Ministry of Defence said the troops acted lawfully. The demonstrations were described as an act of war. And in war there is no compensation.'

'It's unbelievable,' I say.

Muhammad shrugs, smiling at my outrage. 'They were stating what we knew – that they saw us as enemies. So the Committee announced that Israel had declared war against its Arab citizens.' He straightens the front of his tweed jacket and lights yet another cigarette. 'For us Arabs, the spilling of our blood changes everything. I said then and still believe it: the situation of the Palestinians in Israel changed dramatically because of the events of the Land Day. We began to feel that we were united as Arabs and Palestinians and that the land was a matter not of personal but of national value. Before this event, groups of us might have written pamphlets, might have protested against this thing or that, but now we had taken to the streets as a people, fighting our cause as Arabs.'

Despite or because of the brutal reaction to the Land Day protests in 1976, the sense that they were a nation continued to grow among the Palestinian community in Israel. Along with this developing nationalism came the determination and confidence to work together, independently of the state. In the face of discrimination in municipal budgets, for example, leaders in towns like Nazareth organized volunteer schemes to restore and develop their cities' infrastructures. People would sign up for road- or wall-building projects, working for three or four days, listening to speeches and learning about Palestinian culture.

'There had been changes for the Palestinians: military rule had ended, there had been the '67 war, which had brought contact with the people in the West Bank and Gaza,' Muhammad recalls. 'And many more people were better educated and more prosperous too. They were getting active.'

Although there had been Arab Knesset Members from the very first election, they had been Communists or from Zionist-affiliated parties. It wasn't until 1984 that a Palestinian citizen, standing as a nationalist, was elected to the national parliament. That once-new Member of the Knesset sits in front of me now in his living room, surrounded by his library of Arab history and literature. Droll, dapper, debonair almost, it seems amazing that Muhammad has lived through so much turbulence. For all his warmth and charm, he has a steely quality and a reputation for going his own way. By the mid-1980s he had spent a quarter of a century working as an activist and as a lawyer specializing in land-confiscation cases. He had watched his community emerge from the trauma of the Nakba and martial law.

Even so, when the nationalists decided to establish a party, they knew they had to tread carefully to avoid provoking opposition from the government. 'We knew they wouldn't let us register an Arab nationalist party any more than they had done with al-Ard back in the sixties, so we linked up with a small Jewish organization, the Alternative. It was headed by a retired Israeli general,

Matti Peled, and together we formed the Progressive List for Peace.'

There were attempts to stop this party being registered on the grounds that Muhammad was 'a danger to state security', but Matti Peled was a national hero and efforts to ban the group failed. Peled is one of many Jewish Israeli citizens who have used their democratic rights to argue and fight for those of their Palestinian fellows.

Born in Haifa, Matti Peled had served with Jewish paramilitary forces in actions against the British during the Mandate. He was a leading figure in the war of 1948 and one of the founding fathers of the Israel Defence Forces. Though considered at times to be a political 'hawk', he studied Arabic while still a serving soldier and went on to help set up the Arabic literature department at Tel Aviv University.

He moved to the political left and in 1975 was a founding member of the Israeli Council for Israeli–Palestinian Peace. The ICIPP called for Israel's withdrawal from the occupied Palestinian territories and for a sharing of Jerusalem between Israel and an independent Palestinian state. Peled was committed to the Israeli state and always described himself as a Zionist, but he was also a radical politician eager to promote relations between Jews and Palestinians.

'We spoke out about the Arabs' right of return, that Israel must be a democracy with a constitution and proper human-rights laws,' Muhammad tells me. 'We argued that the Arabs should have autonomy for their education system, their lands and so on. We supported negotiations between Israel and the PLO even though the PLO was called a terrorist organization. In 1984 we won two seats, one for General Peled and one for me.'

'*Mish maoul!*' I say. 'That's incredible. Finally you'd got inside the great democracy. How were you received?'

Not cynical but savvy, Muhammad is too much the realist to make any grand statement about his achievement. A Knesset seat wasn't going to change the world. He was still a Palestinian in the Jewish homeland. He shrugs again, purses his lips and says, 'For me it was a mission but I was always an outsider. They called me "the PLO's representative in the Knesset".'

13

The Saddest Room

CARS CRUISE UP AND DOWN HAIFA'S BEN-GURION Boulevard, hunting rare parking places outside the many trendy bars and bistros. I'm sitting with Suha at our favourite watering hole, Fattoush. It's another balmy night and the café's terrace is busy. Enjoying a cool beer, I run over my meeting with Muhammad Mi'ari. He had outlined the path taken by the Palestinian community in Israel from their utter defeat in 1948 to their rediscovery of a sense of national identity and the determination to fight for their rights as supposedly equal citizens of the state. Their reconnection with the Palestinian community in the West Bank and Gaza after 1967 had played an important role in that rebirth, and Muhammad had told me that the first Intifada, twenty years later, had been one of the most important issues of his first term as a Member of the Knesset. It strikes me that Suha would have been around eighteen years old at that time. What was the period like for a young student?

'The first Intifada was an amazing time for us, John –
a very important time. We were all fired up, excited and
committed to helping the cause.' Suha leans forward over
the table as she speaks, her head turning from side to
side, her fork hovering over her food until she waves it
firmly to emphasize a point. 'I was at university here in
Haifa – 1987 was my first year as a student, an amazing
time, anyway, to be away from my village and living in
this city, a new world for me, really.

'There were many demonstrations – but they were
nearly all peaceful. Often there would be Jewish groups
shouting us down, and there were always police, of
course.'

Sitting out on this pleasant evening, on this peaceful
street, talking to Suha, it is hard to imagine the tensions
of that time. Although the Palestinians in Israel had been
finding their feet as a community, they were still facing
widespread discrimination from the Jewish state, despite
all the achievements of people like Muhammad Mi'ari.
And the Palestinians in the West Bank and Gaza had
become increasingly frustrated after twenty years of
Israeli occupation. The Arab world and the international
community seemed to have lost interest in helping
them. The Palestine Liberation Organization (PLO)
had been driven out of Jordan in 1970, then from
Lebanon in 1982. From its new base in Tunis, it seemed
unlikely to make any real progress towards winning a
Palestinian state. In the occupied territories more land
was being confiscated for the construction of Jewish
settlements, and the Israeli military was using

iron-fist tactics to deal with any Palestinian resistance.

The immediate flashpoint for the Intifada (literally 'shaking off', but usually translated as 'uprising') came in December 1987. Four Palestinians were killed when an Israeli military vehicle crashed into them in a Gaza refugee camp. Riots and protests spread in Gaza, the West Bank and East Jerusalem. Although the PLO and other groups were involved they never had full control; the Intifada was essentially a grass-roots movement. It inspired a similar movement among the Palestinians within Israel, as Suha tells me. 'We worked alongside the committees that were set up in every Arab town to co-ordinate the collection of money, food and clothes to support the Palestinians in the West Bank and Gaza.'

While the demonstrations in Israel were often huge, with tens of thousands of people taking part, they were generally without violence, but the abiding images of the Intifada in the occupied territories are of Palestinian youths and children with stones taking on heavily armed Israeli soldiers. The Israeli reaction was brutal, with defence minister Yitzhak Rabin encouraging troops to break protesters' bones.

'As you've been talking,' I tell Suha, 'I've had images in my mind of the stone-throwing and the tear gas. But I didn't really know anything about the Intifada until it was tailing off in the early 1990s. I was underground in Lebanon in 'eighty-seven. It seems weird that the guards never mentioned it. But, then, they never mentioned the fall of the Berlin Wall either – most of the time they didn't want us to know what was going on.'

'Amazing to think you were so near but knew nothing. Maybe for the people keeping you our struggle was just part of theirs against Israel. For people of my generation, the Intifada was our first experience of political action. I went on to become a journalist and writer. Many of my contemporaries and friends continued as activists.' Suha pauses, sips her lemonade, a Fattoush speciality, and stares into the middle distance. 'People weren't just working for Palestinian rights, but for many NGOs that were opening up at the time, concerned with a whole range of issues, welfare, women's rights and so on. I think we were a special generation – we started a revolution to change society here in Israel.'

During the period of the first Intifada and on through the Oslo Peace Process in the early nineties, Palestinian citizens became increasingly active in Israeli politics. Arab parties won more Knesset seats and even lined up in coalition governments. As Palestinian citizens of Israel, they could play a role in the efforts to end the conflict between their state and their fellow Palestinians in the occupied territories. Many of them hoped that a peace settlement between Israel and the PLO would remove a major obstacle to their achieving integration as fully equal Israeli citizens. Once there was peace, their nationality should be less threatening to their Jewish Israeli neighbours.

The Oslo Accords, signed in September 1993, with PLO chairman Yasser Arafat, Israeli prime minister Yitzhak Rabin and US president Bill Clinton, seemed to promise a safe passage towards a resolution of the obstacles to peace. A Palestinian National Authority would administer a territory that would expand as Israeli forces fulfilled various stages of withdrawal from Gaza and the West Bank. Crucial issues, such as final borders, Jerusalem (both sides, of course, claiming the city as their capital), Palestinian refugees and Israeli settlements in the occupied territories, were not ignored, but would be dealt with at a later stage.

For all the hype, there were many critics of the Oslo Accords. Opponents said too much was left vague and that the ethnic cleansing of 1948 had been, in effect, accepted. For the Palestinian citizens of Israel, Oslo did very little. The fact that their situation was ignored in the Accords, and the history of the Nakba 'glossed over', prompted a new round of self-examination and the realization that, as far as the rest of the world was concerned – and even as far as the Palestinians outside Israel were concerned – they were on their own in their struggle for equality within their state.

The failure of Oslo to provide any help to Palestinians in Israel brought an ever greater focus on the need for the community to fight for its own identity. The Islamic Movement, set up in the early 1980s, became a powerful voice for Palestinian, as well as Muslim, rights. In 1995 Balad, or the National Democratic Assembly, was set up to 'struggle to transform the state of Israel into a democracy for all its citizens, irrespective of national or ethnic identity'.

Palestinian citizens were now demanding not only full

equality but also that Israel should recognize them as a national minority and grant them rights of autonomy in areas such as education and culture. One clear, perhaps simple, statement of this confident new nationalism has been the widespread rejection of the state's preferred definition of them as 'Israeli Arabs', in favour of 'Palestinian citizens of Israel'.

That confidence took a severe battering in 2000 when the Israeli security forces once again turned their guns on those Palestinian citizens. 'The atmosphere in the second Intifada was very different,' Suha tells me: 'a different attitude among the Palestinians, especially the leaders, in the West Bank and a very different situation here in Israel. You'll hear more tomorrow.' Suddenly she looks tired. 'Let's go. The stories will be sad.'

'I didn't sleep well,' Suha tells me the next morning, when I pick her up. 'If you know where you're going, maybe I can catch some more rest while we drive.'

'That's fine,' I say. 'I remember the way.'

We are going to Sakhnin, which, along with the towns of Arraba and Deir Hanna, was at the centre of the clashes of the first Land Day in 1976 when six Palestinian citizens were killed by Israeli soldiers. The last time we came here, it was to see Abu Nidal Shalaata, one of the men shot and wounded during the protests. Today we're going to meet relatives of victims of another round of violent confrontations, in October 2000.

Brutal clashes in the West Bank and Gaza Strip in the closing days of September that year marked the start of the second Intifada. Frustrations within the Palestinian community in these Israeli-occupied territories were already running high. The summer's Camp David summit, between US president Bill Clinton, Israeli prime minister Ehud Barak and Palestinian Authority chairman Yasser Arafat, had failed to deliver assurances of a Palestinian state in any real terms.

A visit by Ariel Sharon, then the leader of Israel's opposition, to what Jews call Temple Mount and Muslims call Haram al-Sharif in Jerusalem on 28 September was widely seen as the event that caused frustrations to boil over on to the streets. Guarded by hundreds of Israeli policemen, Sharon declared that 'The Temple Mount is in our hands and will remain in our hands. It is the holiest site in Judaism and it is the right of every Jew to visit the Temple Mount.' As well as being the holiest site in Judaism it is the third holiest site in Islam. Control of and access to the site is a significant obstacle to peace. Israelis and Palestinians both claim the site, along with the rest of the Old City of Jerusalem, as the heart of their rightful national capital.

When demonstrators died in clashes in East Jerusalem, the Palestinian leadership in Israel called a general strike on 1 October. Protests across the north of the country turned violent in various places and continued over the following days. Thirteen Palestinians – twelve citizens of Israel and one from the Gaza Strip – were to die in the clashes.

One of the thirteen was twenty-four-year-old Emad Ganeam from Sakhnin, and we are going to meet his father, Faraj. I find my way to the town square, the scene of violence in 1976. I wake Suha, who looks at her note-book and gives me directions. We take a winding street up a hill past shops, churches and mosques, and then follow a narrow side-road to pull in beside an apartment block.

Faraj Ganeam invites us to join him and a couple of neighbours, who are sitting round a small brazier drink-ing coffee. Faraj, a neat figure in a tight-fitting old brown suit, prepares a brass pot of sharp Arabic coffee, which he pours into a small, handleless cup that each guest uses in turn. The traditional Arab courtesy concluded, he sits and tells us about his son. He insists that Emad was not a trouble-maker but a good man and a devout Muslim, who prayed daily at the mosque. A sociable young man, he enjoyed kung-fu and playing football. And he worked hard with his brother, making aluminium doors and windows. He had built a house and was looking forward to marrying his girlfriend.

Faraj goes into the apartment block and returns with a photo of his boy. Emad was handsome. I'm struck by the size of the black and white photo. It is very large, not something taken from a family album but something to be displayed in public, a poster. This seems to emphasize how the nature of Emad's death transformed him from just another youth to someone who is part of the iconography of his people's struggle for justice. The father props the picture tenderly against the table before speaking.

'There was a big demonstration here against Sharon in

2000,' Faraj says. 'For the young men it was just that, a demonstration.' He pauses and stares into the embers of the brazier. 'Why did the Israelis bring snipers? Why did they train snipers for that sort of situation?' he asks rhetorically. 'They say that this is a democracy, so they shouldn't have snipers at demonstrations. I think there was a plan to kill people from these villages because they were on a black list.'

Between seven and eight thousand people took part in the demonstration at Sakhnin. Emad and one other youth were killed, twenty more were injured.

'I was watching TV when we got a phone call from one of my other sons, Walid. He told me, "My brother is a *shaheed*, a martyr."'

Faraj breaks off again, staring into the coals of the brazier, obviously fighting back tears. I realize that, as an Arab man, he will feel ashamed to display such emotion, so, like everyone around him, I sit quietly as he prods the embers with a stick and regains his composure. Reeling from the news Walid had given him, Faraj spent the next couple of hours on a cruel emotional rollercoaster. A friend of Emad's called from the hospital saying that he was going to be all right. A second call brought the same hope. But when his other sons arrived at the apartment, one look at their faces told him Emad was dead.

This story, yet another example of a young citizen killed by their country's military, chills me to the bone. I can't imagine how I'd feel if my daughter was killed by the security forces in my homeland. Hesitantly, I ask

Faraj how Emad's death has affected his attitude to his state.

'It makes you very, very angry,' Faraj says simply. 'I can't see Israel as my country, my state, after what has happened to me. It is only a democracy for the Jewish citizens and they have taken all our rights.

'Nobody thought that the police would use their guns. I believe they wanted to kill people so that the Arabs would be too frightened to demonstrate. Nobody was charged with the killings. How can we feel safe when the police can shoot us without fear of prosecution or punishment?'

We sit a little while longer with Faraj. His neighbours and I can see him rebuilding his inner strength, putting on again the psychological armour that allows him to continue, despite the loss of his child. A more general conversation springs up around the brazier as he makes more coffee. His neighbours talk of the high unemployment in the town, of the poor facilities in their schools and how the municipal budget is so much less than a Jewish community would receive from the state.

Faraj has the final word. 'What can we do against all this discrimination? Only demonstrate! Even though we know what can happen when we do.'

As we drive on from Sakhnin, Suha and I barely speak. It's another beautiful day in the Galilee, but the sun shining in the clear blue sky seems so utterly at odds with the dark and tragic story we have just heard. My heart is heavy as we reach the outskirts of Arraba, where we are

209

going to see the parents of another young peace activist who was killed in the demonstration.

The Asleh family home, a substantial villa, is set back from the road up a cobbled driveway. The front door is opened by a tall young man, who smiles and nods us in. We say hello over the noise of rock music pounding from his study. He leads us into a sitting room and says his parents will be there in a moment. He goes back to his room and closes the door, sealing the music in with him. Moments later Hassan and Wajiha Asleh join Suha and me. They greet us politely but quietly, with an air of great weariness. Hassan, a little taller than his wife, puts an arm round her shoulders.

We sit down, and they begin to tell us the story of their son Asel, the older brother of the youth who let us in. He had been just seventeen when he was shot dead. As Hassan and Wajiha tell us their son's story, I am struck by their stillness. Sitting on the sofa beneath pictures of Asel they seem almost lifeless. Though there is bright sunshine outside, the curtains are drawn and the room is illuminated by a glaring neon strip light. It is a pleasant house but I keep thinking, This is the saddest room I have ever been in.

'Asel was two things for me,' says Wajiha. 'As my son, he was simply a part of me. And he was the fulfilment of a dream. My personal dream, as a teacher, was to encourage a new generation who were well educated, had a clear national identity and a political conscience.' Wajiha had grown up asking questions, aware that the circumstances of the Palestinians in Israel were not

210

the same as for the Jewish citizens. She had developed a political understanding of the situation in the country. 'So I am not naïve: they have taken our land, destroyed our houses, our dreams and culture. But I couldn't imagine that they would also take my son.'

Wajiha lets her head drop and Hassan begins to talk. Like his wife, he speaks quietly, thoughtfully, and waits patiently as Suha translates for me. 'I cannot talk about Asel as if he is in the past. For me he is still in the present. From when he was young, whenever I played with him or read him a story, I tried to give him the truth – truth and love. As he grew up I felt like an artist who was painting a beautiful picture, and when I saw the finished work I couldn't believe how beautiful it was.'

Hassan has thinning grey hair and deep-set eyes, their shadows pronounced due to the harsh neon light on the ceiling. Wajiha leans forward, elbows on her knees, her hands wrapped around her arms as if she is cold, although it is a warm day. She leaves the room and returns with an electric fire, which she plugs in and places in front of the sofa, pointing towards her. She huddles over it, smoking. Hassan continues to reflect on his son's growing maturity: 'I was very happy that Asel shared my views on the importance of protecting our identity, our roots. Like Wajiha, I felt as if my dream was becoming real. When he went to the USA with the Seeds of Peace programme, I realized how well he had under-stood what we had taught him.'

Seeds of Peace is a US-based organization that, according to its website, 'is dedicated to empowering

young leaders from regions of conflict with the leadership skills required to advance reconciliation and
coexistence'.

Yet for all his delight in Asel's decision to promote an
understanding of Palestinian culture and work towards
building peace, Hassan was always anxious for his boy.
'There was something that I cannot explain, that made
me feel afraid whenever I looked at him.'

On the day their son was killed the couple had visited a
relative on the other side of Arraba. Before they had left
home Hassan had gone to Asel's bedroom; his boy was
still in bed. Full of an unspecified anxiety, he had watched
him sleeping for a few minutes. As Hassan and Wajiha
made their way across the village the demonstration was
just beginning. On arriving at the relative's house they
heard that a cousin was taking Asel to the demonstration.
Immediately Wajiha called him on his mobile. He
answered, saying he was fine and walking to the
demonstration.

'Asel was good at fighting with words, but he had no
experience of violent clashes,' Wajiha explains. 'He didn't
know how to run away. He would have seen that as a
weakness. And that made me more worried.'

The parents decided to look for him and became
separated, searching in the crowds. Asel always wore a
green T-shirt from Seeds of Peace. Wherever they looked
there was no green T-shirt and no reply when they called
his mobile. 'Then I saw some soldiers,' says Wajiha, 'and
instinctively I knew, from the way they were moving, that
they were about to act. They opened fire. Someone fell,

212

lying at the foot of an olive tree and wearing a green T-shirt. It was Asel.'

Suha murmurs, '*Haraam, haraam* [for shame],' as she listens to Wajiha. My friend's usually animated face is, for once, still and pale. As I learn those details I am overwhelmed not only by the couple's tragedy but also by their courage in telling this story. They must have relived it so many times in the years since Asel's death. The phrase my Palestinian friend Ghassan had used in Lebanon many years earlier comes back to me: 'This is not a way.'

Hassan speaks again, almost as if in a dream, his voice a monotone. After all his forebodings, he had found himself in the noise and chaos of the demonstration. He had seen his son standing just a small distance away. 'At that moment I could not call to him. I could not run. I was looking at him and felt something would happen, but I was frozen. I couldn't do anything.'

I have experienced as, no doubt, most parents have the sleeping nightmare of needing to run to help my child and finding myself struggling through quicksand, unable to reach her. For Wajiha and Hassan there will be no release of waking to realize they had been dreaming. Their child was killed before their eyes. How do they bear it?

'To start with I filed the newspaper articles and reports about the October demonstration and Asel,' says Wajiha. 'I kept these cuttings in folders. I sorted out all of Asel's belongings, his drawings from when he was a kid, his school reports and diplomas and so on. I kept everything. I put them all in folders too. One day I looked at the piles of folders. The one with the cuttings about his death and the aftermath of the October killings was getting taller and taller. The one about his life had not grown. Then it hit me: my life had also stopped. I carry on eating, drinking, but I move now in a different way.'

Looking at this couple, sitting in their comfortable home, talking of the horror that befell their family, I think of my own parents when they spoke to journalists about my disappearance in Lebanon. By all accounts they showed this kind of dignity. My mother had died while I was still a hostage but my father was able to see me safely home again from the alien country where I had been held.

My parents never had to worry that I might not be welcomed home: I had that right as a British citizen. Modern Jewish Israelis claim just such a right with a tenacity that can be appreciated, given the treatment they have experienced in other places where they have tried to make their homes. The Palestinians, though, have been denied that right. For the Aslehs there is no escape: their tragedy happened at home and was caused by their state, which shows them no welcome at all. Yet they are still active. My own parents never gave up hope that I was alive; indeed, my mother's determination to see me safely home somehow gave her the strength to maintain her battle against cancer for much longer than her doctors had expected. But Wajiha and Hassan have never had that hope. I wonder what keeps them going.

'We are fighting for our rights, so we never get tired.

We are fighting for all the Palestinians in Israel. We look back and say that our grandparents should have done more to resist Israel. I don't want my grandchildren to look back and think the same about us.'

Wajiha goes on to tell us about the Jewish doctor at the hospital in Haifa who attended Asel's birth. 'She looked at him and said as a casual joke, "Ah, another terrorist!" And she was being friendly!' She shakes her head as she explains that, for all her commitment to future generations, the prospect of more children who will simply be deemed 'terrorists' sometimes fills her with despair. At her daughter Nardin's wedding, she cried and cried and could not stop. 'Everyone thought I was crying because Asel was not there and that he would never be married. That was true a bit, but mostly I was looking ahead to Nardin and her husband having a family and the tragedy they might face if their children met a similar end.

'You need to have Israeli identity papers and passport to stay in your land, but you do not feel that this is your true identity. When you have to fill in the forms and say what you are, it does not feel right to put "Israeli". It is very hard to be a stranger in your own home. You cannot imagine what that is like. It's as if they give you good bread to eat, but it makes you feel sick.'

When they finish speaking, I feel numb and think we should leave them alone, but they insist we stay for coffee. Almost immediately they seem to relax and, like Faraj at Sakhnin, somehow manage to come back from profound grief to normal sociability. As Wajiha hands me a cup of coffee, she smiles the sweetest of smiles and her tragic demeanour transforms into warm radiance.

Hassan jokes that Wajiha was stuck with him instead of someone useful, like a doctor. 'We are a strong couple. We are united against the state. That keeps us strong.'

Then Wajiha laughs. 'But we still argue! Sometimes we are arguing and have to stop for a meeting about Asel, where we will talk together as one. But once we are alone again, the argument continues.'

Hassan's face is serious when he makes what to me seems an almost paranoid statement. 'I believe the Israelis plan to bring about a purely Jewish state. They will do something much, much stronger than in October 2000. They intend to build a wall to separate the Jewish settlements from the Arab villages. They will make all the Arab areas into ghettoes. After that I think they will transfer most of the Arabs out of the country.'

Hassan's premise is that the Palestinians in Israel will be forced to go to the Sinai region of Egypt, where there will be a state that includes Gaza and some of the West Bank. Egypt will give the land and Saudi Arabia will fund the project with American and European backing.

As Suha translates this theory, she says she has not heard it before and I think she shares my doubts about it. We have spoken about the older generation of Palestinians in Israel and how the traumatic memories of 1948 and the military period remain strong within them. Their fear of displacement remains very high, and they believe that their state would do anything to them.

* * *

We head back to Haifa through the dark hillsides of the Galilee, the hillsides Suha loves so much – her home. She is quiet for some time. I assume that, like me, she is reflecting on what we have heard about the deaths of Asel and Emad. Yet it is not the past tragedies she is thinking of but what might happen next.

'Am I living in a bubble?' she asks abruptly. 'Why do I feel safe when so many Palestinians do not? You know, John, it's not just the old generation. Many friends of mine are frightened, and they speak about being desperate to get their children away from Israel as soon as possible. They want to go somewhere where they can get new passports – Canada, Europe or the USA.'

She goes quiet again, staring out at the nightscape. As a car passes in the other direction her face is lit up and I catch the familiar toss of the head as she ponders. I have never heard her talk like this before. She is one of the well-educated, confident Palestinian citizens of Israel, proud to be Palestinian yet comfortable living in her own apartment among Jewish neighbours. She is aware of the indignities and iniquities imposed on her people by her state yet also that she is able to pursue her chosen career as a writer and live an independent life more easily within Israel than she might elsewhere. She is a modern woman in a modern country.

'I am really confused,' she says. 'Why do I feel safe? I know they [the Israelis] want us to go, but I don't believe they will force us. Hassan was so sure, though. Maybe he is right.'

* * *

The violent confrontations of October 2000 marked another watershed in relations between Israel's Palestinian and Jewish communities. The Israeli government set up a commission into the protests under High Court Judge Theodore Or. The findings were published in September 2003. While citing various factors behind the protests, the Or Report looked squarely at the issue of continued state discrimination against Palestinian citizens:

> The state and generations of its government failed in a lack of comprehensive and deep handling of the serious problems created by the existence of a large Arab minority inside the Jewish state.
>
> Government handling of the Arab sector has been primarily neglectful and discriminatory . . . The state did not do enough or try hard enough to create equality for its Arab citizens or to uproot discriminatory or unjust phenomena. Meanwhile, not enough was done to enforce the law in the Arab sector, and the illegal and undesirable phenomena that took root there.

Reading the report, I find myself comparing the events and aftermath of 2000 with what happened in Kafr Qassem in 1956. Has anything really changed? For all this self-awareness little has ever been done to put right the 'neglectful and discriminatory' handling of the Arab sector.

The report also spoke of the effects of Arab community leaders encouraging violent protest and the general radicalization of Palestinian citizens of Israel in the preceding years. It has been the fears of the Jewish majority that have played the dominant role in subsequent policies and attitudes towards Palestinians. Ideas promoting co-existence and mutual development were put back on the shelf, despite the recommendations of the Or Report, as Israel continued to view the Arab population as a dangerous potential 'fifth column'. Renewed fears of the 'demographic time bomb' prompted calls from Jewish Israeli leaders, regionally and nationally, for new efforts to move Jewish settlers into the Galilee in the north and the Negev in the south, the areas with large Arab populations.

In January 2008, Attorney General Menachem Mazuz made a final decision that no police officers would be indicted over the deaths of thirteen protesters in October 2000. Despite the Or Commission having cited the names of many of the police implicated in the shootings, Mazuz decided there was insufficient evidence in any case to indict a single officer or pursue any disciplinary proceedings.

This failure of the state to bring the killers of October 2000 to court, coupled with renewed calls to Judaize Arab areas, reminds the Palestinians in Israel just how utterly vulnerable they are in a state that serves Jewish interests first and treats them as second-class citizens. Integration into a Jewish state is not possible; the only way for Israel to be a proper home for Palestinian as well as Jewish communities is for it to become a state of all its citizens.

For Wajiha Asleh, though, the reports and rulings are too impersonal to mean anything: 'Everyone talks about the people who died in 2000 as numbers, "the thirteen". But for me it is not about numbers. It is my son.'

14

The Negev Bedouin

I'VE COME TO THINK OF THE ST CHARLES GUESTHOUSE in Haifa as a home from home. I always base myself here on trips around Israel, and to return to its ordered tranquillity at the end of long, hard days is a real blessing. In all honesty, the first thing that attracted me to it was the cost. It is incredibly reasonable. But I soon learned that the real appeal is the nuns themselves: Sister Reeta, who runs the guesthouse, tiny Sister Bona, who manages the adjacent hall of residence for girls studying at Haifa University, and Sister Isadora, also petite, who is in charge of the Rosary Kindergarten. Most mornings, while eating breakfast, I watch a trail of parents and children walking around the orchard to the kindergarten at the far side of the property or the nuns gliding through in their habits.

It took me a while to realize that there were just the three of them, all in their sixties. The sisters have seemingly boundless energy and dedication, working from dawn often until the small hours. They are the essential ingredient in the atmosphere of the place I have come to love. Their serenity mixes with the cool, quiet and secure building, peaceful behind its high walls. It offers a neutral and calm space to return to where I can reflect on the many disturbing and confusing stories I've been hearing.

I have learned a great deal about the experiences of the Palestinian citizens of Israel in the first fifty years after the state was formed. The stories people have shared with me have conveyed terrible accounts of violence and oppression, but also a surprisingly uplifting narrative of a people coming out of the shadows of total defeat to find themselves and begin to make themselves heard.

Now I want to discover present-day life. Since my interest in the Palestinians in Israel was sparked by my meeting with the Azbarga family in Lod in 2006, it feels right to learn more about their Bedouin community. Most of the Bedouin live in the south – in the Negev desert – and Suha has worked her usual magic to put me in touch with people there who will show me around.

As I descend the front steps of the guesthouse, a voice calls, 'John!' Turning, I see Sister Reeta framed in the doorway. 'May God bless you for your work,' she says, waving me off.

The drive to Beersheba, the 'Capital of the Negev', is only a little over two hours of very easy motorway travelling. Yet because the journey takes me from the familiar, tree-covered hillsides of the north to the sweeping deserts of the south, where the Mediterranean landscape meets the Arabian, I feel as though I'm on a much longer adventure. As I go south beyond the narrow coastal plain, the horizon opens up into a wide, rolling countryside of pasture and arable land. There is a real sense of space here and, continuing east and south, the desert will become harsher and more arid. The Negev covers 12,500 square kilometres and makes up more than half of Israel, although only 8 per cent of Israel's population live here. There are some 380,000 Jews who are mainly immigrants, and 160,000 Bedouin, whose fore-bears have lived in the area for centuries. Until 1948, the Bedouin constituted 99 per cent of the region's population.

When the motorway stops, so do I. For a few minutes I stand and look out across brown, undulating land. A dry wind plays across my face and I have a prickly feeling on my skin. Though it is very hot a shiver runs down my spine. I am excited to be at the edge of this great space. I've had this feeling in deserts in the Middle East, India and South America. I like the idea of going off into the wilderness, out of my civilized world. On a far hillside I make out the unmistakable black tents of a Bedouin encampment. Although I know that many Bedouin, like my friends the Azbargas in Lod, live in urban homes, my mind immediately fills with images of dark robes, camel trains and oases. In fact, I'm presently standing at the edge of an oasis, but not one with palm trees around a spring: it's just a few wooden tables under shading trees.

A sign announces that this is the 'Yigal Allon Picnic Area'.

I doubt that this is a popular hang-out for the Bedouin, since Allon was the Israeli general responsible for the southern command in 1948. In December of that year, tens of thousands of Bedouin were driven out of Israel – into Gaza, Egypt or Jordan.

My visit to see the Bedouin will reveal another phenomenon I've wanted to investigate: that of 'unrecognized villages'. Suha had mentioned them to me a few days ago, and I hadn't a clue what she was talking about. So, as usual, she had explained what they were.

In a Knesset document dating from 1965, the land on which dozens of Palestinian villages were situated was abruptly reclassified as non-residential agricultural land. This meant the villages were denied official recognition and excluded from any development schemes. Furthermore all buildings in them were, retroactively, denied planning permission. The Knesset had voted officially to designate as 'unrecognized' the homes of tens of thousands of citizens. They became illegal and therefore liable to immediate demolition.

The unrecognized villages, URVs, are all Arab – and most of them are home to Bedouin people. The vast majority of these communities existed prior to 1948. An organization was set up to work for the URVs in 1988, the Association of Forty – forty being the number of villages first represented by the group. Now there are more villages on its books: forty-five in the Negev and nine more in the north of the country. Leaving the picnic area, I carry on to Beersheba to visit the organization's southern headquarters.

After mile upon mile of rolling brown desert, the skyline of the old centre of Beersheba looks to me like a 'proper' oasis town, with tall trees lining streets of stone buildings. The city was redeveloped as an administrative centre by the Ottoman Turks about a century ago. In a wonderful cultural mix, the Ottomans hired a German architect to create something on the lines of an English garden suburb; a kind of Welwyn in a wadi. When British troops led by Viscount Allenby came through to defeat the Ottoman forces in the First World War, they must have felt at home right away.

I find the office of the Association of Forty on the first floor of a drab building on a side-street. I'm welcomed in by Attia El Assam, the organization's co-ordinator for the Negev region. While his immediate neighbours on this floor work for another NGO serving the Arab community in the Negev, Attia tells me that the building is Jewish-owned, and that most of his neighbours are Jewish. Sadly, they rarely exchange anything more than a 'hello' – if that.

Attia's face is sun-lined, neatly framed by grey hair and beard. He has thoughtful, smiling eyes. After each question I ask him, he thinks quietly for a moment before translating his thoughts into English for me. He explains that, as well as helping with more practical issues like putting in water pipes and road improvements, his work for the Association involves arranging social events for the inhabitants of the unrecognized villages. Recently they had a 'Fun Day' with ten buses bringing together children from the Galilee, central Israel and the Negev, an important way of building a sense of identity and community among young Bedouin.

The office is small. Attia's desk holds a computer, while a couple of other tables are piled with papers. Maps of the Negev, showing details of land ownership in 1948 and the modern situation of the unrecognized villages, line the wall – along with a lurid picture of swans in a park. One map catches my eye. Covering much of the northern half of the Negev, some forty-five by fifty-five kilometres, it is divided into coloured zones. Yellow takes up most space. This represents Jewish settlements. Ochre and light mauve are the next largest, marking military zones and an airfield. Then there are pink and purple areas, representing industrial and chemical plant zones. And there are smaller splodges of green. These are the 'settled Bedouin localities'. Black triangles indicate planned Jewish settlements; red squares are for recently recognized Bedouin villages; blue circles are the unrecognized Bedouin villages. Beersheba is entirely yellow on the map.

After making me a strong Arab coffee he says he has arranged a visit to a URV about half an hour away from Beersheba. As we drive through the city I have a strong sense of his wounded pride as he points out fine Ottoman-era buildings, official and private alike. Although this was yet another town designated to be part of the Palestinian state under the UN Partition Plan, the

Israelis took it by force in 1948 and drove out the entire population, all Arab, of course, with repeated bombing raids. They were not allowed back after the war and today there is only a handful of Palestinian residents.

He waves a hand at a grand stone mansion, announcing briefly, 'Arab, before 'forty-eight.' At one point he gestures towards a tree growing high above one of the elegant compounds. 'That tree was there before Israel.' The poignant, almost comical 'claim' to the tree on behalf of the Arab community seems to reflect the endless frustration of being denied a culture.

As we head out of town, Attia points out Um Battin, a Bedouin village.

'It was recognized in 1994 but still they have no electricity.'

'But there are pylons running right over it!' I exclaim.

'Yes,' says Attia. 'Being recognized is just one stage in the long battle to get our rights as citizens.'

I'd assumed that the Bedouin in Palestine were a fully nomadic people until quite recently. I'd imagined they had moved freely across the desert, happily ignoring international boundaries, trading and herding their goats and sheep, up to the establishment of Israel. Yet, while most still lived in black goat-hair tents and had strong connections with relatives in the Sinai, by early in the twentieth century they were already living a far more settled existence, moving within localized areas to provide grazing for their flocks, and growing crops on land owned under a system of unwritten understandings between neighbours. British Mandate records show that nearly all of the region was used by the Bedouin and maps of the period detail tribal holdings.

Today the Bedouin are the most downtrodden section of Israel's population. Their situation is desperate. Expulsions and confiscations have left most Bedouin unable to produce food themselves and there are very few employment opportunities, save for low-paid manual work on building sites or Jewish farms. Much of the community lacks services, such as proper supplies of water and electricity, educational provision or anything like adequate healthcare.

In the aftermath of 1948 only some 11,000 Bedouin, out of a pre-war population of 80,000 or more, remained. Many thousands more were expelled from Israel until the late 1950s. Those Bedouin who stayed were removed from their own lands. They were concentrated in the north-east corner of the Negev, which formed a triangle between the towns of Beersheba, Arad and Dimona. This area became known as the Seyag (Arabic for 'fence' or 'enclosure') and covered some 1,500 square kilometres. As a result of this policy, hardly any Bedouin now live in northern, southern and western parts of the Negev. Lands in those areas were given to new Jewish kibbutzim and *moshavim* (co-operative agricultural communities, similar to kibbutzim but made up of individually owned, rather than collective, farms) or taken for military use.

* * *

Alsara is an unrecognized village on a road that winds across gently undulating desert towards the heart of a vast area reserved for a military airbase. The one-storey houses couldn't be simpler: breeze-block walls with corrugated-iron roofs, some with solar panels perched on them, and a small fenced area for animals. Water comes in a thin hosepipe from the junction with the main road two miles away. There is no electricity supply.

Four children play on the track as Attia drives to the house furthest from the road, which sits on a slight rise in the land. This is the home of Khalil Alamour, the village leader. Chickens peck in the dust as we pass through a neat 'fence' of cacti and climb the steps to his veranda. Under the corrugated roof the terrace is cooled by the breeze, the air scented by the hedge of flowers growing around the veranda.

Khalil Alamour has a big smile, a loud laugh and excellent English. How did it get so good?

'I had to learn to listen fast,' he says, grinning broadly, as we sit looking out over the dusty village. 'Years ago I worked for the local community centre and helped with summer camps. I always volunteered to look after the students from England who came to help. In the morning we had English lessons. In the afternoon the volunteers organized activities. These British guys would always stop and help me understand English grammar. But sometimes they'd speak very, very quickly between themselves. So I'd ask them, "Please speak slowly." So they'd speak slowly for a bit and then speed up again. After a while one guy got mad at me for interrupting him and said, "Would you please listen faster!"'

Despite growing up in this remote place, Khalil is well educated, with a BA in mathematics and education, and a master's in education. His day job is teaching maths in the high school in Kseifa, a 'recognized' town a few miles further east. He continues his own studies, having taken courses in computer science. He has rigged up an Internet connection and runs lines from the router to his relatives living in nearby houses. A diesel generator, augmented by solar panels, powers his connection with the wider world but also keeps a fridge running constantly where the villagers can store medicines.

Khalil, who is in his early forties, takes his responsibilities to his community, both at Alsara and at Kseifa, very seriously. He has studied community leadership and helped set up after-school programmes, and is a long-term member of the local committee.

The Israeli government, from local to national level, takes no responsibility for Khalil and his neighbours. 'The only thing we get from the state is a school bus. It takes the kids to Kseifa, about fifteen kilometres away, in the morning. But for little ones like this,' Khalil points to the young children playing near the house, 'there's nothing. No kindergarten. Kids aged three to five in Jewish villages and settlements go to school. Here they can't.'

The village had no running water until 1998. Fifty years after the establishment of the state, and a very long struggle, the government granted a very small tap – just one inch in diameter – for the whole village. It was not in the village but some two miles away at the main road. They were told to fill cans and tanks of water there and bring them back to their homes.

'Naturally we didn't agree and we fixed up pipes to bring the water to the village. But, of course,' Khalil continues, with a laugh, 'that was an "illegal" action and they tried to make trouble. I showed them what we had done and said, "You can arrest me any time. It's simple – we have to drink water. We didn't harm any of you."'

They have water, just, but no other services. Each large family has a generator, which they run for a few hours every evening. Apart from severely limiting the use of washing-machines and refrigerators, the generators make a lot of noise and, as Khalil says, the lack of power means the children have limited opportunity to use computers, the Internet or even watch television.

'What happens if someone is sick?' I ask. 'What healthcare is there for the village?'

'Nothing,' Khalil states. 'We have to travel to Kseifa for the nearest clinic. But Jewish settlements have everything. Even the smallest one near here in the mountains of Hebron has a clinic. That settlement has just ten families while here we are sixty families.'

And, of course, the Jewish settlements have no fear of eviction. The state security forces are there to protect their homes, not threaten them. For the residents of the URVs, eviction and the demolition of their homes is a constant worry and common occurrence. 'It's routine – nobody takes any notice of what is happening here.'

231

Attia shrugs. 'For Israelis there is building, for Palestinians there is demolition.'

Khalil tells me, his light voice at times trembling with emotion, how it feels when your community is being pushed into a corner: 'About one year or so ago, they came here suddenly without any notice and posted eviction orders up on six houses. A few days later they came and posted them on every other home. There were about a hundred who came. It was terrifying and horrible.'

The forces were members of the Border Police (Magav), which is described as the 'combat arm' of the Israeli Police. They have grey uniforms and are trained by the army but serve with the police force. As well as operating in the occupied West Bank, they are used within Israel to deal with Arab matters.

'All of them were carrying sticks and guns,' says Khalil. 'We had to stand and watch this happen. I took some pictures of them posting the orders. There's nothing more you can do. People were very confused, scared, frightened.'

Villagers have learned not to interrupt or interact with the Border Police. To do so usually results in arrest and probably a beating.

'The second time they came, one village woman heard a lot of noise and opened her door. She was six months pregnant. She collapsed and we took her to the hospital but she gave birth prematurely and her baby died a few hours later. It was a tragedy, really traumatic, you know?'

'No, I don't know,' I say quietly. I can imagine parts of

that experience, having been beaten by gunmen, and having rushed my wife Anna to hospital when she went into labour prematurely with our daughter. Both were profoundly traumatic events. The first I have come to terms with because it was a freak experience at the hands of kidnappers in a place far from my home, committed by young men who were not following orders but having gruesome fun of their own. The second worked out fine in the end as both mother and baby survived and prospered. Once we got to hospital, though still frightened, we were cared for.

While the Bedouin woman, her family and friends had tried to come to terms with the tragedy of losing a child, the gunmen had carried on their brutal operation, posting demolition orders as well as eviction notices.

Khalil gets up and goes inside, returning with a sheaf of papers – a collection of those that have been posted through his door. 'Now every house has a demolition order – that's for all the four hundred people who live here. This village has been here for at least ten generations. We are the indigenous people.' Khalil pauses and his broad smile breaks across his face once more. 'Everywhere else, the indigenous people are the most respected. In this country it is the opposite. I don't hate people. But I do hate the system.'

Attia takes me the long way back to Beersheba, on a swing around the east and south of the great military zone. The main road passes the recognized and long-settled Bedouin village of Kseifa, where Khalil teaches.

I am amazed by how much land there is. It stretches out for miles in every direction, empty brown earth, criss-crossed by all these roads for which there appears to be little traffic. The highway pushes relentlessly on across the desert, ploughing straight through Kseifa's old Muslim cemetery.

'This highway is called Peace Street,' Attia announces suddenly, with a grin, as we turn south on to another main road. 'To mark the signing of the peace treaty with Egypt in 1979. The Israelis pulled out of the Sinai, so the military needed more land at home. They confiscated eighty thousand dunams [twenty thousand acres] for the airbase here. Five thousand Bedouin were moved out.'

Government policy towards the Bedouin was spelled out by General Moshe Dayan. In an interview with the *Haaretz* newspaper in 1963, he said, 'We should trans-form the Bedouin into an urban proletariat – in industry, services, construction and agriculture. Eighty-eight per cent of the Israeli population are not farmers, let the Bedouin be like them. Indeed, this will be a radical move, which means that the Bedouin would not live on his land with his herds but would become an urban person who comes home in the afternoon and puts his slippers on. His children will get used to a father who wears pants, without a dagger, and who does not pick out their nits in public. They will go to school, their hair combed and parted. This will be a revolution, but it can be achieved in two generations. Without coercion but with governmental direction . . . this phenomenon of the Bedouins will disappear.'

The 'phenomenon' hasn't disappeared. Despite extensive immigration by Jewish Israelis, the Bedouin comprise over a quarter of the population of the Negev. The aim of transforming them into an urban proletariat has been partly successful, however, with half now living in modern towns like Rahat. The other half, around 80,000 people, still live on their old lands or, more often, lands they were moved to by the state in the 1950s. The internal transfer of the Arab Bedouin population to the north-eastern Negev has deprived tribes of their land and concentrated them on lands not their own, under increasingly crowded conditions. Today the Negev Bedouin hold only 3 per cent of the land.

Attia pulls off the road and heads up a rough track a little way. Leaving the van we walk up past a water pumping station. Driving around the desert, hearing stories of how pitiful the URVs' supplies are, I keep noticing the pipes running alongside the roads and the big spigots at every junction. It is just as it is with the electricity: if you're an Arab and you won't go where the authorities tell you, you can be just a hundred yards away but water and power are denied you.

At the crest of the hill Attia sweeps his arm in a broad curve. And I realize we're looking out over hundreds and hundreds of square miles of Negev. 'This is the centre of Seyag,' Attia explains. He points out a ruined stone building a few hundred metres away. 'That was a Bedouin place. Not all lived in tents,' he says, planting his feet firmly on the ground and crossing his arms. 'These were permanent places.'

This windblown, arid landscape has a certain stark beauty, yet it seems a cruel irony that, having made such a harsh environment your home, a government would deny it to you. 'How do you feel as you look across this wide desert?' I ask.

After a long pause, he replies, 'Always sad.'

An hour later we are back at Attia's office. While he prays, I read what my *AA Explorer Guide* has to say about Beersheba. It notes the Ottoman renovation of the city but concentrates mainly on the Bible story. The guide tells me that this is where Abraham settled and was told he must sacrifice one son, Isaac, and whence he banished another son, Ishmael.

With regard to the Bedouin people who were once the majority here, the guide advises, 'Bedouin encampments can be seen south of the town; big, dark tents among which human beings, camels and dogs go about their business together under the desert sky.' It doesn't mention picking nits in public, but otherwise I'm sure Moshe Dayan would have approved.

Attia takes me to a meeting of the Bedouin Education Committee at the Tulip Hotel. At times I am over-whelmed by the surreal world of the Arab people in Israel. Here we are, driving through a modern city in a modern car. The people I am with are citizens of the state we are in and we are going to a very normal kind of gathering – about education. Yet somehow I feel we should be meeting in a remote village, in secret, since these people are clearly campaigning against a government whose policies are working against them, sometimes even violently. It doesn't seem right that we go to a normal – frankly, rather boring – hotel for this meeting in a conference room on the third floor.

The forum, of representatives from the various Bedouin communities, is aimed at formulating a plan for the next stage of their campaign for Bedouin children to have equal educational opportunities to Jewish children. The Bedouin are packed into smaller schools, many of which are caravans, not proper buildings, and often lack any outside shade, which just one afternoon in the Negev has told me is a serious matter. At the back of Bedouin men's minds run fears that, with so much to face, their children will turn to drugs, crime or the politics of violence to hold their corner in the world.

Attia drops me off at the Beit Yatziv Youth Hostel and Guesthouse on Ha'atzmaut (Independence) Street. It is quite late and Reception has closed so I am checked in by a rather supercilious youth in the security cabin. He has an enormous pistol on his belt. There is no bar or shop so I go for a walk in search of somewhere to buy water. Under the twilight of Beersheba's streetlights I stroll beside a low wall surrounding a cemetery. Rows of graves march off into darkness beneath palm trees. A carved plaque tells me: 'The land on which this cemetery stands is the free grant of the people of Palestine to whom it was given by the municipality of Beersheba for the perpetual resting place of those of the Allied Armies who fell in the war 1914–1918 and are honoured here.'

The people of Palestine might have been grateful to the British and Australian troops for driving out the Ottoman rulers in 1917. By the time Yigal Allon was herding the Bedouin off their lands, the gratitude may have worn a little thin.

15

How Long Will They Laugh and I Cry?

EARLY THE NEXT MORNING, ATTIA EL ASSAM PICKS ME up from the youth hostel. This is my favourite time of day: the sun is not yet unbearably hot, and its light is fresh and clear. We drive past the British cemetery I saw last night. It's only just after eight o'clock and already two gardeners are hard at work tidying around the graves as sprinklers water the grass.

This beautifully manicured space is in stark contrast to the Muslim graveyard we pass a mile or so away across the Old Town, at the opposite end of Ha'atzmaut Street. For sixty years it has been out of bounds to Muslims, who only occasionally manage to sneak over the fence to clear the weeds. I can see many damaged gravestones and much rough earth; it looks like the site of an excavation, or the aftermath of a grave-robber's attack.

The old city mosque, built during the Ottoman redevelopment a hundred years ago, is also fenced off. No one has been allowed to worship there since the

239

indigenous population of Beersheba was evicted in 1948.

'Some friends and I suggested to the council that rather than leave the building to rot it should be used as a centre for the three faiths,' Attia tells me, his face serious, 'but the idea was rejected. People said, "The Muslims will just take advantage and treat it as their own."'

The walls have now been partially demolished. Fences have been erected for public safety: the mosque is deemed a dangerous structure.

Attia is smiling again as he tells me, 'I want you to meet a real Bedouin, living alone in his tent in the desert. But first we must pick up a friend.'

On the outskirts of Beersheba, behind some serious fencing, is the neat and beautiful Beverly Hills-like suburb of Omer. The streets here are all properly tarmacked with kerbs and pavements. Homes, set back from the street, are shaded by abundant trees and shrubs. Attia tells me this is an exclusively Jewish neighbourhood. We pull up outside a handsome bungalow and he beeps the horn. A tall woman with long, greying hair appears immediately from the front door and is soon shaking hands with Attia and me.

Haia Noach is Jewish and a former secretary general of the Peace Now movement. She set up the Negev Coexistence Forum for Civil Equality in 1997 and is its president. 'We campaign for Bedouin rights in the Negev,' she explains, in a soft voice. 'We've produced reports on the situation here, including one for the UN Committee on the Elimination of Racial Discrimination.'

I ask Haia how she became involved with the Bedouin rights movement.

'Partly it was that,' she says, pointing out of the window.

We're driving through the fence around Omer and Haia is pointing across the road to what looks like a massive rubbish dump. 'That's my neighbourhood, Amra. It's a URV.'

It makes me think of a place at the end of the world, a Mad Max encampment sheltering a few survivors after an atomic Armageddon. It is a wasteland of maybe five acres, with rutted tracks criss-crossing it between shack dwellings surrounded by corrugated-metal fences. Dust and debris drift across this dismal terrain in the bright morning light. A mule, tethered in front of a demolished house, stares dolefully at us as Attia's van bumps across the compound. The spindly framework of a water tower stands over a derelict generator tangled in a mess of iron girders and lumps of concrete. Clearly the local council has been at work here. A little boy scampers across this background to disappear through one of the fences.

Checking my Europcar map, I can find no trace of Amra. Omer, though, is plain to see. Its name was adopted in 1953 and comes from the Book of Leviticus. Presumably it was chosen under the Zionist principle of using names that are very close to those of existing Arab places.

As we drive, I hear more about the Bedouin experience since 1948. The confiscation of their land in the Negev has been, as with other Arab lands in the country, 'enshrined' in laws. While many Bedouin families have land-ownership documents dating back to British and even Ottoman rule, others do not. Under Bedouin tradition land was passed down through generations, the details maintained orally rather than on paper. Without proof that the land was registered under previous regimes, the Israeli authorities throw out any historical claims to ownership. The state even had an answer for those whose land was registered. The Israeli government invoked a regulation that had initially been used under Ottoman rule. This regulation, *mawat*, said that if land was unworkable it returned to government control. As the Negev is desert, Israel has declared it unworkable and 'reclaimed' 85 per cent of the region as state land.

Once that happened the Bedouin settlements and homes on it were automatically illegal and 'unrecognized' and thus denied access to water, electricity, healthcare and education services. In line with the policy outlined by Moshe Dayan, the Bedouin were supposed to give up on their land and their way of life and go to the towns designated for them. Haia points out a grim little place just off the main road. 'That's Hura. It's one of the new settlement towns the government has generously set up for the Bedouin. It was started in 1990. Nearly seventeen thousand people live there and it has an area of less than seven thousand dunams [around 1,750 acres]. My town, Omer, has six thousand inhabitants with a jurisdiction of more than twenty thousand dunams [5,000 acres].'

'They want maximum Bedouin on minimum land,' Attia observes.

The discrimination between Jewish and Arab citizens is barefaced. While the Bedouin have been driven or tricked off their lands, Jewish farmers have been encouraged into the area to settle. For them the land is magically no longer designated *mawat*. One Jewish family ready to settle in the Negev might be granted a thousand or even six thousand dunams. And those new farms inevitably attract Bedouin men who, forced from their own lands and forbidden to graze or farm 'state land', are unable even to achieve self-subsistence so need work.

A half-hour drive from Beersheba, the last fifteen minutes over unmade roads across rolling, dusty hillsides, brings us, as far as I can judge, to the middle of nowhere. Getting out of Attia's van, I find myself standing beside what must be the smallest Bedouin encampment in the world. It comprises a makeshift tent of tarpaulin stretched over a few unmatched lengths of wood. This is the home and campaign headquarters of a Bedouin man named Nuri Elokbi.

Trees dot the landscape and in the distance I can see a herd of goats, attended by a small boy. They are moving around another Bedouin encampment, comprising two or three large black tents. This hilltop is in the heart of Al Araqib, an area that was once entirely owned by Bedouin tribes, including Nuri's family. The tent – in reality it is little more than a sunshade as it has no sides – is furnished with an old carpet, a couple of plastic chairs and a neatly laid out sleeping-bag.

Nuri welcomes us and we sit in the shade. The fierce

morning heat is barely tempered by the stiff breeze that
rolls across the hills, making the tarpaulin snap and the
guy-ropes hum. A slender man, with close-cropped silver
hair, blue polo shirt and white chinos, Nuri looks rather
vulnerable, and certainly not the type of person you'd
expect to be taking on the state and its security forces.
But as he starts talking I realize he has a steely reserve,
coupled with a robust sense of humour.

'I will tell the story in the Bedouin way – so it will take
a lot of time,' he starts, leaning back in a sun-bleached
plastic chair. 'I was born in January 1942, in a house a
hundred metres from this tent.'

I look around the empty hillside: it seems impossible
that there was any solid structure here. Nuri watches me
through narrowed eyes and clearly reads my thought. 'It
was all knocked down a long time ago – nearly fifty years,
in fact – but there was even a school where I studied on
this hill. Until the end of 'fifty-one we used to have a
good life. We were on our own land.'

Late in 1948 the Israeli administration made an agreement with sixteen Bedouin sheikhs. Written in Hebrew
and Arabic, it said that the government would recognize
the Bedouin as the owners of the land and respect their
rights.

'At the beginning of November 'fifty-one, they came
and told us we had to go to another place for six months
and then we would be able to return. And we believed
them! You see, for the Bedouin, if you say something,
you have given your word, your honour. Since the day we
had to leave here, I have not had one happy day in my life.

I lost my school, I lost my home, I lost water to drink. Everything was gone.'

It wasn't long before it became clear that the Israeli government had no intention of allowing them back to their lands. The Elokbis and the majority of Bedouin who had not left or been expelled from the country nevertheless became classed as Absentees. Although they were living in the country, they were not occupying their lands on the date set by the state to determine their ownership status, in this case April 1952. So, although it was keeping them under military curfew in the Seyag areas, the Israeli government cynically defined these Bedouin as 'Present Absentees' – and registered their land as state property.

The machinations of the Israeli land laws tend to make one's head spin at the best of times. In the desert heat I find my mind wandering, trying to imagine anything other than dust, rocks and tumbleweed on this place.

'My father had a house right here.' Nuri has brought out a sheaf of files and produces an old black and white aerial photograph of the area around us. 'The land was all owned by my grandfather who split it up among his sons. This photo shows the people living here in 'forty-nine.'

Clearly visible are a couple of dozen stone buildings, a reservoir and a number of tents. Nuri has other photographs, maps and documents going back to the British Mandate, all showing that the Elokbis owned, lived on and farmed the land. As he speaks, I look at the Bedouin tents just half a mile away. The land around them is clearly being used for farming. 'Who's living over there? Members of your clan who managed to stay?'

'No!' replies Nuri, looking at me as if I'm mad. 'They are from another Bedouin family. They were brought here by the official who forced the original Bedouin off this land. Very likely their own land is being used by Jews or Bedouin from somewhere else. So, those people have a permit. They were given thousands of dunams to cultivate and they have to give the officer the crops. You see the straw bales over there by their tents? That's where my grandfather had his house.'

The area the Elokbi clan was moved to in the 1950s was less fertile than their lands at Al Araqib and represented only a tiny proportion of it. Over the years even these lands were reduced by the state. And as they were never given proper title to the property it has now been declared state land and they are deemed squatters. All their homes, built with the full knowledge of local-government officials, are declared illegal and they are denied public services.

'It is a terrible place – worse than the third world,' says Nuri. 'There's a one-inch water pipe for a thousand people. When they build Jewish settlements, they immediately pave the road and the electricity and water is connected, even if they are in mobile houses.'

The Elokbi clan has been told it must move on to Hura, the little township Haia had shown me on the way here. 'The government wants to treat us like turkeys, giving people no chance to choose.' Nuri shakes his head in disgust. 'Since April 2006 I have been living here because I want us to have a cultural community village here in our own area.'

Most people of Nuri's age – which I reckon to be late sixties – would be thinking of retiring to a quieter life and looking after their grandchildren. Yet here he is, in the middle of the desert in a tent, waiting for the next visit by police carrying papers from the Israel Land Administration (ILA) that say he must be removed because he is on state land. They will arrest him and take him away. Usually after these occurrences he returns to find the tent knocked down, his belongings – car, chairs, food, clothes, medicine and water – confiscated.

Nuri will not spend much time away from his land since he knows the JNF is trying to plant a forest on it. He has been arrested on a number of occasions for obstructing the JNF, by standing in front of their tractors and bulldozers, as they try to enter to prepare for planting. However, when he was in court for obstruction during September 2008, the court accepted Nuri's argument that the JNF had no right to enter and plant the land. This was a rare legal victory for a Palestinian, let alone a Bedouin. Despite that ruling, Nuri is still going to court and presenting the same evidence, the documents and maps, that he has done countless times. He has not won the right to return to his own land, where we sit today.

From his tent he runs his campaign to have his right to his clan's hereditary lands upheld. As he sits under his simple tarpaulin, he writes articles for the Arab newspapers and has produced a booklet about the Elokbi situation. And he writes poetry. 'Love poems I write in Arabic. Protest poems I write in Hebrew, because I want the Jews to feel how they have hurt me,' he explains.

He gives me an English translation of one of his protest poems and then waves us off. As the dust swirls up around the van, his scrawny frame retreats under the shade of his black canopy.

> I had an old grandfather,
> He used to have a house
> He used to have a tree,
> They destroyed the house,
> And burned the tree,
> It was done, really done.
> They stole the wheat,
> They took the land
> They took the goat and the sheep.
> I was left with no bread and no milk,
> And no home.
> They said, 'Nobody was here,
> No living soul,
> Nothing, nothing was here, it was desert.'
> And in my hand I had an olive branch.
> Why did they do it?
> Destroyed the house and burned the tree,
> I was crying, crying.
> How long will they laugh and I cry?

This meeting with Nuri, in the company of Attia and Haia, was one of the highlights of my travels to discover the Palestinian people of Israel. Sitting in that simple tent, talking of politics, pride and poetry, I felt a real connection with the people and the landscape, physical and political, around us. In many ways Nuri's story is a tragedy, another forlorn saga of dispossession at the hands of a rapacious state ruthlessly building a country exclusively as a homeland for the Jewish people. But this trio – Nuri, the brave, quixotic fighter for his family domains, Attia, the caring and committed community worker, and Haia, the campaigner who has dedicated her life to building a country that is a homeland not only for Jewish people like her but also for all the other people of Israel – suggested a brighter future. Their friendship, the shared sense of purpose and moral right, was uplifting.

Attia drops Haia back at her smart bungalow in Omer, then takes me back to his office in central Beersheba to collect my car.

'Good luck, John,' he says, as we shake hands. 'You have seen the unrecognized villages and got an idea of life in the desert. Now go to Rahat and see how Israel wants the Bedouin to live.'

It is only a half-hour drive to Rahat. The only Bedouin city in Israel, it has a population of 45,000. Buoyed up by my recent encounter, I wonder if Rahat will prove less depressing than I expect as I drive into town along a tree-lined avenue. But urban elegance doesn't continue. Plain little houses are screened by ugly metal fences on side-streets that soon peter out into unmade tracks. I go along a couple of streets with villas that appear to be elegant, spacious homes, but around them are areas of wasteland. There is an unfinished atmosphere to the place. Not so much that it is not developing, just that it stopped being built.

I'm given a guided tour of some of the poorer areas of the 'city' by Sleman El Kreny, a social worker. At thirty-one, Sleman is slender, with close-cropped dark brown hair. 'Tribal associations are still very important to the Bedouin,' he tells me, as we drive. 'There are five main tribes in Rahat, with around five thousand people in each. Some, like mine, are smaller. There are a hundred of us. Some tribes have been successful, but others have problems.'

Speaking quietly, Sleman draws a vivid portrait of his people. Perhaps because he is speaking in English there is something very matter-of-fact, almost dispassionate, about how he delivers his description. He tells me that, as well as the stresses brought about by government policies, the Bedouins' traditions often work against them. 'In the old days the tribes had their own lands, so there was space. In Rahat, each tribe has its own neighbourhood, but they are living on top of each other. There is often tension,' he explains, 'and when we have local elections there is always violence. Gun and knife fights between the tribes wanting their man to get elected. They are always fighting over resources, government funds, influence and jobs.'

'And what about you? You're a trained social worker. How did you do that?'

'I worked as a labourer for two years to pay my way

through university. I got a degree in social work and just recently I finished studying at the Mandel Leadership Institute in Jerusalem.' He pauses and goes on proudly, 'I am a fellow of the Mandel Institute.'

As he directs me around the dismal streets of Rahat, Sleman leans forward, keeping his hands on his knees. When he wants me to turn off, he points with the appropriate index finger, saying, 'Here.' This oddly furtive signalling system means that I have to watch the street and his knees at the same time – not ideal for maintaining road safety.

As we drive tentatively around town, the call to midday prayers sounds from a mosque. Built with private donations, this is about the only imposing public building in Rahat. For a city of more than 40,000 the services are pitiful. There is only a small market area with a few shops around it. There is one post office and one bank. There are no factories or business centres, no social spaces, theatre or cinema, not even a library or a swimming-pool; nowhere, as Sleman says, for anyone to go and do anything. I think of my home town of Woodbridge, less than a quarter the size of Rahat, and soon lose count of the facilities, shops and entertainments that our community has.

'The state supports the Jewish sector but gives nothing to the Bedouin except a small amount of money in National Insurance.' A smile flits across Sleman's face but he carries on speaking with intensity. 'Take the Jewish new town of Lehavim near here. They have community centres, swimming-pools, clean streets, public celebrations, a hospital and a big clinic.'

Just across the main road from Rahat is Kibbutz Shoval. Home to some six hundred people, it was set up in 1946 and now has a thriving economy based on a plastics industry and agriculture. It has one of the largest dairy farms in the area and vast tracts of arable land – taken from local Bedouin families, who were forced to move east in 1956.

The cruel irony is that the Jewish settlements, the small agricultural communities and co-operatives like the kibbutz and *moshav*, would be an ideal model for the modern Bedouin.

'You know, John, Rahat and the other seven Bedouin towns in the Negev are all on the list of Israel's ten poorest municipalities.' Sleman pauses to point left and says, 'Here.'

As I turn the car he carries on with his litany of despair, and I feel the optimism inspired by Nuri Elokbi and his friends seeping from me. The statistics Sleman is reciting seem insurmountable: 'Fifty per cent of the adult population and sixty per cent of the children live below the poverty line.'

We arrive in one of the poorer districts, home to a thousand people. Here there are no villas, and the homes are smaller and basic, some little more than tin shacks. Pathways are uneven and dusty, and the air is full of the noise and smells of chickens and sheep kept in pens rigged up outside the houses.

'The people have no hope,' Sleman tells me, as he guides me along dusty lanes. 'They have no money and no work, and as there are no factories or anything here, their children will be caught up in the same cycle. They get just two thousand NIS [New Israel Shekel; less than £300] a month from the state. And that is to cover every-thing the family needs.'

As we pull up at a shack, we are warmly greeted by Sleman's uncle. At thirty-seven Salem Abu Jaber is just six years older than his nephew, but from his careworn face I'd have put him in his late forties. His four young children join us as we sit in the shade outside their simple home.

'Until ten years ago I lived in my father's house,' Salem explains. 'Then I got married and had to move out. I bought a little piece of land but cannot afford to build a house, so we have to live here. I earn five thousand NIS a month as a building labourer, in Ashdod. I have to get up at five every morning to get there. It is very hard work. My wife is unemployed. Money is very tight for us.'

The prospect of saving enough money from his meagre wages ever to build a proper house on his land is so remote that Salem seems to have given up on the plan.

'What's the point of me saving so I can finish the house when I am seventy? This house is illegal so we have no services from the municipality. I get water and electricity by cable from my brother's house. I bought a computer for the kids because I think that's important. My father was against me carrying on at school, but I want mine to get a better education. The school is their future.'

The children walk to a school nearby and work hard there, their father announces proudly. The oldest girl, who is nearly eight, says she wants to be a nurse. Salem is keenly aware of how his lack of education has limited his prospects. Other members of his family continued their education, studying medicine and law. One of his brothers now works in Frankfurt in IT. Salem doesn't speak of escaping the limitations of his life in modern Israel but he does yearn to leave Rahat.

'I grew up in a big wide open space and feel I can't breathe on this little three-hundred-metre plot,' he says. 'I moved here in the mid-1980s when I was fifteen, and found it very strange. The state did nothing to prepare us for the transfer from the open lands to these towns and the new lifestyle. My parents' generation took it very badly. Suddenly they found themselves cooped up in little houses without their land around them, without their flocks of sheep. Now they may have one sheep and a couple of chickens. The social life collapsed in many ways. When they lived out in the open, people visited each other. All the encampments were open house. After the move they guarded their little bit of space and didn't welcome each other. They are stuck in the past, always looking back.'

After a moment of quiet Salem shrugs, looks intently at me, then at his nephew and then, one by one, at his four children. His next words are addressed to them as much as to the visitors: 'It was a crisis for our people. Before the move we didn't have stress, we were healthy. The government promised us a paradise here, where we would live well. We got nothing.'

* * *

Once, sitting round a campfire under the star-filled sky of the Sinai desert in Egypt, I spoke about Paradise with another Bedouin. Wearing traditional clothes, he talked of his belief in God and his vision of Paradise as a vast, green, fruit-filled oasis. He wasn't educated, he wasn't rich, but he was totally at one with his environment; he belonged there.

Rahat is nothing like that and the Bedouin here are living a life that is a long way from that of their Sinai cousin, who was then still tending his flocks in the great wide spaces of the desert. From what I have seen of it, Rahat is not a place to live in. It isn't a real city, just a government plan. The people here are caught like the Native Americans were and forced to live in reservations. No wonder they want to get away from the place.

Sleman, who is one of fifteen children and married with four offspring of his own, tells me that the Bedouin of his generation don't necessarily want to give up on modern conveniences to live in tents. They want their land back to farm and live on, and they want to pursue the careers on offer in a modern country like Israel.

As they try to come to terms with an abrupt and enormous shift from their traditional lifestyle, the prospects of the Bedouin winning their rights or building a future on their old lands seem remote. All around them they see Jewish settlers who are provided by the state with every assistance and amenity as they take over the con-fiscated Bedouin lands. The state offers the dispossessed indigenous community no alternative but to languish in the new towns with minimal infrastructure and no chance of economic development.

Yet despite all that, just as has happened in the broader Palestinian community in Israel, the Bedouin are developing an independent, educated leadership. The likes of Khalil, Sleman, Attia and Nuri are thwarting Moshe Dayan's prediction that the phenomenon of the Bedouin would disappear.

'So are you Bedouin, Israeli or Palestinian?' I ask Sleman.

'Our identity is Arabic. We are Arabs first, then we are Palestinians and finally we are Bedouin. Bedouin is a way of life.'

16

Location, Location, Location

A FTER A COUPLE OF DAYS IN THE NEGEV I FIND myself looking forward to a glimpse of the Mediterranean, as I drive north and 'home' to the nuns in Haifa.

If I lived in Israel I would want a home by the sea. To be able to look out over the blue waters and visit the almost endless beaches would be very good for the soul. Before 1948 Palestinian Arab villages were dotted all along the coast. The UN Partition Plan of 1947 allocated the proposed new Arab state well over a third of the 215 kilometres of shoreline. After 1948, though, the Palestinian territories had just the forty kilometres of the Gaza Strip.

Apart from sizeable communities in the old coastal cities of Acre, Haifa and Jaffa, the Palestinian presence on Israel's shoreline is now limited to just one location, the romantically named town of Jisr al-Zarqa, or Bridge over Blue Water. It takes up only a couple of hundred metres of the sea's edge. All the other Palestinian villages on the coast were 'cleared' by Israeli forces during and after the 1947–8 war.

This place has often intrigued me when I've been driving north from Tel Aviv to Haifa. After the urban sprawl of Tel Aviv, the landscape has a real sense of freshness and vitality, with thousands of acres of banana plantations, fish farms and light industrial parks. Every couple of miles there is a slip-road with a sign to a new housing development. Blue and white Israeli flags fly everywhere, from buildings and telegraph poles.

Except at Jisr al-Zarqa. Here the skyline changes: tall, white, green-tipped minarets replace the blue and white flags.

Passing it on my way back from Rahat I look, as I always do, for a turning from the highway but can't see one. Frustrated, I decide to ask Suha, pull into a lay-by and phone her. I tell her I've just passed Jisr al-Zarqa and that I'd like to visit it. Before I ask, 'Do you know anyone who could help?' I'm confident of her reply.

'Of course I do,' she says. 'I'll call my friend Khawla in the morning and let you know. Get some rest – you must be tired.'

A couple of days later I'm approaching Jisr al-Zarqa with Khawla Rihani sitting beside me in the passenger seat. We met earlier and had coffee at her office in Haifa. She has one of those voices that seem to run all over the tonal scale and are very attractive in an eccentric sort of way. A mass of tightly curled hair falls to her shoulders.

As we drive along, she laughs at her English, which is very good, and I laugh at my Arabic, which is atrocious.

Khawla works for Economic Empowerment for Women (EEW). This is a joint Jewish–Arab organization, which provides education and assistance to women from Jewish and Arab communities in setting up small businesses. Khawla's enthusiasm for her work is infectious, and she is soon telling me more about it. Her clients are at the very bottom of the economic and social scales. For many poor women, Khawla tells me, especially within the Palestinian community, it is very hard to break out of the traditional roles of mother and housekeeper. Lack of education, marrying very young and lacking the opportunity to travel from their villages and towns, the women can do little to boost family income. Later this morning Khawla has a meeting with one of her groups.

The low-rise apartment blocks of Jisr al-Zarqa have none of the 'brand-new' shine of the other places that line the main coastal highway, and even though the town sits right beside the dual-carriageway, there are neither slip-roads nor signs to it. The only way in is from the old road, a mile or two inland. One approach swings over a bridge to the northern edge, but to reach the town centre you enter via an underpass. At the last minute the side-road narrows to a gravel track and dips down as you go under the highway. Nestled on the Mediterranean shore this should be a dream location, yet as we arrive at the entrance to Jisr al-Zarqa I realize that something is wrong, distorted, with this dream.

'It's weird!' I say to Khawla. 'It feels as though we're being squeezed into another place.'

'Exactly!' she replies, with a wry laugh. 'Maybe it says something about how the authorities see the inhabitants.'

I find myself taking a deep breath as we 'bob' under the highway, and when we come up on the other side of the bridge the sense of breathlessness continues as the buildings crowd in on all sides.

Although Jisr has a total area of just over 1,500 dunams, only 600 (150 acres) are designated for housing. The town's population of some 12,000 must all live in a space less than half the size of London's Hyde Park.

We stop and pick up cousins Khalil and Muhammad Ammash, who take us on a tour of the town. Both men are young and dynamic: Khalil, a graduate of Haifa University, works for Jisr Council running training courses and activities for youths, especially those who don't finish their schooling; Muhammad works with a youth programme in Jaffa.

As we drive around, Khalil and Muhammad point out the civil amenities, consisting of a very modest council building and a simple two-storey community centre. The streets are close-knit and apartment blocks sprout half-completed top floors. Khalil tells us that one such building is home to a hundred people. 'It's a neighbourhood in its own right,' he jokes. 'Several generations of one family live there, four children in each small room.'

Khawla summarizes some of the key factors that

generate social problems in towns like Jisr: 'Women will often get married at fifteen or sixteen years old, so families get larger and so do their economic problems. Hardship and overcrowding lead to trouble between men and women; there are drug and alcohol problems and domestic violence. Such troubles at home tend to affect the children's socialization and behaviour. They have difficulty concentrating at school. Something like thirty-three per cent of students in schools here cannot read or write.'

The world continues to close in as I drive around the town. Not only is there limited housing space but the local planning authority won't allow the people of Jisr to build on any of the little open land remaining in the town. Also, it has refused permission for the town to expand beyond its existing area.

While around seven hundred new Jewish communities have been founded since the formation of the state, not a single new Arab community, aside from the state-sponsored and unwanted new towns in the Negev, like Rahat, has been established in Israel. This means that close to 1.5 million people live on the same amount of land as 160,000 did in 1948.

Ninety-three per cent of Israel is held as public domain under the control of the Israel Lands Administration, which is heavily influenced by the JNF. The JNF was established to acquire and develop lands exclusively for the benefit of Jewish people residing in Israel.

In addition to there being a lack of land for Palestinians to build on, getting permission to build on existing lands is practically impossible too. This problem isn't limited to the unrecognized villages, which have no official development plans. Fewer than half of the country's 128 recognized Arab towns and villages had had master plans accepted at the end of 2009. In some Arab communities any buildings erected over the past six decades might be deemed illegal, so their owners live in constant fear that their homes will be demolished.

We stop off for coffee at the home of eighty-six-year-old Anis Jarban, whose children and grandchildren share the building. Anis is rather deaf, so the conversation, which includes Anis, various sons and neighbours who drop in, as well as Khawla, Khalil, Muhammad and me, is carried on at great volume. As everyone tries to make themselves heard above one another and the blaring television mounted high on the wall, I tune out and take in the immediate surroundings.

We sit in a corner of a large room that serves as a family living room and, judging by the large bed in one corner, a bedroom to one of the families. As well as the bed and seating area, there are wardrobes, cupboards and piles of clothes everywhere. Khawla tells me that the Jarban home is typical of Jisr. Like the town itself, it has the air of a place of transit, not a permanent home.

After coffee we head to the beach. Surely the Mediterranean waves lapping across the sand will offer a sense of hope and space to counter the depressing confines of the town centre? But no: although there are waves and sand, the Jisr shore is neither an enticing beach nor a busy harbour. It is desolate. There is none of the bustle I would expect to find in a fishing waterfront on the Mediterranean shore. There are no bars or cafés and just a few tatty fishing boats bobbing in the harbour. Khalil tells me that only twenty-five families, a tiny fraction of Jisr's population, can make a living from the sea.

The beach is designated as state land. Many other open areas in Jisr are designated as of archaeological interest – for example, the town's Roman ruins – or have been taken as a national wildlife park. Although such features would be a great draw for a burgeoning tourist industry, any development schemes proposed by the local population to capitalize on these assets are rejected. It's a great shame – I can easily imagine a couple of bijou hotels set back from the beach and a café beside them named after the al-Zarqa stream, but such ideas would never fly.

As we watch a fisherman cleaning his sparse catch beside a shack knocked up from driftwood and rusty corrugated iron, a party of Jewish schoolchildren come walking along the beach with their teacher, who is dressed in the black clothes and hat of an orthodox Haredi Jew. The group goes on to look at the Roman ruins with but the briefest nod between the fisherman and the teacher.

The two cousins want to take us to see one of the few 'developments' that have occurred in the area. We drive back inland and Muhammad directs me down a

side-road to the southern edge of town. We pass a couple
of half-built breeze-block structures and the road peters
out as a massive embankment rears up in front of us.

We leave the car and clamber up the ridge. I follow
Khawla, Khalil and Muhammad to the top. To the north
is Jisr, to the south Caesarea. None of us speaks. The
view across Caesarea is filled with the bright green of the
well-watered gardens that surround each villa. Managed
by a private organization, the Caesarea Development
Corporation, the town's five thousand-odd inhabitants
can spread out over 35,000 dunams, so swimming-pools
sparkle outside many homes and there is a golf course
and country club. The ancient port and Roman theatre
are developed as major cultural attractions and there is a
large business park. The community has two direct links
on to the highway. Up until the expulsions of 1948,
Caesarea had a predominantly Arab population; now it
is entirely Jewish. It is a very wealthy community, home
to some of Israel's leading figures, including Prime
Minister Binyamin Netanyahu. Looking the other way, I
see Jisr: a drab, grey, densely packed urban environment
where no swimming-pools reflect the Mediterranean sun.
The town's minarets stretch up to the sky like funnels
desperately seeking fresh air. The difference between the
places is shocking, but how had this dividing rampart
come to be built?

Khalil explains that in November 2002 the neighbouring Jewish community began piling up the earthen
embankment between itself and the Palestinians of Jisr.
The people of Jisr were not informed that the barrier,

which stands four or five metres high and runs 160 metres from the highway to the shore, was to be built.

'The people of Caesarea said they need the barrier,' Khalil explains, 'because they didn't like the noise of the call to prayer from the mosques. They also claimed that the embankment was to stop thefts they blamed on young people from Jisr.'

Muhammad joins in: 'That's nonsense! Look how easy it was to climb – anybody can just walk over it. The real reason for this barrier is that the rich Jewish people of Caesarea are racist and don't want to see the poor and overcrowded Arabs next door.'

People say that the Palestinian citizens of Israel live 'behind a glass wall'. At first sight it looks as though they live in the same space as their Jewish neighbours, but that impression is a distortion of reality. Jisr seems to epitomize this distortion. Caesarea has space, money and power. Jisr al-Zarqa has none of those. Caesarea is, of course, featured in my *AA Explorers Guide*. Jisr al-Zarqa, of course, is not.

Muhammad and Khalil explain how profoundly the barrier has affected their community. Even though there is no legal backing for it, children dare not cross it and adults, too, feel it as a real limit on their lives. The psychological effect has been to make residents afraid and ashamed.

'We are very angry and feel very isolated,' says Muhammad, making a fist of his right hand and slapping it into the palm of the left. 'It makes us feel we are second-class citizens, less valuable than Jews.'

Khalil nods. 'It's like the Wall round the West Bank, except that we are meant to be citizens of Israel.'

With the town hemmed in by the national park to the north, the embankment to the south, the highway to the east and the sea to the west, Khalil is fearful for its future. 'Sometimes it's hard to feel alive in Israel,' he tells me, squinting into the bright sun. 'We need more land. Otherwise, as we have more children, I think we will have a disaster here in a few years' time. With no jobs and too many people, the place will explode.'

It is time for Khawla's meeting with the women's group so we drop off Muhammad and Khalil. Muhammad asks me to wait while he goes into his house. He emerges a few moments later carrying a small plastic bag. It contains a handful of pebbles. 'Here, John, a few stones from our Palestinian beach for you. Please come again one day.'

On the way to the women's group, I ponder the nature of Israel once again. It presents itself as a democracy, and in many ways it is. Yet any claim that the Jewish homeland aims to be a homeland, too, to its non-Jewish population is hard to defend.

This is particularly the case when one examines the distinction that Israel makes between 'citizenship' and 'nationality'. Although all Israelis qualify as 'citizens of Israel', the state is defined as belonging to, owned exclusively by, the 'Jewish nation'. Jews in the diaspora who may be British nationals, for example, can claim 'owner-ship' of Israel as part of the Jewish nation, but indigenous

266

non-Jewish inhabitants can lay claim only to citizenship of the place; they cannot claim it as their national home.

Israel and its territory are defined as the inalienable property of one ethnic group, so any other group does not, by definition, really belong there. If one accepts that the basic requirement of a democracy is to guarantee everyone equality before the law, can Israel really claim to be a democracy?

One of the most notorious modern pieces of legislation that specifically discriminates against Arabs is the Citizenship and Entry into Israel Law, of 2003. This law prohibits an Israeli citizen's Palestinian spouse from the occupied territories acquiring citizenship by marriage, and also from residing in the country. So, in effect, Israeli citizens are prevented from marrying the spouse of their choice and living with them in Israel if that spouse is an inhabitant of the West Bank or Gaza. Of course, this only applies to Palestinians. If an Israeli wants to marry a Jewish settler from the occupied territories, that is completely acceptable. The law discriminates dramatically between Israeli Jewish citizens and Israeli Arab citizens.

When we get to the small community centre on the east side of town, Khawla goes off to chair her meeting, and I have a chance to talk with one of her colleagues in Jisr, Salha Ammash. Dressed in a black headscarf, top and trousers, Salha has a kind face and speaks softly. She tells me that her family came from Wadi al-Hawarith, a village about ten miles south of Jisr al-Zarqa. During the fighting of 1948 her father moved to the West Bank, where Salha was born and raised. After the war the old village was destroyed by the Israelis.

'I wanted to come back to my land, to feel I belonged. Some of our family managed to stay in Israel and came to live in Jisr. Twelve years ago I found a man here and married him.' Salha laughs shyly and then her expression changes to one of exasperation. 'I am married to a Jisr man and we have two children who are Israeli citizens but still I do not have citizenship. The government is worried that if they let people in, there will be more and more and then more children – more Arabs. So they stopped letting people in.'

Salha shakes her head at the madness of this. Any Jew from anywhere around the world enjoys the right of return but she is denied citizenship even though she is married to an Israeli citizen, is the mother of Israeli citizens and her father and grandfather were born in what is now Israel. 'I am fighting,' she tells me. 'I have a lawyer. I try to reassure my children – one is nine and the other four – that whatever happens we will stay together.'

But such reassurance is not based on experience. In the state's view Salha is living here illegally and could be expelled at any time.

'I have been deported before. It was awful, like having knives in my heart. I still feel it now. Two soldiers took me to the border with the West Bank. But I am not afraid. They may take me out again but I will find a way back. I want to stay within the law, but I know that there will be no justice. Never.'

* * *

Driving back to Haifa I am depressed. Naïvely I'd thought that Jisr al-Zarqa would be a little jewel. But, as I've seen, it is a very sad place. Its beautiful location on the Mediterranean shore seems to emphasize the tragedy of the Bridge over Blue Water. It should be a little paradise. The reality is hell.

For a while Khawla is busy making and taking calls on her mobile. When her phone goes back into her handbag we talk. She tells me that her husband is an accountant and a Muslim. Khawla is a Christian.

'Khalil said it was hard to feel alive in Israel. Is that how you feel?' I ask.

'In some ways I do feel connected to the reality here, to the daily life. I work in an organization with a mix of Jews and Arabs and I live in a Jewish neighbourhood. But I think there are two elements to life here. There's the formal one, where I am a citizen just like the Jewish people – but perhaps I can say that because I'm more empowered than many Palestinians. I have been to university, I have my home and I am comfortable to go and vote in the Knesset elections. For people who live in a village and have a simpler life, it is harder to feel any connection. They don't have the language, education or experience.'

Khawla looks out of the window and up at the wooded slopes of Mount Carmel. She runs her hands through her curls. 'The second element is that you always feel that you do not belong one hundred per cent to this country, what it says and does, its symbols and so on. Usually I feel much more comfortable with my people, with my language. I think this is very normal.'

'After a day in Jisr – and what I've seen in the Negev over the past few days – the situation looks very bleak,' I say. 'Any ideas of Jews and Palestinians enjoying co-existence are just fantasy, aren't they?'

'We have a big problem with using the word "co-existence" because the establishment in Israel has given it very bad connotations. If the idea is used and practised properly, with all groups having the same rights, it could work. I think there must be a way for everyone to live here. But it is a very long road to get there. '

With so much discrimination, and with so large a proportion of the Palestinian community stuck in the rut of poverty, even this guarded optimism is impressive. 'How do you find the energy to keep on fighting the fight?' I wonder.

'I have learned a lot from living in this environment. If you face all this discrimination you can be destroyed by it or you can develop and get stronger,' she says. 'Empowered people like me have a duty to support the others, those who don't have the same chances.

'Many of the problems we've been talking about in Jisr are common to the Palestinian community in Israel,' Khawla tells me, as we pull up at her office. 'But it is extreme. It would be good for you to get an idea of what's happening in other towns.'

As she gets out of the car she pauses, laughs her throaty laugh and gives me another tip: 'If you want to get the best *manakeesh* in Haifa, go to George's shop. It's just round the corner from here and it's very good.'

17

Dealing with Discrimination and Defining Identity

THE AFTERNOON IS VERY HOT AS I HEAD NORTH AND east from Haifa. I pass Jewish and Arab towns. It's easy to spot the difference. In the Jewish towns the roads are well maintained, the streets lined with footpaths and flowerbeds. In the Arab towns they are not: kerbs are rarely maintained and there isn't space for the luxury of flowerbeds. Also, on the outskirts of most Jewish towns there are neat industrial parks of varying sizes. These are absent around Arab communities. The population of the Galilee is split almost exactly 50:50 between Arabs and Jews, yet the government allows far more land for industrial development to the Jewish local authorities.

The main roads run through large, neat, European-looking farms and market gardens. The smaller roads wind up hillsides covered with olive trees. Often I come across an Arab man with a *keffiyeh* on his head walking with his sheep or goats, or Arab women in headscarves with their children. I have the car windows wound down

271

but it is so hot that, even driving at speed, I feel as though I am in an oven. When I slow down on reaching the town of Kafr Yasif, where I'm to meet some high-school students, I think I'm at risk of self-combusting. And the temperature seems to reinforce the sense of Kafr Yasif as another cramped, overcrowded Arab town. As soon as I turn off the main road I lose my bearings. The scribbled directions in my notebook become smudged by my sweaty fingers, the letters soon as hard to read as the few Arabic street signs. After a few minutes of pushing on, in the hope of spotting a landmark that features in my disintegrating guide, I accept that I am lost and phone Hilani Shehadeh, the teacher who is to host my visit. With fresh instructions I find my way eventually to the Yanni Yanni High School.

Hilani stands on the pavement. A young woman with a winning smile, her English is excellent. The school is deserted and the gates are locked, so we have to make do with looking through the fence at the small, bare compound. A two-storey classroom block runs around two sides of the courtyard, where weeds grow through the tarmac. It is so run-down that one would assume it was about to be rebuilt. It certainly does not look as a high school in a town of more than eight thousand people should.

Hilani takes me across the road to a café in the middle of a roundabout. Once inside I am surrounded by ten teenagers, some of Hilani's sixteen-year-old students, who all appear remarkably fresh after a morning of exams. They also seem quite suspicious, asking a great many questions about me and my project. Hilani reassures them that I am not some sort of spy and, after ordering cold drinks, we all seem to relax a little.

Although they are wary, these young people are not fearful. Their age and situation makes them so vulnerable that I have decided not to use their names here, even though they gave their permission for me to do so. One young man wears a blue T-shirt and often takes the lead, speaking in a low voice. Much of the time he sounds angry. He starts off talking about how they discover their history and culture, how they learn about the creation of Israel and their society's place here.

'We are not taught about the Nakba at school,' he tells me. 'We have to learn about our history from our parents, youth organizations and the Internet.'

A girl picks up the theme: 'It's weird. They must think we're stupid, because we know they're telling us lies about the history of this country and about our people. We came to school to learn, not to be lied to. The Israelis try to hide us . . .'

There are only three mixed schools in Israel. Otherwise they are segregated: Arab children attend schools where they are taught in Arabic, as they are at Yanni Yanni High School, and Jewish students learn in Hebrew. A few years ago an enlightened minister of education approved a textbook that talked about the Nakba. It was only to be used in Arab schools, though. A subsequent minister had the book taken off the syllabus. The history of modern Israel and of the Palestinians, when taught in school, is twisted by the establishment's agenda.

However, government policies don't seem likely to break the will or sense of identity of the group sipping their drinks with me in Kafr Yasif. They tell me that they have no intention of leaving the country for Europe or the USA. This is their home. One boy, who tells me he wants to be a doctor, says, 'If we move out then the stake of the Arab people in Israel will go down and down. Of course the Jewish people have advantages, but we will go to university; education is very important.'

The boy in the blue T-shirt speaks up again: 'The only revolution that we can make is with learning. If we have an education, maybe we can make a difference in politics or something.'

These teenagers are already thinking about the political struggles they face within Israel and in the occupied territories. I ask them about the Palestinians in the West Bank and Gaza.

'We feel very connected to them,' answers a girl in a bright yellow shirt. 'It hurts to see people suffering. Maybe if the leaders spoke without the violence, the world would listen more. The Palestinian leaders need to be united to beat the Zionists.'

How do they feel about the Zionists, about their Jewish fellow citizens? The heads around the table nod as another girl leans across the table to me. 'When we go to a Jewish town we can tell that the people there want to stay away from us. They think we are dangerous! Sometimes you feel you are being watched, but we are not frightened.'

Sadly, the Jewish students are frightened. They are taught to be afraid of the Arabs, and this fear leads to discrimination. According to a poll published in February 2010, nearly half of Jewish Israeli high-school students believe that Arab Israelis should not be granted the same rights as their Jewish counterparts, and more than half say Arabs should be prevented from running for the Knesset.

Given this context, the atmosphere among the group in Kafr Yasif is surprisingly positive – but with a strong dose of realism. The last word goes to the young man in blue: 'We know about sorrow, but we keep smiling. The Israelis shouldn't be smiling. They can get up in the morning and shoot Palestinians in Gaza, have lunch, then shoot more Palestinians and go to sleep. That is not right. But we smile because we know there might be a better tomorrow. Our people here are getting stronger, so there is no reason not to smile.'

Still smiling, the students head home. Hilani doesn't look so happy, though. While she has been good company and is clearly pleased to see her students talking about their lives, her mood has changed. She now seems quiet and depressed.

'It must be tough keeping the energy up as a teacher,' I say, 'when you know the facilities available to your students are so limited.'

'It is partly that,' she replies. 'At times, even though I like my work and know it is important, I get depressed because everything is in a mess. The teachers here haven't been paid for two months. But it's even worse for the council workers, like my mother. They have not been paid for fifteen months.' While she reminds me that Arab towns get smaller budgets than Jewish municipalities, she surprises me with the anger she directs at the local Arab leadership. 'It was better when the Communists were running the council – the people we have now are fools who cannot manage things.'

Hilani's opinion is common among Palestinians I have met. The state's discrimination against Palestinian communities is a given, but the responsibility of Arab councils for the deprivation their communities face is admitted too. There is often a failure of leadership at a time when communities are facing crises over funding and land usage. Many councils eventually go bankrupt. The establishment then installs a Jewish committee to take over. Many aspects of Palestinian society are still dominated by traditional attitudes. Loyalty to clan, or *hamula*, for instance, leads people to vote for family ties rather than ability or honesty.

Back on the highway I look across the Zvulun Valley, stretching away to the south, am carried away by the beauty of the countryside. I'm on the road to Acre and, on a whim, decide to go for a swim.

I find a likely bit of beach just south of the old city of Acre looking south across Haifa Bay. All the beaches seem to be 'managed' so I park where I can and go through the first gateway I pass. The changing rooms seem spartan. And I notice that a couple of little boys are staring at me as if I've just landed from Mars. Then they start laughing.

By the time I get to the water's edge I realize why. I've barged on to a beach segregated for orthodox Jewish men. Feeling ever-so-slightly out of place, I have a quick dip and depart.

Having spoken to the high-school students in Kafr Yasif, I want to find out about the political life for Palestinians who are in higher education. Suha puts me in touch with two brothers, Nasri and Jawad Dakwar, who live in Tarshiha, the Galilee town I visited with her to hear about events during the Nakba.

Meeting the brothers at their family home, an apartment in the town, I ask them how interested their generation is in Palestinian history and culture.

'We had a few friends at school we could talk to, but most weren't interested. The Israeli state has worked hard to create this new identity of the "Arab Israelis" and for many it has worked. People in the village still ask why we are involved in politics – what will it gain us? They say we'll end up in gaol.'

Nasri Dakwar speaks with a slight stutter as he concentrates on getting his point across in English. In his early twenties, he is studying dentistry at the Hebrew University in Jerusalem. His younger brother, Jawad, is studying occupational therapy. A few years ago they launched a local paper, with the aim of telling young people about Palestine and its history. Jawad is wearing a T-shirt with a cartoon figure on it, a character called Handala. A small child who witnesses events in the Palestinian experience, Handala was the signature of

Palestinian cartoonist Naji al-Ali, and remains an iconic symbol of Palestinian identity and defiance.

'We grew up with pictures of the first Intifada on the television,' says Jawad. 'We were only little kids but it became part of our background. Our grandmother told us about the Nakba. As we got older we realized that Kafr Vradim and Ma'alot [neighbouring Jewish towns] were confiscating thousands of dunams from Tarshiha. So we got involved with demonstrations and learned more.'

The municipality of Tarshiha was founded in 1920 and had a great deal of land. It was re-established as Tarshiha-Ma'alot to include the Jewish settlement of Ma'alot, which had been set up in 1957. In this way the Jewish community gained control of the municipality and of 70,000 dunams of public land that had belonged to Tarshiha. Nasri and Jawad explain that if a new road is built through the Tarshiha-Ma'alot area, it will be constructed alongside Tarshiha, the Palestinian neighbourhood. The rest of the land – on the other side of the road – will be in the Jewish Ma'alot area. The Palestinians will be surrounded.

'We have only a little bit of land left here that has not been taken by the Jewish towns around us.' Nasri points out of the window to some trees and open land a hundred metres or so distant. The new road will run there. 'We demonstrate to keep these areas,' he continues. 'It is our land, but their country. If we don't fight, the Israeli state will take it all.'

Clearly, though, the views of the Dakwar brothers are

the exception rather than the rule, as Jawad explains: 'People in the village, people we were at school with, know that there is racism against the Palestinians, but they would rather live here than in another Arab country. I have friends who sympathize with us and don't like Israel but they won't go to demonstrations.'

As was the case for their parents and grandparents in the Military Period, stepping out of line can still damage employment prospects for young Palestinians. Although the Dakwars study hard they know the university will be monitoring their activities, which include organizing protests, lectures and showing films. There is a risk their grades will be deliberately marked down to make finding a job more difficult.

So how do they see themselves fitting into Israeli society?

'There is a problem of belonging,' Jawad answers. 'We don't have a football team we can support; we don't have a flag we want to wave or a national song that we want to sing. We don't believe that we belong to the blue and white of Israel. And we know that we are the indigenous people.'

The brothers describe Tarshiha-Ma'alot as a microcosm of the whole country, showing up the situation of the Arabs in Israel. Tarshiha has no basketball teams, no football teams, no Scouts or social clubs. Ma'alot has taken all the Arab land and gets the lion's share of public funds yet still tries to promote the idea that the two communities are living side by side in happy co-existence.

You Can't Hide the Sun

'When the Mazuz decision [that no policemen would be indicted for the shooting of civilians] closed the book on the October 2000 killings, you felt worthless in this country. It seems like a green light for the next atrocity against the Palestinian people.'

Nasri nods. 'It kills the whole concept of co-existence. How can we live happily together when our blood has no value? All they want is to destroy our culture and let us all turn to drugs.'

With so much against them, and widespread apathy among their fellow Arabs, why do the brothers keep campaigning?

'You can sit in your room all day and do nothing, or you can try to make a difference,' Nasri says. 'It gives your life a meaning.'

And, says Jawad, they are making progress. 'We know that we must keep struggling, even if it takes another twenty-five years. Eventually we will win our rights. Someone said, "As long as you are struggling, you are winning." Here in the Galilee and at the university in Jerusalem, people are beginning to think and understand. When you start to look you learn fast – it is all so obvious. You can't hide the sun!'

280

18

Finding a Way Forward

'ARE YOU ORIGINALLY IRISH?'
'Well, yes,' I say, smiling, surprised at the question. 'I'm an Irish Mac, not a Scottish one.'

'Good. I was in Dublin last year staying with friends. I liked it very much.'

The questioner is Fadi Shbeita, a twenty-nine-year-old man with close-cropped hair, black T-shirt, trainers and combats. We're talking in his office in Jaffa, the old Arab city just south of Tel Aviv. He works for Sadaka Reut, an NGO that brings together Jewish and Arab youth. Speaking rapidly, in fluent English, Fadi explains what drives his work: 'To get anything constructive out of the conflict we have to look at the deep roots and how we take responsibility for what has happened. Our approach is that the winners write the history books and that history will always depend on who is telling it. So then we say, "Here we have two narratives, the Jewish and the Palestinian." So we are not coming as "educators with the truth", but we come, saying, "Let's see how each side tells their story and we can then think about it." '

Working with students from Jewish and Arab high schools, Fadi and his colleagues set up debates and use theatre and role play. Courses run over two years. So, for example, a Jewish class might be divided into two groups: one to enact the Zionist narrative and the other to play out the Palestinian one. These students will know the Zionist account well so they will be given some facts and figures about the Palestinian story, including information about the villages destroyed in and after 1948 and so forth.

'That must be quite a revelation to them,' I say.

'Yes, it is,' replies Fadi, 'but we give them this information without saying, "What you've been taught before is bullshit." That way we're not criticizing them in any way. And we find that they look at it and really get into it.'

As with the Jewish students, Arab classes are divided into two, with one group enacting the Palestinian and the other the Zionist account. Of course, the Palestinian youths will be well aware of the Zionist narrative as it is the foundation of the national curriculum.

Groups from Arab and Jewish schools will then be brought together. In the first year the national groups will often work separately, thinking about their own identities and group attitudes. In the second year, once they have a better awareness of themselves and some of the concerns of the other community, the students are encouraged to take on some responsibility and maybe start projects – like looking at house demolitions.

I can see that Fadi is very closely connected to his students, committed to guiding them to a better understanding of themselves and the community they perceive as 'others'. When I ask how the dynamics of bringing together Jewish and Palestinian youths work, his first reaction is to smile and raise his eyebrows. 'It can be complicated. Usually they start out quite apart, and then they recognize their similarities, age, interests and worries. There is euphoria in the group – "We are all the same, all human beings."' He pauses, glancing at his mobile as it pings to announce a text. 'Then it gets more complicated. As they get deeper into the identity issues, there is a kind of crisis in the group. Here the national differences come out again and people are very disappointed – "We thought they were nice but now we see they are not . . . There is no way of dealing with these people."' Fadi pauses again and rolls his eyes. 'That's when the critical work can really start. That's when people start to think really seriously.'

The aim is to break down the false attitudes that each community, Jewish and Palestinian, has about the other. Fadi says that in many ways this is more difficult for the Jewish group because they have to try to look past their Zionist-dominated education. Also, they begin to realize that, contrary to the constant message they have received, which says the Jewish population is vulnerable, that they are, in fact, on the privileged and powerful side. For the Palestinians the course outcomes are more oriented towards empowerment and discovering identity.

It is the only joint Jewish–Arab youth movement in the country and sounds like a very positive programme. It has been running for a number of years, and I ask Fadi if he thinks it has been successful.

'Well, I hope so! After studying with us, many young Jewish people choose to do civilian national service rather than go into the military. They don't want to use force against people they now understand better. That's an interesting development.'

'And what about the Palestinian youth?' I ask. 'Where does empowerment take them?'

'It is still difficult. For mainstream Jewish society it can be very frightening if you define yourself as Palestinian,' Fadi acknowledges. 'That's because they are taught that Palestinians are the enemies. So how do you define your identity as a Palestinian in a way that is not saying, "Drive the Jews to the sea"? As an activist how do you deal with this in a way that is constructive? While recognizing that a lot of bad things happened, how can we make something positive now? What am I fighting for?'

Fadi grew up conscious of this difficult set of questions. His family was politically aware; he joined a youth group and, very unusually, he studied in a Jewish high school from the age of fifteen. Although he had been especially selected to go there, it was a challenge for him, as a Palestinian, to be accepted in the school. It was a difficult experience, despite his having a pretty good grasp of the situation between Jews and Palestinians.

The phone rings, and Fadi takes the call. It is from a

Jaffa family who are being threatened with eviction from their home. 'I have to go round for a quick meeting.' he says. 'Would you like to come?'

Alongside his day job, Fadi is a volunteer on the Popular Committee against Evacuations and House Demolitions. As we drive he gives me a brief overview of the situation facing many Palestinian inhabitants of Jaffa. By the 1950s neighbouring Tel Aviv had grown into a city and was declared a full municipality. Jaffa, on the other hand, was now deemed a small suburb of Tel Aviv, and stripped of its municipality status. The new municipality of Tel Aviv stated clearly that the plan was to Judaize Jaffa and break down its old Arab identity. Run-down districts were to be evacuated and rebuilt. Around 3,250 buildings, houses, schools and hospitals, including some of particular historical interest, were demolished. This process continues today.

'If you have a good lawyer and a good case,' Fadi tells me, 'you might get compensation and be able to buy an apartment somewhere else. But most of the cases are declared illegal. Some three hundred out of five hundred families are currently under threat of eviction. They will get nothing.'

Fadi is made very welcome when we reach our destination: a large old house inhabited by a very old man and several of his descendants. Theirs is a common story, Fadi tells me. The family have lived in the house since 1948. They moved in when they were driven from their own home in another district. The owners of this house ended up as refugees in the West Bank. Now the housing

authorities want the building empty as part of its redevelopment plan. The family is being sued for massive
amounts of rent they are supposed to owe and also for
making additions to the property without planning permission. They seem remarkably cheerful despite the
threat to their home.

Once Fadi has gone through some documents with the
family, we leave. On the way back to his office he shows
me around some of old Jaffa. There are large building
sites where either new apartment blocks are going up or
old buildings are being refurbished. All will be beyond
the means of the Arab residents who hang on in their
poor, decaying homes. Many, like the family we've just
visited, are under threat of eviction. Others live in overcrowded tower blocks in areas with few employment
opportunities. Drugs are a major problem. According to
Fadi, the threats faced by the Arab population – poverty,
discrimination, crime and home demolition – represent a
continuum from 1948; he calls it the 'ongoing Nakba'.

Fadi's family home was in Miska, a village about thirty
kilometres from Jaffa. It was destroyed in 1948. How
does it feel to be able to go and see the place, but not be
allowed to live there or work in the fields, to know the
state will never let you belong there again?

Running a hand over his head, Fadi shrugs a little.
'Well, it really gets on my nerves, of course.' He pauses,
and we burst out laughing, amused at the gentility of the
phrase. 'A lot of times there is a load of anger too. But
you need to see how to use this anger in a more constructive way, maybe. For me I still feel very connected to

the place and feel it is mine. It was taken by force and I cannot accept that.'

When one of the Jaffa families was evicted and their house demolished, Fadi and other members of the Popular Committee rebuilt the foundations. A few days later the authorities destroyed the foundations and also a neighbouring house. As soon as the site was cleared a truck arrived laden with mature olive trees, which were planted to create an instant park.

'Turn right here and you'll see. Perhaps you can guess where the trees came from.'

It is a spiteful little park. The neat lines of short, heavily pruned olive trees look grotesque. I can imagine them spread across a hillside, part of a timeless scene, their gnarled trunks and branches at one with the rugged terrain. Here, on this flat urban space, they look bizarre and alien. I could guess where they came from. As the Israelis build their illegal barrier, the 'Wall', around the West Bank, they appropriate a great deal of Palestinian land. Often the route of the barrier tears through old olive groves. Some of those trees are reported to be 'reclaimed' and sold on to Israeli developers wanting instant antiquity for a site.

A couple of years ago Suha and I met a farmer in the West Bank village of Jayyus. He showed us where bull-dozers had ripped through his land. Before us was a scene of devastation. Everything natural and good had been uprooted to flatten the terrain and prepare it for the complex of razor wire and electronic sensors that make up the barrier. It was grotesque. In tears, he said that he looked at the splintered remains of his trees and felt he had lost part of his family.

Fadi works hard, professionally and as a volunteer activist, to promote the Palestinian cause. For all the sadness he witnesses, he has seen some progress, some movement towards understanding between Jews and Palestinians. What is his long-term hope?

'I define myself as a Palestinian citizen of Israel,' he says. 'I am a part of the Palestinian people. I don't need to explain it. And I am a citizen of Israel, someone having the full rights of a citizen of the state today. In the future, I want my identity to be less a national definition. When we have moved beyond who controls who, and one nation fighting off another, it will be more of a cultural thing. That's what I hope for.'

After dropping Fadi back at his office, I head into the centre of old Jaffa and wander the streets. Clock Tower Square, surrounded by small restaurants and stores selling all manner of things, is just a few hundred yards from the sea. As I wander uphill I find alleys and lanes leading off between high stone buildings. This would once have been teeming with Arab life. Now it is being transformed into a Jewish area of smart restaurants, cool art galleries and private apartment blocks. Walking along the cliff road, I take in the wonderful view out over the Mediterranean and appreciate why people are ready to pay a great deal of money for a home here.

Just off Clock Tower Square I find a restaurant looking towards the sea. It is run by two women: the owner, who does the cooking, and a waitress. The place is packed, though, for the good food and the lively banter that flows between the two women. A party arrives – from the noisy greeting, they must be regulars. There is much hilarity around their attempts to say '*Salaam alaikum*,' the Muslim greeting. They get it horribly wrong and swiftly return to Hebrew. Arabic is the second language of Israel but few Jewish Israelis bother to learn it.

I am tired and frustrated. This place, Israel, simply does not make sense. As I sit in this restaurant surrounded by happy and, no doubt, decent, caring Jewish citizens, my thoughts keep turning to that nasty little park of olive trees. Are my fellow diners aware that the balmy atmosphere they are enjoying is being built on so much distress and loss?

These people are ordinary; they are not inhuman. But when will they see Palestinians as physical and cultural neighbours, rather than as people to be feared and controlled? Though tensions often run high here, especially in mixed neighbourhoods, no Palestinian I've spoken to wants to see more violence. In this state, which loudly proclaims itself a democracy but clearly falls well short of that ideal, the people suffering discrimination are eager to win their rights through democratic means rather than by force.

Fadi Shbeita raised the question of how he should define his Palestinian identity within the Israeli framework. It is a debate that runs at both personal and national levels, the Catch-22 of Palestinian citizens of Israel. How can they be loyal to their state when it is so often at war with the rest of their nation?

The Palestinian community has gradually come together to find a way of expressing who they are and to demand that Israel become 'a state of all its citizens', not just a Jewish state. In late 2006 it found expression in four documents: *An Egalitarian Constitution for All*, *The Democratic Constitution*, *The Haifa Covenant Project* and *Future Vision of the Palestinian Arabs in Israel* share many themes.

Future Vision is the most comprehensive. It was produced by the High Follow-up Committee (an organization that, though not officially recognized as representing the Palestinian community, deals with the state on a national level and is made up of elected figures, such as Arab mayors and Members of the Knesset) and the National Committee for the Heads of the Arab Local Authorities in Israel. It attracted great interest and criticism. The introduction lays out its ambitious aims: 'These documents focus on affiliation, identity and citizenship of the Palestinian Arabs in Israel. They also focus on the legal status, land and housing, economic and social development, educational vision for Arab education, Arab Palestinian culture and on the political and national work of the Palestinian Arabs in Israel.'

The central demand is that the 'State has to acknowledge that Israel is the homeland for both Palestinians and Jews (the future Israeli constitution and state laws should reinforce this point by adding an introduction [*sic*] paragraph)'. *Future Vision* also calls for the state to acknowledge its responsibility for the Nakba and for reform of land laws to end discrimination against Arab citizens.

Some Arab commentators in Israel have criticized *Future Vision* and the other manifestos for effectively arguing in favour of the ghettoization of their community rather than focusing on gaining equality. Since they call for such an absolute change in the nature of the state, they have also been viewed as pointless.

These documents enraged and alarmed much of Jewish Israeli society: they were seen as evidence of intent to destroy the very nature and purpose of the state. Some commentators believe that they frightened the Israeli government. Its recent insistence that Israel is acknowledged in all international discourse as a Jewish state – not just that it has a right to exist – is ascribed to the growing influence of the Palestinians in Israel.

What is certain is that the state's ambition to create a new identity for the indigenous people, that of 'Israeli Arabs', has failed. What the Palestinians in Israel are now saying is that the state is unworkable and that its basic premise goes against human rights and international law. It has to change, especially as the demographic balance continues to shift. By 2015 it is expected that Arabs will constitute 25 per cent of Israel's population.

Hassan Jabareen is a key figure in the new Palestinian élite in Israel, a successful lawyer fighting for

Palestinian rights through the state institutions. He founded Adalah (translated as 'Justice'), the Legal Centre for Arab Minority Rights in Israel, in 1996 with his Jewish American wife and fellow lawyer, Rina Rosenberg. The organization deals with everything from land expropriation, challenging the Citizenship Law, discrimination in services and restrictions on political parties to representing the families of the victims of the October 2000 killings. Adalah drew up one of the four 2006 documents, *The Democratic Constitution*.

We meet in Adalah's offices, a few yards from my regular base at the St Charles Guesthouse in Haifa. The organization is based in a refurbished stone mansion, its interior air-conditioned and elegant, with marble floors. A map of the world hangs on the wall.

Hassan is in his mid-forties and wears a trademark flat black cap and thick beard. He tells me more about *Future Vision*, and the beliefs behind it. 'Our document and the *Future Vision* were part of an attempt for us to imagine the future based on the borders between Israel and a Palestinian state being those that had been the boundaries up to 1967, and based on the Oslo Accords of 1993. The concepts of Oslo were two states, two entities with self-determination.

'After Oslo and the Israeli agreements with the Palestine Liberation Organization in Gaza, the West Bank and East Jerusalem – and with Egypt and Jordan – the issue of national identity became very important to us Palestinians here in Israel. Before then we didn't think about it: the peace made us more nationalist.'

292

Until 1993 the Palestinians in Israel had seen themselves as part of the Palestinian nation as a whole, but when the Oslo Accords did little, if anything, to address their needs, they became more determined to assert themselves as a national minority within the state. They pursued group and citizenship rights through Israel's legal and parliamentary system as well as in general public debate. New political parties flourished and leaders began to speak on behalf of the whole community. A growing Arab middle class, with more intellectuals, shaped the national character of the struggle. People began to speak about 'national dignity, identity and the right to their own land'. The increased authority of the High Follow-up Committee as the representative of all the Palestinian people within Israel made strike action possible. For Hassan this is terribly important. Though the Palestinian community has little financial strength or military power, the ability to call a strike gives it some muscle.

Despite the clear aims articulated in *Future Vision* and other documents, Hassan points out that, until a final agreement is reached between Israel and the Palestinians in the West Bank and Gaza, there is no satisfactory definition of where people belong physically. 'We are a minority whose borders are not clear,' he explains, in his low, well-modulated voice. 'And the borders matter because they can help people to conceptualize their struggle. What borders am I struggling for? 1948, 1967? Are we under occupation or are we oppressed citizens? How do we imagine the future? Although Israel doesn't give answers for the borders, what is clear is the fact that the occupation of the West Bank and of Jerusalem has become part of Israel's legal system.'

Without a decision on borders there can be no clarity for the Palestinians in Israel. However, Hassan believes that the national-minority concept is well established. The struggle for recognition of this will continue. 'We will take strength from the masses, with strikes, yes, but I don't think this will be an armed struggle. Historically, since 1948 there has only been very marginal support for armed struggle.

'The Israeli right wing perceives this kind of Palestinian identity as treacherous and believes that oppressing it is legitimate. That's what they are doing with their legislation – directly anti-Arab legislation – and this trend will continue.'

The authors of *Future Vision*, and the other documents, recognize that their ideals will take many years of hard discussion and political activity to achieve. The key point is that they are looking forward in a strategic and proactive way, as opposed to dealing only with the present and responding to Israeli actions.

The Arab community is not working in isolation, of course. As the government continues to restrict the civil liberties of Palestinian citizens, many Jewish Israelis are alarmed that their state is losing its way on human rights. Outside establishment circles, many Jewish people join forces with their Arab neighbours to create a more equal state. Nearly all of the Palestinian activists I have met in Israel are working in or alongside organizations that include or are funded by Jewish Israelis.

Hassan Jabareen's Adalah has Jewish staff and the organization works with many Jewish human-rights organizations. Yet, given that they face the right-wing reactionary political situation at present, is Hassan in any way optimistic for the Palestinians in Israel?

'As Israeli citizens, we do not have to fear transfer or genocide. So that gives us confidence,' says Hassan. 'When you have the security that you are not going to die in battle, you can struggle with less fear.'

In recent years the international political situation has changed and the world is more aware of the Palestinian situation. This is due to an improved international media, particularly the increasing role played by the Internet in disseminating information. The Palestinians of Israel have become better mobilized and are taking part in international conferences to present their case to the world.

'The Israel project has failed,' Hassan states. 'The desperate effort to legitimize what is being done in East Jerusalem and the West Bank, with a raft of new laws, shows that it has failed. It cannot continue. So there could be a new movement, of secular Palestinians and secular Israelis working together.' However, he predicts a decade of impasse before any new situation starts to emerge in Israel. In the meantime, he points out, 'Since 9/11 there has been a perceived legitimacy for the state to emphasize security and use oppressive measures. This will limit the rights of freedom and liberty of Arabs here in Israel. We may see more direct apartheid. At the moment it is creeping apartheid in the West Bank and East Jerusalem.'

19

Occupation

THE LITTLE CAR IS VERY PINK AND IS TRAVELLING VERY fast – directly at us. At the last moment there is a screech of brakes as the driver executes a handbrake turn and brings the vehicle to a stop right beside us, as neatly as if we were in a car park. As the dust settles, I maintain as impassive an expression as possible and look into the eyes of the driver. They are wild, glittering with excitement and, I am sure, drugs. No one seems to take any notice of this crazy, dangerous behaviour at a junction busy with cars and pedestrians, including children. Normally I would be shaking with shock at such a near miss, but this morning I am too angry and frustrated, too hot, even to feel fear. My only response is to mutter a weary expletive.

I'm much more concerned with the conversation going on between my passenger and guide, Rana Bishara, and the man standing by her window, whom I've dubbed 'the Cowboy'. Rana and I are trying to find a family who, we think, live somewhere near by. For at least two hours I have been driving around a very small, very dusty and very confusing patch of the earth's surface, crossing between the West Bank and East Jerusalem, between supposedly Palestinian territory and supposedly Israeli territory.

Israel conquered both areas from Jordan in the 1967 war and has occupied them ever since. While it says it is prepared to negotiate over the area now designated as the West Bank, in a peace deal that would see the formation of a Palestinian state, it insists that East Jerusalem is part of Israel. East Jerusalem includes not only the Old City of Jerusalem itself, but also an extensive area north, east and south of the city. Israel annexed this area soon after the '67 war to be part of the municipality of Jerusalem. In 1980 Israel declared that Jerusalem, 'complete and united', was now, and would be for ever, 'the capital of Israel'.

At the moment we are in the West Bank, just, in the little town of Az-Za'im. We went through the checkpoint at the foot of the hill twice before we found the little slip-road that brought us to the edge of town. The Cowboy seems to be an authority figure, albeit an unlikely one. He wears tight black jeans, a black string vest and a vast Stetson, which appears to have been fashioned from sheer black silk and wire. It is a very camp look, though he was looking anything but camp when we arrived a few moments ago. He was up a ladder casually hooking up thick power cables to an overhead pylon, unfazed by the massive sparks flying in all directions. After a couple of passers-by proved unable to help us with directions, he dismounted his ladder and sauntered over. Now he barely glances at the boy racer in the pink car.

Rana is talking on the phone to the man we are looking for and is repeating his words to the Cowboy. My nerves are frayed. I find myself snapping, 'Give him the phone. If we're anywhere close they'll work it out.'

My hunch proves right. In moments we're heading off again with allegedly clear directions to follow. Then we hit a wedding. It looks as though the town's three thousand inhabitants are out celebrating. I feel self-conscious, trying to nudge the car through the throng of vehicles and people who are blocking the road. People make way, though, happily waving us on.

Many Palestinians have told me that if my interest is in the Palestinian citizens of Israel, I should not include those living in East Jerusalem because the area is not part of Israel. This view is fully endorsed by the international community. Israel's occupation of the Palestinian territory of the West Bank, including East Jerusalem, is illegal under international law. As ever, Israel takes no notice of international law.

Although I know that legally East Jerusalem is not part of Israel, it is the one area of the Palestinian territories that Israel says it will never hand back as part of a peace agreement. I want to see how Israel treats this community, which appears to be living in a very literal limbo land.

Rana has volunteered to act as a guide and translator for me because Suha has been laid low with a vicious bug.

Having met her before, I am very pleased to have her company as well as her help. Picking her up at eight this morning, I thought we'd get to our destination, the home of the al-Qumbar family near Abu Dis on the south-east side of Jerusalem, in about an hour. Even with rush-hour traffic, it's no distance. Now I'm remembering Suha's warning that the place might be tricky to find.

But Rana is endlessly confident. We have contact numbers for the al-Qumbars. She also has a friend who is a taxi driver. He spends his life working around East Jerusalem and into the West Bank. If we lose our way she can call him for advice. By ten o'clock and our encounter with the Cowboy, Rana has already spoken a number of times to her cabbie friend without getting us where we need to be. My frustration at the extended journey is mollified by the chance to get to know her better.

Rana is an artist and a highly expressive, passionate person. She has a very warm personality and is an interesting, sometimes confusing mix of serenity and intense emotional outbursts. Her frustration and anger at the way the Palestinians are treated, in Israel and in the Palestinian territories, drives her every breath and certainly her art. She says there are many young and increasingly prominent Palestinian artists whose work, like hers, has a political edge.

Rana was born and brought up in Tarshiha in the Galilee. She tells me about her father, describing him as a loving but withdrawn man, traumatized by his experience of the Nakba and the Military Period. And she explains how the situation affects her today. 'I mean, how can you

300

deal with it?' she says, rolling her eyes in frustration. 'They put you in this endless feeling of restlessness – I have lived all my life this way. However much they increase their violence, their vandalizing of the homeland, I feel they want us to feel that there is more to come. You always have to expect that something bad is going to happen to you.'

'You mean,' I ask, 'that when you might be thinking it can't get any worse, their idea is "Just you wait"?'

'Exactly. Time is very significant. You feel something is deteriorating and disappearing out of your hands. *Saber* [cactus] is important as a Palestinian symbol because it will grow up again and again, no matter how many times you cut it down. I use it a great deal in my art as a symbol for me of Palestine, of resistance and existence. In Arabic *sabara* means "to be patient".'

Becoming agitated, Rana moves around in her seat, using her hands to emphasize her point. 'The Israelis stole that symbol too! The Jews who were born here before 1948 are called Sabra.'

Other young activists have spoken of taking advantage of knowing Israel from the inside. Rana does that too. 'I see myself as from both sides. In a way it's an advantage to live in Israel. We understand the situation from the viewpoint of the Palestinian struggle but also as so-called citizens. As Palestinian citizens of Israel we understand what they think, what their so-called democracy is trying to take from us.' Her eyes flash as she says, 'We are the indigenous people here – but they want us to feel so grateful all the time for what they've given us.'

Since getting through the wedding party at Az-Za'im, we have been heading south-east. Our destination, near Abu Dis, is two or three kilometres from the Old City of Jerusalem. We race along the highway towards the massive Jewish settlement of Ma'ale Adumim. The scale of the construction, the roads and the settlement, is astonishing. It still shocks me, no matter how many times I travel here, that all this has happened on occupied land. This landscape is supposed to be at the heart of an independent Palestinian state, as laid out by the United Nations Partition Plan of 1947. But Israel has continued to develop all this for the Jewish settlers, regardless of international law and criticism.

We turn off the highway and take a lesser road south to Abu Dis. The town is home to one of the campuses of the al-Quds University (al-Quds being the Arabic name for Jerusalem). Rana says we'll have to pass close to the university to find the checkpoint we need. We seem to be following smaller and smaller roads until we turn a corner and I hear myself say, 'Oh, my God, the Wall!'

An eight-metre-high concrete slab rears up in front of us, heading off in both directions. It is ugly, threatening and utterly oppressive; a brutal edifice designed to dwarf human spirit. The Israeli separation barrier was started in 2002 and runs around nearly all of the West Bank. The public premise for the huge structure, which is concrete wall in some places but fence and ditches in others, is to prevent suicide bombers entering Israel. But the Wall (and to talk about it as a fence doesn't convey the absolute nature of this barrier to human movement and

302

communication) does not follow the 1967 boundary lines between Israel and the West Bank. Almost twice the length of those lines, it makes deep inroads into the Palestinian territory to go around the Jewish settlements and is widely seen as a means of annexing ever more land. The Wall has been broadly condemned by international opinion; the International Court of Justice has found that it is illegal, and the European Union considers the route of the barrier, where it is built on Palestinian land, to be illegal.

Since the Wall was built, al-Quds University has lost a third of its land to the Israeli side. It takes a long time to find our way through the Wall, so we can cross back from the West Bank into the East Jerusalem district where we think the al-Qumbar family lives. I like to know where I am and take pride in getting my bearings in a new location. This morning I feel as though I'm veering around with a very faulty compass. Nothing makes sense. Eventually we find a gate where the Wall runs right through a residential district. We park and continue on foot.

My heart is in my mouth even though I know nothing will happen to me. An Israeli soldier stares at us as we walk past his little bunker. Hemmed in by crash barriers and metal-link fencing, I feel like an animal being herded to slaughter. There is an ominous stillness in the hot morning air. Two Palestinian youths walk through in the opposite direction, their faces blank. I hate places like this because you are so utterly exposed and vulnerable to the whim of the man with the gun. He can nod and smile, he can ignore you, he can keep you waiting for hours, or he can beat you.

Rana says that she is shocked by the place too. Everything has changed since her last visit a few months ago. A call to the al-Qumbar home confirms my fears. We are in the wrong place.

After another hour's driving we get it right. The fence and gate we face now are very low-key compared with most checkpoints I have encountered. It could easily be the entrance to some private land. Beside the gate, though, there is an army building with security cameras. We have barely stopped the car when a jeep races up behind us and two soldiers jump out. I smile and explain that we're visiting a family here. The first soldier, with wraparound sunglasses, doesn't smile back and asks to see my passport. The rest of the conversation, carried out in Hebrew between the soldier and Rana, has no more joy in it. As far as I can judge both lose their tempers immediately and I know we'll have no chance of access. When I ask why we cannot enter he just tells me to talk to my friend: 'I've already told her in Hebrew.'

I can't help thinking that if Suha was here we might still be talking. She is used to negotiating her way through these situations and never loses her temper. Rana is more volatile and may have let her feelings towards the soldier get in the way of trying to talk our way through the gate. Maybe the other soldier would be more approachable. He has gone into the small check-point cabin just off the road. I walk towards him, still smiling, and begin asking him what the problem is. He half raises his rifle.

'Go out of the compound now, please.'

The discussion, such as it was, is clearly over.

While I turn the car around, Rana calls Muhammad al-Qumbar. Minutes later a young boy appears on a bike from the other side of the gate. He gives a half-wink to Rana and heads off down the road. We follow in the car until we are out of sight of the soldiers. The boy tells us to follow him. The track deteriorates to the point where my little hire car has had enough. It's time to go by foot.

As we walk across the steep, rocky hillside, the boy on his undersized bike waiting up ahead, I am panting and nervous. A family has simply invited me to meet them at their home, yet I feel I am doing wrong. I expect another aggressive confrontation at any moment.

This must be what it was like during the Nakba, people scuttling across hillsides fearful of meeting Jewish troops; ordinary roads and paths fraught with danger and familiar places suddenly off limits. We clamber up to a decent road, the one we were forbidden to use by the soldiers at the gate, and pass a couple of villas set behind high fences. The boy tells us that these belong to Jewish settlers. A couple of hundred yards further on, our young guide knocks on a door, then cycles off.

After the hellish journey, the al-Qumbar home seems remarkably normal. The family, Muhammad, his parents and his son Iqab, greet us with great warmth and offer tea and coffee. We sit in a plain room at the front of the house. Relieved to be here at last, I realize I have no idea where 'here' actually is. Are we in the Jerusalem municipality or the West Bank?

'We are in the municipality of Jerusalem,' Muhammad explains. 'We are right on the edge of Jerusalem and the West Bank. This place is called Abu Mjeira and the West Bank towns of Abu Dis and al-Izzariyya are very close to us. But we pay our taxes to Jerusalem. Our community here is made up of thirty West Bankers and a hundred and twenty Jerusalemites.'

The word 'Jerusalemite' sets up a biblical frisson in me. The justification for the theft of so much Palestinian land is that the Jewish people have a right to the place as recorded in the Bible. The Palestinians are nothing better than the ancient indigenous Canaanites or Jebusites, who were supposedly 'trespassing' on the Israelites' divinely granted property. Modern Israelites are not coming in across the Jordan, of course, but from Brooklyn, Buenos Aires and Barnet.

With Rana's help the al-Qumbars give me a quick introduction to the intricacies of identity papers operating here. Palestinian West Bankers have green ID papers. Jerusalemites have blue ID papers. Which ID you carry determines where you can and cannot go and which checkpoints you can pass through. Israeli citizens can, of course, go wherever they like.

Muhammad explains that although he is a West Banker, he does have a permit for Jerusalem, so he can stay in his house. The permit has to be renewed by the military every six months. He has been living like this for twenty years. Even though the Israelis have built the

Wall, which physically keeps him in the Jerusalem municipality area, he has never been allowed a full Jerusalem residency permit. He is handicapped and uses a wheelchair, yet the soldiers will not allow him to pass through the gate at the end of his road in a car. He has to get out and go through in his chair, a cruel indignity, even though he has a Jerusalem permit. It doesn't seem to help much when he visits West Bank places like Abu Dis.

'If I go to Abu Dis or al-Izzariyya, I can pass through any checkpoint easily enough, but coming back they won't let me through at the nearest crossing, Az-Za'im. They make me go to the one at Ras Abu Sbeitan, which is only for pedestrians,' he explains.

The physical distance between these places is very slight. Although I was frustrated with Rana earlier, as we were going through the pedestrian checkpoint on the outskirts of Abu Dis, I have to acknowledge that she had brought us very close to where we are now sitting. Because the Israelis have sealed off this little area, any journey is a roundabout one, on a mix of small roads in the Palestinian areas and on huge, sweeping Israeli highways. You end up feeling as though you have travelled halfway to Amman, rather than round the corner.

Because of the Wall, the al-Qumbars and tens of thousands of other Palestinians are denied access to their neighbouring communities where they have lifelong friends and have done business all their lives. 'The thirty people here who have no Jerusalem IDs are only allowed to go to the nearby town of al-Izzariyya,' Muhammad tells me. 'They have to go on foot as there is no public transport and West Bank cars are not allowed to come in here as this is deemed to be Jerusalem.'

Muhammad and his family are smiling at me and I realize my face must be expressing my total confusion. Nodding in understanding, Muhammad continues, 'Food can only come from Jerusalem with those who have the papers to go there. So, because al-Izzariyya is in the West Bank, no food – milk, eggs, fruit – is allowed to come in through the gate from al-Izzariyya. The thirty people without Jerusalem papers cannot bring anything in with them. Everyone is registered at the gate.'

Muhammad, like his father Hussein, wears a long robe, or *galabieh*, and a skull cap. Hussein speaks for the first time: 'I am eighty-five and my wife is seventy-eight. We have lived here all our lives but we cannot go to Jerusalem to pray at the Dome of the Rock because we don't have a Jerusalem ID. Some of our children have Jerusalem ID and they have cars with Israeli licence plates. But they are forbidden to take us, their parents, because we are West Bankers. If they catch them with us they confiscate the car for forty days and they have to go to court and will be fined five thousand shekels.'

I feel another surge of biblical frisson and outrage. Your property is confiscated for forty days – and presumably forty nights – when you try to take your parents to worship where they have worshipped all their lives.

Unable to travel in the area where they have ID and denied ID in the place where they live, they are humiliated at every turn, despite their age and disabilities.

Muhammad sums up their existence with a shake of the head: 'We are living in a gaol. Al-Quds was our city and we live just five minutes from it yet we cannot go there any more. We never have guests coming to see us. Even my daughter, who is married and lives in Abu Dis, is not allowed to come here without a special permit. She is here at the moment. She was given a permit to visit for one day, just one day! It was her first visit to see her family for a year even though she's just a couple of miles away. She is sick, so couldn't go home on the same day. She has stayed and we, her parents, are looking after her. It's only been two days but she is breaking the law.'

Israeli policies, most dramatically and harshly enforced with physical facts on the ground, like the Wall, are astonishingly inhuman. As well as severing links between communities of all sizes, the Wall has meant that access to health care has been seriously limited. Many of the key hospitals that once served the population of the West Bank are now sealed within the expanded Jewish metropolitan area. For those without Jerusalem ID, special permits are required to visit hospitals in the city – regardless of how urgent the medical case may be.

Muhammad points out that, as well as creating appalling logistical problems for the Palestinian healthcare system, the Israeli authorities hinder other help coming to them. 'They won't even let the Red Cross in.' He pauses and smiles. 'John, if you hear too many stories of the Palestinian experience, you will have a heart attack – but don't have one here. There are no services – even though we pay taxes. Our children go across the hillsides and walk to school. A car picks up the kindergarten children, but all the others have to walk.'

Even when they get to school, Palestinian children in East Jerusalem face disgraceful conditions. There is a desperate shortage of teaching space with around a thousand new classrooms needed. Many schools rent inappropriate buildings, like apartments or business premises, to bridge the gap.

Rana points out that the situation for the people of East Jerusalem, and especially in isolated communities like this, where the al-Qumbars live, is similar to that in the unrecognized villages, the URVs, within Israel's 1948 borders. The people pay taxes but get no services.

In another parallel with what has happened across Israel since 1948, the state uses its specially created laws to 'legalize' its theft of Arab land. Muhammad tells me that all the land on the hillside used to belong to Abu Dis, but since the Wall was built, Israel has expropriated everything that belongs to the people stuck on the West Bank side. The Absentees' Property Law of 1950 is still doing sterling work.

The al-Qumbars used to get water from Abu Dis, but when the Wall was built, the supply was cut. Muhammad complained and petitioned for a new supply. Eventually, after three years, he was allowed a connection but had to pay 200,000 shekels to have the supply hooked up. The meter is in the grounds of the Jewish settler house we passed on the way here.

Ateret Cohanim, a religious settler group, bought that

house and another near it. The organization has a long-term plan to develop a new settlement here, called Kidmat Zion. This is part of a project to build settlements all the way around Jerusalem, a Jewish 'shield' around the city. Sites like this, right up against the segregation Wall, are important to their plan. Should the Wall ever be moved, a barricade of Jewish people will be living along its route.

'So they want us out,' Muhammad explains. 'One of the houses up the road was built in the seventies. The Jews said the land had been sold to a Jewish family in the 1920s. After a long court case the Palestinian owner was given the option of having it destroyed or accepting compensation and leaving. So he left. The settlers have a lookout there, watching the whole area.'

Grandfather Hussein begins speaking and soon becomes very agitated. The family and Rana smile as they calm him down. They tell me that he has forgotten who I am and is asking whether I might be able to issue him with the necessary ID. His anger will burn itself out, though, as he lists again all the iniquities that he and his family face.

And the thing is that this is a lovely place with views across the hillsides to other villages. Burned brown now by the summer sun, the landscape is austerely beautiful; in the rainy months and spring it will be softened by the green of shrubs and wild flowers. On the horizon, glittering eternally, is the Dome of the Rock, a building of huge spiritual importance to the family and to which they are denied access.

Hussein's wife, her face and head wrapped in a white

scarf, says they feel abandoned by the world. 'It is real humiliation, it is torture,' she says. 'I walk all the way into the town. I am seventy-eight and my sons and grandsons cannot drive me to the gate, even in their Israeli cars. In this summer heat I walk a little and sit down to rest, then go a little more. It is torture.'

Having seen the attitude of the soldiers at the gate, I can only assume that their manner is even more aggressive and rude to the inhabitants than it was with us.

Muhammad says, 'It is a situation of total despair and frustration. We only hope that something is resolved. Either they will give us to the West Bank or allow us to be a proper part of Israel. We cannot continue to live as we have since the Wall was built in 2005. Do we feel safe? No! But we have no alternative and we will stay here, whatever happens. We would rather die than leave.'

Iqab saves us another hot walk across the barren hills and runs us down to the hire car in his four-by-four. Then he leads us back to the Jerusalem suburbs that even I recognize. After the tortuous route we followed this morning, it is amazing that we are there in minutes. He parks at a junction and comes to say goodbye. A tall young man with a mullet haircut that would have been a seventies footballer's dream, he seems determined to make the most of his life. Even though work is difficult to come by now, he says he's sure he'll get by. Unlike his father, at least he has his Jerusalem ID and the ability to escape the confines of that fenced hillside.

* * *

It is mid-afternoon and Rana and I are both hot and hungry. We've a meeting in the Old City so decide to have a late lunch at Abu Shukri's café. A visit to this place, a series of rooms with arched ceilings leading off the narrow cobbled street where the Via Dolorosa meets al-Wad, is one of the pleasures of a trip to the Old City. It's as popular with locals as it is with tourists. Rana and I eat in companionable silence, enjoying the hummus for which Abu Shukri's is famous, with pickles and falafel.

Out on the street all sorts of people pass by: Hassidic Jews in their black suits and hats, Arab women wearing headscarves, and Israeli soldiers, sauntering, rifles cradled in their arms. Groups of young Palestinian men bustle past, talking loudly in Arabic. These youths, the *shabab*, all seem to wear trainers, jeans and white T-shirts, and have close-cropped hair. A grey-suited old man is a permanent fixture. He sells fresh fruit juices from highly polished silver urns perched on a small stall. One or two customers stop briefly. Then another, even older, man comes by. He is wearing a dark brown jacket and a *keffiyeh*. Prayer beads dangle from his hand. He stays for a longer chat.

I guess that these two would have been boys when the British were still running Palestine. They have seen the great colonial power depart, leaving their Palestinian community in violent conflict with the Jewish one. Then after 1948 the Old City of Jerusalem – and the whole of the West Bank – was annexed by Jordan. Two decades later it was seized by Israel, which continues to occupy it today. So much turbulence and distress between people vying for control of their home town. And these two old men have lived through it all and are still here, selling juices and chatting, just as their fathers and grandfathers would have done before them.

20

Not Complicated, but Simple

RANA LEADS ME DEEP INTO THE MUSLIM QUARTER OF Jerusalem's Old City. We follow the cobbled streets, turn off on to a little pathway that appears to be a blind alley and discover a doorway opening on to a courtyard.

We stand for a moment, looking into this small stone-flagged space. Lines of washing hang between the surrounding walls, which rise for a couple of storeys to frame the blue sky above. A man appears from a doorway and greets us with a smile and a handshake, introducing himself as Awni Ahmed Iryashi. He is small with slumped shoulders and, though very polite, he seems distracted.

Awni tells us that this is his family home and that in Ottoman times it was the neighbourhood prison. Though he was born and brought up in it, he has lived and worked in Amman since his mother died some eight years ago. His Jordanian wife and their nine children are still in Jordan while Awni fights to have his residency permit for Jerusalem restored by the Israeli authorities. As he shows us around the courtyard, I sense that he is not only angry that he has to battle for the right to be a resident in his native city, and that he is bereft without his family, but also ashamed to live like this, supported by his brothers, since he is unable to work while in Jerusalem.

For the past two months he has shared a room off the courtyard with one of his brothers. The brother's wife and their five children live in a room above. 'Room' is a generous description. It is little more than a cell. He tells me that eight families live in this little place. Aesthetically it is very attractive, particularly with the sun filtering down to warm the old stones, yet it is very cramped. There is only one bathroom for everyone and they share the small, very basic kitchens. But for the style of clothes – and the heat – I could imagine this might be like the Marshalsea Prison in Dickens's *Little Dorrit*, full of people living in a kind of parallel world where, oppressed by the establishment, they maintain the social graces as best they can in the midst of absolute poverty.

Awni seems much confused by the world. His rounded face is etched with tiredness. He asks us to sit in the courtyard while he makes coffee. Two little girls chatter and giggle with Rana while a bird twitters in a cage. Awni returns with coffee and a sheaf of papers. In a quiet voice he explains that they are from the East Jerusalem Regional Population Office, a branch of the Israeli government's Interior Ministry.

For Jerusalemites like Awni, who have lived away from home for a while, it can be very difficult to hold on to their 'Blue Card'. If someone cannot make it back within an allotted period, the government revokes their ID papers – even though Jerusalem is where they were born or grew up. Between 1967 and 2008 the Ministry of the Interior revoked the status of more than 13,000 Palestinian residents.

Awni explains that he had intended to return at various points in recent years but could not leave his family or his work in Jordan. When he came back to renew his ID it was revoked under the rule – which was brought in while he was out of the country – that to retain your residency you have to return once every three years. He had not done this and the authorities now argue that Jerusalem is no longer the 'centre of his life'. The Israeli authorities aren't interested in his reasons for being unable to come back regularly: the policy is designed to keep people out.

Awni has a Jordanian passport but had hoped to apply to the Israeli authorities for family reunification so that his family in Jordan could all have Jerusalem ID. But even without the huge obstacle of his own ID having been revoked, I've learned that family reunion is now little more than a pipe dream for people like Awni. In the past it was possible. It took a great deal of time, but in the end, if one of the spouses was a Jerusalemite, the family would eventually be granted permanent residency. But in 2003, the Citizenship and Entry Law (Temporary Order) came into force. It prohibits Palestinians who are married to Israeli citizens from receiving Israeli citizenship, and Palestinian citizens of Israel are also not entitled to family reunification with foreign (i.e. also Palestinian) spouses or children. I've already met one victim of this law: Salha Ammash in Jisr al-Zarqa. Although she is married to a Palestinian citizen of Israel and mother of his two children, she is deemed an illegal alien. Though not full citizens of Israel, Palestinian Jerusalemites are definitely covered by the law. The policy is that there should be no family reunions.

Awni's main objective now is simply to regain his Jerusalemite ID so that he can at least travel between Jerusalem and Amman. 'I do not understand what this is all about,' he tells me wearily. 'I am a simple, down-to-earth person and am not interested in politics. I just want to live a normal life and be able to earn money to look after my family. If I'd done something wrong or created problems, I'd understand that they might want to take my ID from me. But I cannot understand this. They have never given me one good reason why they are doing this.'

Without his Jerusalem ID he cannot stay or work in the city. And if he cannot get his Jerusalem ID restored, the Jordanian authorities have told him they will not renew his Jordanian passport. And if that happens, not only Awni but also his children will be stateless, since in Jordan citizenship has to come from the father. Unable to do anything – get work, travel or marry – they will be condemned to live in a bureaucratic no man's land. As we talk, Awni's mobile phone rings: it's his wife calling from Amman. After he has spoken to her, he explains the impact of these calls: 'It breaks my heart. Some of my kids are still very young. When we speak on the phone they cry for me to come home. One of them was asking, "Daddy, when are you coming back?" He wants me to bring him a bicycle. What can I do? If I go to them I may never get back to Jerusalem. I may not even be allowed back into Jordan. I have to go back to my family. Whatever happens to me I will have to accept. There is nothing else I can do.'

Somewhere near by, church bells start ringing. I try to take it all in. In this ancient city, the holiest of places for so many people, this man, and tens of thousands like him, is forced to live in a physical and moral vacuum.

'I was born here and raised here. I have papers to show that. How can they take that away from me? Do I not have the right to live in freedom and dignity? Why must I suffer like this? Am I not a human being? Are my children not human beings?'

Having felt so at home staying with the nuns in Haifa, I was pleased to get a room at St George's Cathedral Guesthouse in Jerusalem. It's about a mile north of the Old City. Like my Haifa 'home', St George's is a simple establishment. Tourists and pilgrims are staying here, but I notice, too, a number of clergy among the guests – here for conferences.

The next morning I walk down the quiet back-streets, past the US consulate, where people are always queuing for visas, past various art shops selling paintings and ceramics. The architecture is a mix of old and new but there are few blocks of any great height. It is a predominantly Arab area and the sense of being somewhere

Oriental rather than Western becomes stronger as I approach Damascus Gate on the edge of the Old City. Once I've negotiated the noise and fumes of a bus station I am surrounded by shops and stalls selling mainly food. Old women in black dresses and headscarves sit on the pavements behind baskets of fruit or vegetables.

Despite the bustle around this great stone gateway, the economy of East Jerusalem is in terrible decline. It has been devastated by the Wall. As goods and people are no longer allowed in from the Palestinian side, business in these markets, which were once the focus of the West Bank economy, is very limited.

As I walk among the stalls I am aware that some of the goods will have been smuggled in from the West Bank. I've heard that even some of the old women sitting by their baskets will have crawled through sewage pipes to get under the Wall to market.

A semicircle of wide staircases leads down to Damascus Gate. It is everything a medieval gateway should be: massive, elegant and castellated. There is a throng of people to negotiate as I follow a dog-leg path under the huge portal, past tables laden with cheap shoes, and kiosks offering tourist tat or paraphernalia for mobile phones. Then I'm inside the Old City, on a cobbled street running between yet more stalls.

Drifting through the narrow lanes I relish the sense of mingling with the whole world. There are Arab men and women in traditional clothes, Jews in black hats or skull caps, Christian monks in long robes, tourists in shorts and T-shirts, and soldiers with guns; everyone

320

squeezing past one another in extraordinary intimacy.

Some stalls are no more than a niche in the old stone walls; others, deep caverns. Some are full of tourist offerings, toy camels, menorah, hats and T-shirts, jewellery and artefacts; others are crammed with junk, wonderful piles of scrap metal, ancient light fittings, taps and old tools with brass ornaments mixed in. There are many clothes shops, cafés – tiny places, some of them. Little arches lead into small Islamic prayer halls. One alley is full of butchers' counters where the smell of flesh turns my stomach and I increase my pace across the treacherous stone slabs, worn slippery and shiny by millions of feet over thousands of years. Then my nostrils are refreshed as I pass the beautiful spice and herb shops with their fantastic pyramids of paprika and *zatar*.

Space is so limited that all the goods are moved through the maze of ancient stone on small carts. Made of wood, these basic barrows have wheels set exactly wide enough to roll down the central ramp of the stone stairways that make up the highways and byways of the city. These machines have no engines and no brakes so the operator, sometimes with an aide, will sweat uphill, often with sacks of flour or rice piled high and teetering, then bounce down, standing on the rudimentary brake – an old tyre fixed to the cart with a chain – hoping his weight will provide enough drag to slow his Holy Land bobsleigh sufficiently to avoid disaster. Sometimes one winces in anticipation and there are many cries of '*Imche!*' (Get out of the way!), but I've never seen a crash.

One man I see today strikes me as the quintessential heroic failure. He is doing his rounds on one of these precarious carts, making his deliveries and collections, even though one of its tyres is flat. So, as well as pushing, he is half lifting his load as he goes up, and on the way down he is hanging off the side with the good wheel in a surely doomed effort to keep the contraption upright and moving. His intense concentration removes him from the world, where his plight appears both tragic and comic. But only someone desperate not to lose the morning's work would carry on rather than stop to mend the puncture. Whatever the odds, you keep going. In a life of uncertainty and oppression, a flat tyre isn't such a big deal.

Passing a café, I see a family group enjoying drinks and cakes. The mother wears a headscarf and long coat, and cradles a baby in her arms. The father and his little boy are making faces at each other and laughing. I think of Anna and Lydia back in England and wish they were here to enjoy this place. The thought has me feeling homesick even though I know I'll be going home in a week or so. What must it be like for people such as Awni Iryashi? What does it do to you to be held in permanent limbo? My years as a hostage taught me all I'll ever need to know about frustration and the misery of distance from home and family. But the people holding me against my will in another country never pretended they were serving anything other than their own ends. I wasn't ensnared in this cruel, cynical and surreal world of identity games and legalistic ploys.

At one point in the Old City you can get up above the narrow streets and walk on the rooftops. Up there, out of the throng, I wander between small domes and barrel-vaulted roofs and wonder what is going on below my feet. There is a sense of real peace as church bells ring and muezzin call the faithful to prayer. Yet the political tension is unavoidable. As I scan the beautiful array of stone roofs, towers and domes, my eye is jarred by a small metal watch-tower. One or two Israeli flags fly from it. I know I'm looking over the Muslim Quarter yet the Israeli flag and watchtower show that a property is in the hands of a Jewish settler group.

I find it confusing that the settlers put so much effort into taking over small buildings in a Palestinian area, given they already have so much power here.

'No, it is not confusing at all. It is the easiest, most coherent and successful part of the Israeli strategy. In East Jerusalem the name of the game is demography – the percentage of the population that is Jewish, and the percentage that is Arab. East Jerusalem was annexed to Israel and the aim is to make a united Jerusalem not only the capital but as much a Jewish city as possible. In 1967 the Arabs were just below one third of the population of Jerusalem. This is supposed to be the magical figure. More than a third and we are moving towards a bi-national city.'

I've walked out of the Old City into West Jerusalem for an early meeting with the Jewish writer, and co-founder of the Alternative Information Centre (AIC), Michael

'Mikado' Warschawski. He has a lively, open face, with bright eyes, a high forehead and a luxuriant grey moustache. He smiles as often as he lights a cigarette. He is a chain smoker.

'Through very well-coordinated policies, the number of Palestinians in Jerusalem has been kept to around one third.'

As he speaks we are inspecting the rather ancient air-conditioner in his office. It is on the blink, but as it is not quite nine in the morning we decide not worry about it. The summer heat isn't too intense yet. Settling at a table, Michael reviews the four policies used to keep Palestinian population numbers down.

First there are the planning regulations, not permitting any new building by Arabs outside the existing villages. This is the same as it has been within Israel's 1948 borders. Second, the identification documents (IDs). I've learned a good deal about the way the Israeli state uses them from the al-Qumbar family and from Awni Iryashi. Most countries let foreign visitors have permanent residency rights on certain conditions. If you behave badly you can be removed, and if you cannot show that the country is your main home, maybe you won't be allowed to return. The 250,000 Palestinians in East Jerusalem are treated in this way.

'But,' cries Michael, with a mix of anger and outraged humour, 'East Jerusalemites are not foreign visitors. They never left anywhere. They are in their own home!'

The third aspect of Israeli policy has been to remove all the Arab political and cultural bodies from the city.

Palestinian national institutions and anything to do with the Palestine Liberation Organization have been pushed out.

'The Wall is the fourth factor,' says Michael. 'It is a way of closing off Jerusalem from the West Bank. It is like disconnecting the heart from the rest of the body. There is no blood supply and it dies. Hospitals are dying. Theatres are dying because people cannot come in to them.'

The Palestinian areas of East Jerusalem are decaying rapidly so, like Arab Jaffa, they are turning into large slums. Social breakdown leads to the death of the community. People want to keep their ID so that they can move around and have social security. They keep their heads down to protect these small privileges.

Michael tells me there is no nationalist movement in East Jerusalem. The Palestinian community in Jerusalem is the least politicized, militant or active part of the broader Palestinian community. Through *farok tassod*, divide and rule, the East Jerusalemites become another isolated minority, estranged from their fellow Palestinians, desperately clinging to some Israeli-given 'privilege' to stay in their homes. This is just as I imagine life in Israel during the Military Period.

'There are many identical syndromes,' Michael agrees, 'with one big difference. The Palestinians who remained in Israel after 'forty-eight accepted, within a few years of their defeat, that they were part of an Israeli state. But even if they are not very politicized, the Palestinians of East Jerusalem, like those of the West Bank in general, more than forty years since it was occupied, still don't accept Israel.'

Turning from East Jerusalem to the situation in Israel proper, Michael argues that the biggest threat to Israel does not come from the West Bank or Gaza, or from other countries, but from the Palestinian community within Israel. A wall can be put around Gaza and the West Bank. Talks about the Palestinian refugees around the world can be put off for ever, but the Palestinians in Israel are seen as a real and present danger. Michael sees the killing of the thirteen demonstrators in October 2000 as the end of the illusion that there could be some kind of integration. In his eyes, the Establishment was telling the Palestinians very bluntly that they were becoming too confident and must remember their place as secondary citizens.

'Zionism is a philosophy of separation: Jews cannot live among non-Jews and should live in their own ethnic state,' Michael continues. 'The ethnic cleansing of 1948, and the permanent drive to see Palestinians as a strategic threat, is part of this philosophy. Even in 'forty-seven to 'forty-eight, most of the strategic thought was on the demographic issue – not on how to counter the Syrians, Egyptians and so on. And it is still the main concern for national strategy, not Iranian missiles, not Syria or Hezbollah. It is an obsession.'

Israel's first prime minister, David Ben-Gurion, argued against seeking final settlements of Israel's borders. His idea was that Israel would be defined not by international agreements and not by what is written in the Bible, but by 'facts on the ground'. Ben-Gurion said, 'Our border is where we dig the last furrow.' Michael says that that thinking is still dominant.

Walking from Michael Warschawski's office, back towards the Old City, I start thinking back to when I saw the Wall for the first time. During that visit, I heard a powerful expression of the importance of separation to some Jews. In 2003, I visited the West Bank settlement of Alfe Menashe and was shown around by the mayor, Hisdai Eliezer. Founded in 1983, the settlement was home to seven thousand people and, set some three miles into Palestinian territory in the hills of the West Bank, looked across the coastal plain to Tel Aviv. Walking around, I was struck by the sense of security and tranquillity: from people tending their gardens in neatly laid-out suburban streets to children exercising in the school playground, there was a powerful atmosphere of permanence. Alfe Menashe appeared to be anything but an endangered community in a hostile landscape.

But Hisdai told me that his community felt so vulnerable to attack from Palestinian militants that they had campaigned to have the Wall diverted from the original ceasefire line of 1967 to enclose their location, which was inside Palestinian territory. If the Wall had gone around the other side of the town they would have felt cut off from Israel and isolated in alien land. The mayor said that he believed that it would be a suicidal mistake for Israel to accept a Palestinian state.

He took me to see the monumental 'fence' being

erected around his town. As massive machines rolled back and forth across the hillside, I was sickened that such a beautiful landscape was being destroyed: a landscape that by all but Israeli accounts belonged to another people. But Hisdai had no such sentiment. He insisted the Palestinians had been there for only a hundred years or so and were therefore unimportant. The widely held belief that modern Jews had a right to be there because their ancestors had been there in biblical times wasn't of much importance to him either. For him the importance of Jewish settlements was that they brought greater security through the capturing of land. 'Settlements like Alfe Menashe act as an insurance for the state of Israel,' he told me.

Yet capturing the land was the reason that Israelis were the target of Palestinian militants. 'Why is it necessary,' I asked him, 'not only to control the territory but also to exclude the native population and put walls and fences around everyone, including yourself?'

'I represent the second generation of Holocaust survivors,' he answered me, staring intently into my eyes. 'Jewish people suffered the greatest loss that humans can suffer and we still live with the trauma of genocide. So our main motivation is security and that is why I am here.'

Hisdai was clearly a successful mayor and an effective campaigner, yet as he spoke I knew I was listening not to a smooth politician but to someone with a profound and sincere motivation.

'I am here to say to anyone that such a thing as

328

happened in Europe will not happen again to the Jewish people,' he told me. 'We are here in the land of Israel for ever. People who are prepared to concede to the idea of a Palestinian state remind me very much of my father's family in Greece. On the day they were told to get on the trains to Auschwitz, they got on, naïvely. They said, "The Germans are an enlightened nation. They won't do us any harm. In a couple of weeks we will be back." They had a kind of trust in mankind that comes from a great deal of naïvety. And I'm glad to say that the majority of the Jewish people managed to rid themselves of this innocence and naïvety.'

Remembering his words now, I think of all the Palestinians I have met in Israel who echo those thoughts on their previous generations' innocence and naïvety for believing that, 'after a little while', they would be allowed back to their homes.

I could understand Hisdai Eliezer's ideology, and appreciated that it could not be shaken. But though he spoke of the innocence and naïvety of others, history has shown that simply building walls never guarantees lasting security. For all his ruthless determination to ensure his community's safety, I suspect all the Wall will do is breed ever deeper and ever more violent mistrust between the people on either side of it. Retreating behind a wall doesn't reflect confidence, but fear.

Entering the Old City through the Jaffa Gate I wander through the Armenian to the Jewish Quarter. There has been a great deal of building and rebuilding in the Jewish

Quarter. In 1948 when the Jordanians captured the Old City, all the Jews were driven from it to West Jerusalem. At that time there were some two thousand Jewish residents. Today there are around four thousand, compared with an Arab population of at least 35,000 in the Old City. As well as rebuilding houses and synagogues that had become derelict or were demolished between 1948 and 1967, many new buildings have gone up. For Jews there is little difficulty in getting building permission, whereas for Palestinians in East Jerusalem, it is well nigh impossible.

The heart of the Jewish Quarter is the Western (or Wailing) Wall Plaza. The wall is the holiest site in Judaism. It is hard to imagine the great space of the Plaza filled with stone buildings and all the bustle of the old Mughrabi Quarter as it would have been before 1967 and the ensuing eviction of its Palestinian inhabitants and the demolition of their homes.

To the south of the Plaza is the Dung Gate. Leaving the Old City through it, I head downhill. This road has long been called Wadi Hilweh, 'Beautiful Valley', by Arab residents. In the latest round of redrawing maps to suit the Zionist agenda, the name has officially become Maalot Ir David, or King David's Ascent. The road, whatever you call it, leads to Silwan, the biggest village in Israel and the Palestinian territories combined. A large number of Palestinians moved here in 1948 as refugees from the new Israeli state. Now, with more than 55,000 Arab residents, Silwan represents at least a fifth of the population of the East Jerusalem area.

As well as Palestinians, there are now a few hundred Jewish settlers living here. That's because Silwan is believed to be the site of the fabled City of David, the place where King David would have had his palace in the heyday of the kingdom of Israel in the tenth century BCE.

Going down the hill I pass the 'City of David' settlement and its tourist complex. A modern stone wall protects the site with the words 'City of David', in Hebrew and English, emblazoned on it in large gold letters. I've visited the site before and was told, as are all visitors, to believe that this was, without doubt, the political centre of David's empire. It is guarded by heavily armed men, which does not generate a good feeling for what aims to be a tourist attraction.

The settlement group Elad (in Hebrew, El Ir David, 'to the City of David') runs the whole set-up, above and below ground. Beneath Silwan there is an extensive and growing complex of tunnels, which are part of the group's archaeological project to discover evidence of the ancient city of King David's time. They are doing this even though most of the archaeological community sees David as a partly mythical character and reports that no solid evidence has been found that he ever lived in Jerusalem.

A senior Israeli archaeologist told me once that after years of working on the site he had plenty of pottery evidence for occupation in the eighth century BCE when Jerusalem was the capital of the Kingdom of Judah. But between then and a thousand years earlier, when the place was Canaanite, there was no evidence whatsoever of occupation by Israelites.

So, until evidence is found to the contrary, it would seem that Jerusalem only became associated with a state called Israel in 1967. But as a Zionist politician once told me, it isn't right to let archaeological 'nitty-gritty' cast doubt on the veracity of the Bible stories and their use by modern Israel to claim precedence over another people's lands.

There are regular clashes between Palestinian residents, Jewish settlers and police in Silwan. In 2010 a settler leader drove into two boys when his car was stoned. Another Palestinian resident was shot during an argument with a settler. Sometimes the clashes escalate into full-scale riots. The Palestinian community here, just like the Palestinian communities in Israel, know they are under threat and that the state wants to move them out.

Past the City of David complex, I continue down Wadi Hilweh Street until I reach the Silwan community's protest tent. In its shade I meet Jawad Siyam, a social worker and a leader of the residents' protest movement against the settler actions. 'The Elad group was set up in the mid-eighties and they used various methods to get their hands on Arab properties,' Jawad tells me, as we sit on plastic chairs with cold drinks. 'They claimed that some people didn't own the houses they were living in and that the real owners were overseas. They got permission to take over the properties under the Absentees' Property Law. In 1991–2 the settlers started to come.'

Jawad speaks quickly, telling me of the lengths settlers have gone to in pursuit of Palestinian homes: 'When my grandmother died, the settlers managed to get someone local to take her fingerprints and put them on a document to make it look as though she had sold them her house and land! It took eight years in court but eventually we won.' Nobody involved in the fraud was fined, imprisoned or punished. And the settlers who had moved in after the forged transaction remain in the house. 'The settlers are very powerful. They are digging new tunnels under the village. This causes subsidence, which is damaging the houses. The municipality does nothing to stop the digging. All they do is close down a house or building when it becomes unsafe. So we lose out.'

In recent years the municipality has become ever more open in its support of the settlers and their drive to take control of Silwan. Jerusalem's mayor, Nir Barkat, has put all his weight behind the development of another tourist site in the valley, the King's Garden. He has agreed to the destruction of twenty-two Arab homes to make way for the biblical theme park. It will be linked to the adjacent 'City of David' site, which, in turn, via the ever-expanding Elad tunnel network, will lead excited tourists underground from the 'King's Palace' to emerge in the Plaza by the Western Wall.

Next to the plot where Jawad's protest tent is set up, an Israeli flag flies over a settler excavation site. 'One day a settler came on to this field. I was here with a group of fifty or so people, having a meeting. He started shouting at us. We asked him to leave. He wouldn't, so I called the

333

police. They came and told me to go to the police station to make a complaint. I went with my cousin who owns this field and an Israeli friend who was there. At the police station, they arrested us, saying we had attacked the man!'

All this influence is wielded by only three hundred settlers. Yet even though they can tunnel and cause problems for the community, they cannot drive out 55,000 Palestinian inhabitants. 'They do not have the same connection with this place that we do. We are connected with the land; they are connected with an idea only.'

Jawad, a tall wiry man of thirty-nine with a shaved head, shows me the small community centre he has helped set up and takes me around this part of Silwan. As we walk, he explains some of the issues facing his community. If residents in West Jerusalem fail to pay their local taxes, the *arnona*, they get a letter. If the Palestinians in East Jerusalem don't pay, they get sent to gaol. But less than 2 per cent of what they pay comes back in services. There are no sports clubs or a community centre. The few kindergartens are privately run and, as elsewhere in East Jerusalem, there is a serious shortage of classrooms in Silwan. After ninth grade, students have to go to schools outside the village.

Jawad points out that the settler properties are built too close together, in contravention of the planning regulations, yet nothing is done about them. When a Palestinian breaks a planning regulation, a demolition order is almost certain to follow. 'Every second Arab house has a demolition order. Every family has at least one lawyer to deal with demolition orders and issues like subsidence. The costs are huge and, with unemployment at sixty per cent here, our problems keep growing.'

Though Silwan is a particularly important cultural site for Jews, the way Palestinian homes here have been subjected to demolition orders is not unusual. Such orders are issued against Palestinians throughout the municipality. In 2009 eighty homes were demolished in East Jerusalem, leaving three hundred people homeless. New building is almost exclusively for Jewish residents. Until 2007 more than 50,197 housing units had been built for the Jewish population (on land expropriated by the government since 1967). No homes were built for Palestinians during that time.

Jawad knows that his community must look also to its own failings when trying to deal with the situation. 'The Israelis create all these problems as a way of breaking our society and social life, and we are letting this happen,' he says, exasperated. 'People have started to behave as they do in big cities, not talking to each other. We have to recognize that there are problems between families here, and the settlers and the authorities play on these weaknesses. I am optimistic that we can keep going with non-violent protest, but for how long I don't know. Violence may happen. I don't know what the future can hold.'

Leaving Jawad at the tent, I walk back up Wadi Hilweh pondering the potency of the King David story. The idea that people somewhere beneath me are burrowing for evidence of something that, by all accounts, never happened is disturbing. Wearily, I wander through the narrow streets of this most beautiful and troubled Old City of Jerusalem to St George's Guesthouse. I can't understand how people become so self-absorbed in religious obsession and nationalist fervour that reality becomes unimportant.

There are so many Palestinian campaigners, like Jawad Siyam, struggling for their rights, for their land and for the world to acknowledge their story. There are many Jewish activists, like Michael Warschawski, who are trying to bring the truth to the light. Yet ancient fable and modern myth still seem able to convince the majority of Jewish Israelis, and much of the international community, to support Israel in its relentless expropriation of another people's land and heritage.

21

'Happy Nakba'?

M̲Y NEXT VISIT TO ISRAEL OPENS WITH THE USUAL
questions at Passport Control at Ben-Gurion
Airport. Why am I here? Where will I be going? Whom
will I be meeting? Sometimes this takes a couple of minutes, sometimes longer. It is tedious and irritating, young
officials talking down to you, using a script that will provide no useful intelligence, and serves only to create an
unsettling start to a trip.

Palestinian citizens of Israel coming in or out face
lengthy questioning and delay, but as a white Westerner
I'm unlikely to get any prolonged hassle. This time the
passport officer, a strikingly beautiful young woman,
smiles and asks what I do.

'I'm a writer,' I reply. 'I am writing a travel and history
book about Israel.' I decide not to mention that I am
researching the situation of the Palestinian citizens of
Israel over the past sixty years.

She asks what the purpose of this visit is.

I think a little before I answer her, then say simply, 'For Independence Day.'

She nods her mane of wondrous curly hair, and dazzles me with another smile. 'For Ha'atzmaut, of course. Welcome!'

Arriving in Israel two days before the state's sixtieth-anniversary celebrations, I can sense that the excitement is building. Even at the car-rental desk the urbane manager in his dark green jacket is more friendly than usual.

It is mid-afternoon and as I drive out of the airport, intending to go north to Haifa, I see a sign to Lod and decide instead to visit the Azbarga family, who sparked off my journey to discover the story of the Palestinians of Israel. Twenty minutes later I knock at the door and hear, '*Mien?*' (Who is it?)

This is a word I heard many times as a captive in Lebanon. Whenever there was a knock at the door, the guards would all go quiet in their room and one would call out, '*Mien?*' I always imagined their hands reaching for guns in case the visitors were not welcome. Never daring to hope that there would be anyone coming to help us, I was worried that the visitor would be the precursor to a terrifying move to another prison.

For the Azbargas there is a similar tension. The knock at the door might be the police telling them to get out or a lawyer bringing good news.

Today it's just an unannounced Englishman. Saud opens the door in T-shirt and shorts and greets me with a kiss of welcome as he ushers me in. His daughters,

Jenna and Nowa, and his son, Annis, crowd in to see who is visiting. Saud makes me a sandwich and fills me in on family news. His brother Moadi, the engineer, is planning to get married, and the wife of Muhammad, the brother whose wedding I attended, is now pregnant. Saud explains that the demolition order on their house is still in abeyance. 'And I am starting my own business!' he announces. 'I want to show you.' As Rania is out he calls a niece and asks her to pop round and look after the children. He disappears for a moment and returns in jeans and shirt. 'Follow me, John. It is on your way to Haifa.'

I feel flattered and excited that he wants me to see his new undertaking. We drive some ten kilometres north and east of Lod to the new Jewish town of Shoham. Dual-carriageways, lined with lawns, flowerbeds and trees, sweep through the exclusive development. What will be Saud's pharmacy is currently an empty unit in a brand-new mall.

He takes me inside and, beaming with pride, talks me through his plans. Setting up on his own has needed capital and that meant borrowing money but Saud, in his quiet way, sounds confident he will make a go of it. 'It could be a very good business here,' he says, looking around the shop. 'I had to give up my last job. Nobody has had a pay rise for ten years.'

From the picture window at the front of the shop we can see the high-rise blocks of Shoham. Founded in 1993, the town has just over 20,000 residents and an area of just under six thousand dunams (1,500 acres). There are 250 dunams of green parks and gardens alone. The new town's prosperity should provide a good start for Saud's business.

'*Mabrouk!*' I say. 'I hope you do very well.'

Saud shrugs and turns his head to one side. 'I hope so too.'

I leave him fitting up some shelves and head on to Haifa and my home from home with the nuns at the St Charles Guesthouse.

Surprisingly, the diminutive figure of Sister Isadora stands at the top of the steps holding the door open for me. Usually Sister Reeta is in charge of the guests but I'm told that she is on a pilgrimage to Fatima in Portugal.

When I tell Sister Isadora that I'm here for the anniversary celebrations and plan to go on the Nakba, Right of Return march, at the village of Saffuriyya, she becomes quite animated. She is more outspoken than Sister Reeta has ever been about the situation of their fellow Palestinians. Originally from Jerusalem, Sister Isadora tells me that much of her family emigrated many years ago. 'They had to go,' she says. 'All my brothers and sisters left. They were well educated but there was no work for them here. In 1962, they left our beloved Palestine.'

When I ask what she thinks of the preparations for the sixtieth-anniversary celebrations, she fixes me with sharp eyes. 'We are citizens. Why don't we have equal rights? What are people supposed to do when the Israelis knock down our houses, cut down our olive and fruit trees, and take away our living? People naturally will try to defend themselves. But wherever you go in the world now, people believe what the Israeli government tells them. If you say you are an Arab they think you are a terrorist.'

Next morning I find Sister Isadora at the reception desk and ask if she knows whether banks or *bureaux de change* will be open today. She says she has no idea.

'Sister Reeta deals with all those things,' she says, with an apologetic smile.

An hour later, having found a *bureau de change*, I am on my way back to St Charles. Suddenly the cars in front of me stop. Their drivers get out and stand still, looking ahead. I hear a siren, and wonder if there has been an accident. Checking my watch, I see it is eleven o'clock and realize that the people standing silently by their cars aren't looking forward but back. It is Yom Hazikaron, Memorial Day, when Israel observes two minutes' silence for those who have died fighting for their country or as victims of terrorism.

Later on, I read that Prime Minister Ehud Olmert, attending an official ceremony in Jerusalem, said, 'There is no one in Israel to whom the price of war is alien . . . This special day wipes away our divisions. The feeling of unity and shared destiny is stronger than ever.'

While all Israelis, whether Jewish or Arab, know the cost of war, it seems unlikely that they share feelings of unity. One of the consistent themes of my meetings with Palestinians in Israel has been their sense of exclusion from full membership of their state. They often say that they feel like strangers in their own home.

All the parades, street parties and Israeli flags on cars, buildings and lamp-posts enforce the impression of one solid national identity. Yet Palestinian citizens know that the state has consistently ignored, denied and even tried to destroy *their* national identity.

Prime Minister Olmert had spoken of Memorial Day as sad, and so it is. To me, the sadness seems compounded by the fact that many Israelis think it is inappropriate that their Palestinian fellow citizens should want to acknowledge and express their sorrow for what happened to *their* community: the 'price of war' as paid by them. The planned Palestinian Nakba Day march has been condemned by right-wing politicians as a subversive challenge to the existence of Israel, and they are calling for it to be banned.

This evening, as I saunter down side-roads off Ben-Gurion Boulevard, I see Palestinian families on their balconies watching fireworks, little children squealing with delight. A few floors above the street a man, perhaps in his mid-forties, holds his young son and points at the explosions of colour in the sky. The boy's eyes are wide with excitement. I wonder what thoughts are running through his father's head. Suha, and other members of her generation, have told me how, when they were children, the authorities required them to stand in the street and wave the Israeli flag on Independence Day. Now that they know about the Nakba they are angry that they were made to do that.

The Israeli flag was inspired by the *tallit*, the blue and

white striped Jewish prayer shawl. With the Star of David at its centre, it was a key symbol for Zionism, prior to being adopted by the new state in late 1948. For the other Israelis, though – the Palestinians from both Muslim and Christian communities – it is an emblem of loss.

Independence Day dawns beautifully. After an early, solitary breakfast I head toward Ben-Gurion Boulevard to rendezvous with Hisham Naffa. Suha, who is away in Europe at a film festival, has arranged for me to meet Hisham, an award-winning writer, novelist and journalist who works for *al-Ittihad* (the Union), the Communist Party newspaper.

On the street the world has turned white and blue, from puffs of cloud against the bright Mediterranean sky to the thousands of Israeli flags that fly from every conceivable position. Ben-Gurion Boulevard is closed to traffic, and the holiday crowd saunters up and down, enjoying the perfect spring atmosphere. Looking at the people – elderly, very smartly dressed couples, younger couples pushing buggies, groups of teenage boys and girls – I sense the national pride, confidence and unity that the prime minister was speaking of yesterday. Yet I know that while all can feel the sun on their skin, not everyone on the street shares the inner warmth generated by the anniversary. Many of the staff, and on most days many of the customers, at the cafés up and down the avenue are Palestinians. Several of the young waiters I have met here speak of home not as the area of Haifa that they grew up in, or the village where their parents lived, but the village that their grandparents remembered living in before 1948.

I settle at a café and am met within minutes by Hisham, a slender man in his late thirties with a beard and long, thick black hair tied back in a ponytail. We sit in the shade sipping fruit juice and watch the throng walking up and down. I wonder how it feels to be a Palestinian in this very happy atmosphere.

'Sad. Sad for the Jews as well as the Arabs,' answers Hisham. 'These people are happy celebrating but most of them don't know what they have yet to face up to and own up to. I used to hate Independence Day. Four or five years ago I had to have Arabic music blasting out in my apartment to obliterate the Ha'atzmaut sound! Now I'm not really bothered. And more and more people are saying that there should be a new discourse – "not my Nakba, but our Nakba, all of ours".'

Hisham's English is fantastic. He is attentive, serious, with a sense of humour, reflective and self-deprecating. I like him immediately. He grew up in a political household, where both parents were activists. His father, Muhammad Naffa, is secretary-general of the Israeli Communist Party and a former Member of the Knesset. The situation of the Palestinian people and their relations with Israel was a constant topic of conversation.

'My parents argued that we couldn't let the state turn us into a new community, one that had no ties or relations with its history and its consciousness. So they taught me that we faced a struggle that was deeper than a clear-cut fight for civil rights.'

Hisham is a Druze, one of around 100,000 in Israel. Though most Druze see themselves as part of the Arab people, the Israeli government designates them as a distinct ethnic community, as well as a religious group. Historically the Druze have had a closer relationship with the state than most Palestinians in Israel. Some Druze men are conscripted into the Israel Defence Forces (IDF). Hisham says that conscription is an extreme statement of *farok tassod*, Israel's policy of divide and rule towards the Arab community.

'I went to a military centre in Tiberias and told them that I would not be a soldier in the army, for political and national reasons. They said, "But you are Druze, not Arab!" They really believed all Druze are keen to collaborate with the Zionists. They were shocked.'

Shocked and also angry: Hisham was sentenced to a year in prison. Although he was a civilian, he was sent to a military prison, the ominously named Prison Four in central Israel. For all his political awareness he was unprepared for the conditions in prison, which were tough and violent. His captivity was in 1989 at the height of the first Intifada. The prison authorities ran an extreme form of boot camp, which aimed to 'break' those who had dared to refuse to serve in their country's armed forces. Hisham was unusual in that he was a civilian; most of the other inmates were 'refuseniks', Jewish soldiers who had refused to continue their military duties.

For all his suffering at the hands of the authorities, Hisham, like most people I've met who are fighting for their community's rights, has no desire to generate another human tragedy to achieve his goal. 'I don't want to create a mirror of the terrible Israeli policies,' he tells me, raising his voice slightly as the Israeli national anthem 'Hatikvah' (the Hope), a surprisingly mournful tune, begins playing over the PA system. 'I learned from my parents that you should keep sight of everyone's humanity. I live with Jewish people here and to be realistic is to think, How can we change this situation without creating another tragedy? I don't want to improve things for the Palestinians if the price is to make life worse for the Jewish people. I think we should take responsibility for the two peoples.'

I point out that Israel's leaders don't seem keen to encourage a broader understanding of how the Arab minority has been treated. Just yesterday President Shimon Peres was reinforcing what is now known to be a myth, that the Jewish leaders at Independence, David Ben-Gurion and the others, wanted the Arabs to stay in 1948.

'Oh, sure, all the time the Israeli establishment tries to keep the story of the founding of Israel very clean for the young Jewish people. Otherwise they will start thinking and that . . .' he pauses, opening his eyes wide in mock-horror '. . . would be very dangerous!'

I ask Hisham what he thinks of the thousands of Israeli flags flying today, the physical emblems that mark out allegiance and territory.

'Do you think there are enough?' He laughs. 'You know, chanting slogans, waving flags makes people sound certain, but I think it's a hollow certainty because it stops them looking at the reality that lies behind those symbols. We should be looking for ways of dealing with uncertainties and fears. Everyone here, Jews, Arabs, left and right, hides behind their flags and slogans.'

Leaving the blue and white of Israel's flag behind on Ben-Gurion Boulevard, we head off to meet the bus for Saffuriyya. For eleven years now the Palestinians in Israel have gathered on this day at or near the site of one of the five hundred or more villages that were destroyed by Jewish forces.

Walking through the narrow lanes of Wadi Nisnas, I see no flags at all. I assume that flying a Palestinian flag would cause problems with the authorities – and, of course, I don't expect the Palestinian people living here to be flying the state flag.

Following the Six Day War in 1967, when Israel occupied the West Bank and Gaza, and until the signing of the Oslo Peace Accords in 1993, the Palestinian flag was banned in Israel. Under a 1980 law, artwork of 'political significance' using the flag's four colours, red, white, black and green, was also banned. Although the ban has been relaxed it is still occasionally enforced.

But not this afternoon. When we arrive at Haifa's Arabic-language theatre, al-Midan, the rendezvous for people getting buses out to Saffuriyya, we are greeted by a couple of dozen Palestinian flags. And while these few are heavily outnumbered by Israeli flags, I haven't seen any in blue and white to match the size of the banners that are unfurled as we walk to the buses. Laughter and cheers greet the stares of utter disbelief, turning quickly to anger on the faces of passing Jewish motorists.

The small convoy of buses makes its way through the narrow side-streets of old Haifa, then heads south-east on Highway 75 with the slopes of Mount Carmel rising on our right. Then we take a turn north-east towards Nazareth and Saffuriyya across the rolling hills of Lower Galilee. Every time I drive through this landscape I am overwhelmed by the scenery, with its mixture of wide, fertile valleys and rocky hillsides. Even allowing for roads and pylons, it remains soft on the eye.

Given they are marking the Nakba, I'm surprised by the 'holiday' atmosphere on the bus. People have rolled up their Palestinian flags and are chatting amiably as we drive through the farmland and hills beneath blue skies. Among the Palestinians I've met in Israel, their continued optimism, their robust sense of humour and the ability to laugh at life, the world and themselves never cease to impress me.

'This state created refugees, created victims – not just Palestinian victims but also Jewish victims,' Hisham reflects. 'The Palestinians are the main victims. They are stateless refugees – a people of refugees. There is always the feeling that something was stolen. The people who use these lands now are not criminals but ordinary people. If they would think and recognize what has happened maybe I could forgive them. After all, they were refugees too.'

As we drive along we see many Jewish groups and families enjoying Ha'atzmaut in shady picnic spots just off the road. The distance between the two communities seems to be summed up by those Jewish families lying confidently on the Galilean grass while the people who were once the majority and considered this their home-land pass by on the bus, looking on like tourists.

As we are carried past another group, sitting at tables under trees, Hisham speaks again: 'Every side can keep their political ideas and beliefs, can hold on to their ideas of their right to be here. But if there comes a day when the Jews can begin to see and acknowledge the pain of the Palestinians, it could help the Palestinian to accept the situation, that his land was taken.' He shrugs. 'But, of course, we must never forget.'

The Survey of Palestine Map from 1946 shows Saffuriyya a mile or so to the north of the main road, but on my Europcar map only the modern Jewish village of Tsipori and the Tsipori National Park are shown.

The plan for today's event, which has been approved by the police, is to march to the old village well, which was fenced off by the Israeli authorities years ago to prevent former villagers going there. Seeing a field full of cars by the road on that side I immediately assume that this must be the car park for the marchers. Then I see all the Israeli flags. This is not the Nakba gathering, but a counter-demonstration by a group of Israelis. Instead of turning left, we turn right. We learn that the march will now take place across the hillside facing the old village site. No one seems in the slightest bit surprised that the presence of this relatively small protest means that thousands of Palestinian citizens of Israel have to alter their course for a few Jewish citizens of Israel. I also notice that the security forces are on the Jewish side of the road facing the Palestinians.

We step off the bus into a sea of purple, the designated colour for this year's march. Purple T-shirts, baseball caps and flags are everywhere. There are children with banners and flags – black flags for Nakba Day, and Palestinian flags. I see people greeting each other with big grins, big handshakes and bear hugs. There is much laughter in the crowd and many family groups. Youths, *shabab*, on horseback, take in the scene from their vantage-point up among the trees of the hillside behind us. Cars and buses arrive, depositing more and more people. I'm impressed by the numbers, and the family atmosphere.

'It is getting bigger every year,' says Hisham. 'It's become part of the way we sustain the collective memory. As you say, it is a family thing – and that is unique to this march. It passes the message on from one generation to the next.'

There's a gasp from the crowd as hundreds of black balloons are released and float up into the blue sky. It is hoped that Jewish Israelis seeing the balloons will acknowledge, at least, that this is a day of mourning for one fifth of their fellow citizens.

As the crowd moves across the hillside the leading banners disappear into the tree line. The dust from thousands of feet lends the scene the quality of a mirage. Various chants are taken up along the length of this huge crocodile of memory. The hillside is rocky, but the trees provide shade. People laugh and sing and children ride on fathers' shoulders.

We meet up with Hilani Shehadeh, the high-school teacher from Kafr Yasif. She is wearing a wide-brimmed straw hat and looks as though she may be attending an English garden party rather than a nationalist march. Hilani tells me how she feels as a Palestinian on Independence Day.

'I respect their right to protest, to demonstrate, I respect their right to celebrate the independence of their own country and on this particular date I actually envy them – to be able to celebrate the existence of their own country, their anthem and their flag. But what about me? The only solution left for people in this country is co-existence.'

The path changes direction across the hillside and the rival demonstration can be seen beyond the main road. The security forces are lined up in between.

'I hope there won't be any clashes,' says Hilani, 'but from experience, when I see those Yassam, the Special Forces, I expect something bad to happen. They are fierce people, they have no mercy.'

Chants run through the Palestinian ranks. Hilani translates for me: 'We are ready to die, to give our blood and souls for Palestine'; 'Long live Palestine'; 'We are all one people.'

She returns to the subject of the Israeli protesters we saw. 'Yes, it's their right to demonstrate against our march. But why the hell do they have to do that here and now, in that specific spot? It is provocative. Sometimes I believe we are heading towards an irreversible point with no way back.'

Despite the opposing rally, the mounted police and the chants of being ready to make the ultimate sacrifice, most people are still smiling.

The crowd spreads out through the trees. There is a wide clearing with a stage set up at one end. Speakers address the gathering. Looking around, I imagine that many people here are, like Hilani, thinking of incidents they have witnessed on the screen or in real life. Yet they recognize that, for all their military might, the Israelis are not so strong. They have guns, but they cannot control minds.

I know about this myself, from my time as a captive. The people with the weapons can stop you moving and they can beat you, but they cannot stop you thinking.

Hilani and I stop to talk to an elderly man, Mahmoud Saleh Taha, who was born and brought up in Saffuriyya. He is walking slowly, with the aid of a crutch, and tells us that he is seventy-nine. Wearing highly polished brown brogues, smart suit trousers, yellow shirt and a white *keffiyeh* with black *agal* (rope band), Mahmoud looks every inch the senior Arab gentleman. Sitting in the shade of some of the European trees planted by the Jewish National Fund, he tells us of his memories of Saffuriyya before the Nakba.

'I was born in 1929. There were nearly five thousand of us living in the village then. It was over there on the other side of the main road. They've planted trees where the place used to be. Most of the people went to Lebanon by foot following the attacks by the Israeli forces.'

Mahmoud was the only one of his immediate family who stayed here, coming back with his grandparents. His parents went to Damascus and died there so he never saw them again. 'This was my land and it is very painful to see immigrants coming from all over the world who are given the right to settle and get citizenship, while the original inhabitants of this land are living just a few kilometres away, most of them across the border, and cannot even get to see their old homelands.'

I'm cheered when I see Daoud Badr from al-Ghabisiyya. As a member of ADRID, the Association for the Defence of the Rights of the Internally Displaced, he has been involved with the plans for today's march and for all the preceding ones.

'In 1998 ADRID set up a Nakba Day march to be held on the site of a different destroyed Palestinian village each year,' he tells me. 'The first return march was to al-Ghabisiyya.'

The march, like that commemorating Land Day, has become an important event in the Palestinian calendar. Like many of his generation, Daoud refuses to see the passing of time as any valid reason to accept their eviction from their homes. 'We must keep working to let the world know the truth, the human truth, about what happens here.' He continues, in his soft voice, 'They tell us every day that this is the only democratic country in the Middle East. It is a democracy only for one side, for the Jewish side. For the Palestinians there is no democracy. They tell us that this is a Jewish state. We do not agree. We think it is the state of all its inhabitants. If you have a right and keep fighting for it, eventually it will be returned to you.'

Once the speeches are over, musicians take to the stage. People listen, wander and meet friends. Children run about between the thousands of people in the dappled shade. The atmosphere is very positive and happy. After all, while they are marking the sixtieth anniversary of their people's worst catastrophe, they are also celebrating the fact that they are here still.

Hisham and I join the growing stream of people heading back to the buses. Overhead, a helicopter with a huge camera on its snout continues hovering above the scene, as it has all afternoon.

Then, suddenly, there are the loud cracking sounds of tear gas being fired. We run down to see what is happening. On crossing a wide clearing, we see police on foot and the mounted Special Forces in their grey uniforms, helmets and black flak-jackets sweeping up the hill from the main road, chasing people through the trees. Small groups of police, maybe five or six strong, run along throwing stun grenades and tear-gas bombs ahead of them at the fleeing people.

The beautiful countryside has turned into a nightmare of acrid fumes, drifting smoke and noise. The menace is intense; I feel fear and confusion racing through me as I watch the squads of police come up towards us through the woods. One policeman is filming the scene. He stands fifty feet in front of a young Palestinian woman. She, too, has her video camera up and is filming. They stay there in a strange kind of standoff, cameras held at arm's length as they record the other's actions. The woman doesn't flinch. The policeman falls back with the rest of his unit.

I catch up with Hisham, who is kneeling on the ground beside an old lady. She sits on a rock, breathing heavily. Her scarf is wrapped around her face against the tear gas and smoke. Hisham speaks quietly to her, asking if we should call her an ambulance. She shakes her head. 'They were shouting, "Dirty Arabs!" as they charged at us,' she gasps. 'One of them came right up to me screaming that I had to keep moving, but I told him, "No!"' She shrugged. 'I have a bad heart and I'd rather risk a beating than a heart attack trying to run through this wood.'

There is an eerie quiet around us now as members of the Yassam move away, back down the hillside, through the trees towards the road. Spread out through the wood are other small groups like ours, waiting to see what will happen next. The woman seems very calm, as does Hisham. I am panting heavily, not so much from the exertion of running over the uneven terrain but from shock at what I have just seen.

Now I look at the old woman, into her lined face. She must be in her seventies and I realize that her whole life must have been punctuated with incidents like this, being chased and threatened in her own homeland. How many more times, I wonder, will she have to scurry for shelter across this landscape that once was part of her village land?

I am angry. It is unbelievable that so-called 'security' forces should so threaten civilians. Parents are still cowering with their children behind trees and parked cars at the foot of the hill as others run through the woodland, scattering, terrified, fearful that live ammunition could be used at any moment. I, too, have been frightened, intimidated by the harsh glint of violence in the eyes of the men on horseback.

We learn that four people were arrested and at least five taken to hospital. An elderly man, bleeding profusely from a cut to his head, tells us he was standing by his car when a couple of soldiers ran over. One hit him on the head and the other kicked his car. There is a large dent and a dusty boot print in the driver's door. 'I was about to head home when I saw a policeman beating someone,' he tells us. 'I got out of the car and policemen came over and started to beat me. They fired a tear-gas bomb at the car. There was no reason for any of it.'

Moments earlier this had been the epicentre of the violence. Now the spot is strangely quiet, with most of the police and demonstrators still spread out across the hillside. The man stands beside us looking placid, calm even, blood running down his face. It is remarkable how quickly people regain their composure and how smiles and conversation come back among the Palestinians. Within minutes the immediate tension begins to subside.

We leave the injured man and walk in silence for a moment before Hisham says simply, 'This is our reality.'

* * *

Just before we heard the stun grenades we'd been talking to a Palestinian TV producer. She was laughing with a young couple and their two little children, as she leaned against a TV satellite truck, headphones hanging round her neck. Recognizing Hisham, she had beckoned us over. 'Americans! They just don't understand, do they?' she said. 'We were doing a live interview with this family. The anchorman in the States kept on about how happy they must be as it's Independence Day in Israel. The dad was trying to explain that for Palestinians it's a day when they remember what they lost in 1948, when they think about all the people who became refugees, all the villages that were destroyed.

' "For the Jews this is Yom Hatzmaut, Independence Day, but for us Palestinians it's the Nakba, the Catastrophe," the father explained.

'The anchor guy couldn't understand – obviously couldn't get his head round the idea that there were Palestinians in Israel and that they could be anything other than delighted. He sounded more and more confused until he ended the interview saying, "Well, thank you very much and, er . . . Happy Nakba!"'

Witnessing the violent end to this peaceful demonstration, seeing old women and children cowering from police truncheons, choking on tear gas, seeing the bloodied face of an innocent man and feeling my own heart race as the mounted troops stormed this way and that across the forested hillside has given me probably my

357

sharpest insight into the experience of the Palestinian citizens of Israel.

Sitting at the back of the bus as we return to Haifa, I feel depressed: how can this miserable story of oppression ever end? I remember my friend Ghassan in Beirut: 'This is not a way.'

Israel claims to be a modern democracy, but its treatment of its Palestinian citizens shows that claim to be massively flawed. The Palestinians here are not an insignificant minority, but make up one in five of the Israeli population. They are an indigenous people with a profound love of the land they live on. Yet, though they have this deep connection with the place, it has been impossible for them to develop any such bond with the state of Israel, which continues to see them as outsiders. By now they should be living in a 'state for all its citizens', but just as in 1948, they are treated still as strangers in their own home.

Then I look round at Hisham and the other passengers, their flags carefully rolled away, ready for the next rally. As the chants of 'We may die, but Palestine will live!' had shown, they are not going away.

The journey to this point, from a cowed and broken community in 1948, has been a long one. It started on hillsides, like those of Saffuriyya, when the people were running from the soldiers for the first time. The oppression may continue but so, too, does the determination of the Palestinians of Israel to maintain their national identity and connection with the land.

The political horizon in Israel in the early years of the

state's seventh decade does not offer much hope of any sudden move towards genuine co-existence between Jewish and Palestinian citizens. Zionist ideologues and policies of reaction and defensiveness have become dominant. Their insistence that Israel, as a homeland for the Jews, must be exclusively Jewish has encouraged open demands that non-Jewish citizens be banished by a redrawing of geographical boundaries. Any statement that promotes the idea that Israel should be also a home for its indigenous Arab population is denounced as treasonous. The state's intransigence over the occupation of the West Bank and the sealing off of Gaza is reflected in a belligerent attitude to its allies as well as real or perceived enemies.

But for all that a growing number of Jewish voices within and without the country is calling for justice for the Palestinians in Israel and outside. And, more broadly, the international community is learning more about the nature of the Israeli state and can appreciate that much of the information that it has relied on in the past, which portrayed Jewish Israel always as the injured, threatened party, has been unbalanced to say the least. Modern communications – the Internet and satellite television – have allowed a wider audience to understand that the issues of the Israel–Palestine conflict are far from black and white.

But there are many still who faithfully accept Zionist propaganda, and in many ways the Palestinian community in Israel offers the clearest perspective on the nature of the injustice that has dominated the Holy Land since 1948. The efforts of this group of people to maintain a sense of identity and community within the Jewish homeland have not involved PLO attacks or Hamas bombings; there has never been a serious militant Palestinian movement within Israel.

That absence of violence in the face of their state's belligerence, I believe, gives the struggle of the Palestinians in Israel great potency. They cannot be written off as terrorists. The state's attitude towards them cannot be justified on grounds of security; it will be seen clearly as discriminatory. The Palestinians of Israel will have a crucial role to play in the future of the Israeli–Palestinian debate. Indeed, they are already emerging as an important voice in it: a voice to remind Israel and the world that 'You can't hide the sun.'

Chronology

Fifteenth–Nineteenth Centuries
Palestine under Ottoman rule as part of (southern) Syria.

1896
Publication of *Der Judenstaat* by Austrian Zionist leader Theodor Herzl, advocating creation of Jewish state in Argentina or Palestine.

1897
August: First Zionist Congress, meeting in Basel, Switzerland, issues the Basel Programme on Colonization of Palestine and establishes the World Zionist Organization (WZO).

1917
2 November: British foreign secretary, Arthur Balfour, sends letter (the Balfour Declaration) to Baron de Rothschild pledging British support for establishment of Jewish national home in Palestine.
9 December: Surrender of Ottoman forces in Jerusalem to Allied forces under General Sir Edmund Allenby.

1920

Jewish paramilitary organization Haganah, 'the Defence', founded in Palestine.

25 April: San Remo Conference awards administration of the former Turkish territories of Syria and Lebanon to France, and of Palestine, Transjordan and Mesopotamia (Iraq) to Britain.

1922

30 June: US Congress endorses Balfour Declaration.

24 July: League of Nations Council approves Mandate for Palestine without consent of Palestinians.

October: First British census of Palestine shows total population of 757,182 (11 per cent Jewish).

1923

29 September: British Mandate for Palestine comes officially into force.

1931

October: Irgun Zvai Leumi (National Military Organization) founded by dissident members of Haganah.

18 November: Second British census of Palestine shows total population of 1,035,154 (16.9 per cent Jewish).

1933

October: Riots in Jaffa and Jerusalem protesting against British pro-Zionist policies.

1935

November: Sheikh Izz al-Din al-Qassam, leading first Palestinian guerrilla group, dies in action against British security forces.

1936

April: Arab Higher Committee established.

16–18 April: Revolts all over Palestine, largest confrontations in Jaffa.

20–30 April: National Committees established in all Palestinian towns and large villages. Great Rebellion begins.

1939

February: Round Table Conference on Palestine at St James's Palace, London, followed by 1939 White Paper restricting Jewish immigration and land buying.

3 September: Outbreak of Second World War.

1940

10 October: British government authorizes the Jewish Agency to recruit 10,000 Jews to form Jewish units within the British Army.

1945

26 June: United Nations (UN) established, San Francisco.

September: British government issues Defence Regulations, authorizing military rule in Palestine.

1946

22 July: Irgun and Stern Gang Zionist groups blow up King David Hotel, Jerusalem.

24 July: British issue special White Paper on Terrorism in Palestine, accusing Jewish Agency of being involved in acts of terrorism with Irgun and Stern Gangs.

1947

18 February: British foreign secretary, Ernest Bevin, announces British submission of Palestine problem to UN.

15 May: UN Special Session ends with the appointment of an

eleven-member Special Committee on Palestine (UNSCOP), the eleventh commission of inquiry appointed since 1919.
8 September: Publication of UNSCOP report: the majority of members recommend partition, and a minority a federal solution.
29 September: Arab Higher Committee for Palestine announces rejection of UN Partition Plan.
2 October: Jewish Agency announces acceptance of UN Partition Plan.
11 October: US endorses UN Partition Plan.
13 October: Soviet Union endorses UN Partition Plan.
29 November: UN Partition Resolution 181 includes the recommendations that Jaffa be part of the proposed Palestinian state and that Jerusalem and Bethlehem be a *corpus separatum* under a special international regime administered by the Trusteeship Council on behalf of the UN.

1948
2 May: The Jewish Agency completes mobilization of Jewish manpower.
14 May: State of Israel proclaimed in Tel Aviv at 4 p.m.
15 May: British Mandate ends.
– The Arab States dispatch around 25,000 of their armed forces to Palestine.
– The Haganah, made up of 60,000 to 70,000 trained members, becomes the backbone of the Israeli Army.
1 September: Palestinian National Conference in Gaza. Formation of All-Palestine government.
1 October: All-Palestine government announces Palestinian independence.
11 December: UN General Assembly Resolution 194 (III) passed, acknowledging the right of Palestinian refugees to return.

1949

February–July: Armistice agreements signed in Rhodes, without prejudice to the settlement of the Palestine Question, between Israel and Egypt (24 February), Lebanon (23 March), Transjordan (3 April) and Syria (20 July).

May: Israel conditionally admitted to UN.

12 May: Lausanne Protocol signed by Israeli and Arab delegates.

31 June: US grants *de jure* recognition of the unification of the two banks of the River Jordan.

13 December: The west part of the City of Jerusalem is declared the capital of Israel.

19 December: UN General Assembly Resolution 303 is passed: Internationalization of Jerusalem.

1950

14 March: Absentee Property Law is passed, whereby any person who on 29 November 1947 was a citizen or resident of the Arab States or who was a Palestinian citizen who had left his/her place of residence, even if to take refuge within Palestine, is classified as an 'absentee'. Absentee property is vested in the Custodian of Absentee Property who then 'sells' it to the Development Authority authorized by the Knesset.

24 April: Unification of the West Bank and Jordan; Gaza Strip comes under Egyptian administration.

27 April: British government recognizes the union between the West Bank and Jordan.

1 May: UN General Assembly establishes UNRWA (UN Relief and Works Agency) based on Resolution 302 of 3 December 1949.

July: 'Law of Return' passed by Knesset, whereby any Jew, from anywhere in the world, is entitled to full Israeli citizenship.

1952
11 August: The Law of Nationality affirms the Law of Return and legislates that resident non-Jews can acquire citizenship only on the basis of residence if they can prove they are Palestinian or by naturalization. Palestinian Arabs remaining in Israel literally become foreigners in their own country. Proving residence is in practice often impossible as most Arab residents have no proof of citizenship, many having surrendered their identity cards to the Israeli Army during or after the war.

1956
26 July: Egyptian President Nasser nationalizes the Suez Canal.
29 October: Israel, in collusion with Britain and France, invades Sinai Peninsula.
31 October: Kafr Qassem Massacre.

1959
January: Fatah is established by Yasser Arafat and associates; al-Ard group starts to publish an Arab nationalities periodical in Israel.
15 June: UN Secretary General (Hammarskjold) Proposal A/4121 for absorption of Palestinian refugees by the Middle East states.

1964
28 May: The First Palestinian National Council (PNC) meets in Jerusalem.
2 June: Palestine Liberation Organization (PLO) founded.

1965
1 January: First military operation of Fatah in Palestine.

1966

Military Period in Israel comes to an end.

1967

5 June: Six Day War: Israel begins military occupation of West Bank and Gaza Strip of Palestine, Sinai of Egypt and Golan Heights of Syria.

28 June: Israel annexes Old Jerusalem and begins Jewish settlement in occupied Palestinian territories.

4 July: UN General Assembly Resolution 2253 (ES-U) calls upon Israel to 'rescind all measures taken [and] to desist forthwith from taking any action which would alter the status of Jerusalem'.

22 November: UN Security Council Resolution 242.

1973

6 October: Yom Kippur/October War: Egypt and Syria fight to regain the Arab territories occupied by Israel in 1967.

22 December: Geneva Conference for Middle East.

1974

14 October: UN General Assembly recognizes the PLO as the representative of the Palestinian people in its Resolution 3210.

November: UN General Assembly reaffirms the inalienable rights of the Palestinian people in Palestine.

1975

13 April: Start of the 1975–90 civil war in Lebanon.

1978

12 March: Israeli Army invades South Lebanon.

19 March: UN Security Council adopts Resolution 425, calling for an immediate Israeli withdrawal from Lebanese territory, and establishes a new UNIFIL to be dispatched to southern Lebanon.

1979
22 March: UN Security Council Resolution 446 calls on Israel to dismantle the settlements, 'those having no legal validity', in the occupied Palestinian territories, including Jerusalem.

1980
30 June: Israeli Knesset adopts the Jerusalem Basic Law 'officially' annexing the pre-1967 Palestinian eastern part of the city of Jerusalem.

1982
4 June: Israel invades Lebanon for the second time with estimated 100,000 troops.
21 August: The evacuation of PLO troops from Lebanon begins as 400 board a ship to Cyprus.
16–18 September: More than 1,000 Palestinian refugees are slaughtered in Sabra and Shatila refugee camps in Beirut.

1987
25 June: More than 400,000 Palestinian citizens of Israel join in general strike to demand equal rights and an end to discriminatory practices.
9 December: The Intifada begins in Gaza; four Palestinians are killed and at least seven wounded when an Israeli truck collides with two vans of Palestinian workers returning from work in Israel; 4,000 demonstrators attend funeral of those killed.

1988
19 January: Israeli defence minister, Yitzhak Rabin, announces new policy for dealing with the Intifada – 'Force, might, beatings.'

7 February: In New York, US veto defeats UN Security Council Resolution demanding that Israel abide by terms of Fourth Geneva Convention and calling for international conference on Arab–Israeli conflict.

5 December: After a year of the Intifada 318 Palestinians have been killed, 20,000 wounded, 15,000 arrested, 12,000 jailed, 34 deported and 140 houses demolished. Eight Israelis have been killed (six civilians, two soldiers).

1990

22 March: US Senate adopts by voice vote resolution recognizing undivided Jerusalem as capital of Israel.

27 March: Israeli Knesset adopts resolution that united Jerusalem is under Israeli sovereignty and there will be no negotiations on its unity or status.

19 April: Robert Dole tells his Senate colleagues they made a 'dangerous' mistake in passing resolution recognizing undivided Jerusalem as capital of Israel.

20 May: Israeli gunman massacres seven Palestinian workers and injures scores more at Iyun Qarah.

1991

9 October: Hundreds of Jewish settlers invade Silwan, on outskirts of East Jerusalem, and occupy eight Palestinian homes.

23 October: Members of the Jewish Ateret Cohanim Seminary move into a house in the Muslim quarter of East Jerusalem.

13 December: Israeli police evict settlers from one of the homes they occupy in Silwan following Jerusalem court ruling.

20 December: Some 3,000 Israeli Palestinians demonstrate against occupation of six homes in Silwan.

1992

February: Israel Interior Ministry expands area of Jerusalem municipality by annexing some 15,000 dunams (approximately 3,750 acres) of land south and west of the city.

You Can't Hide the Sun

12 May: US State Department says USA supports UN General Assembly Resolution 194, passed 11 December 1948, which upholds right of Palestinian refugees to return to their homes.

13 May: Responding to US statement on Palestinian refugees' rights, Israel prime minister, Shamir, states, 'There is only a Jewish "right of return" to the land of "Israel".'

1993

8 March: *Jerusalem Post* reports on quota for Palestinian population of Jerusalem set by government in 1973 and consistently enforced through housing plans. In 1967, Palestinians were 26 per cent of total population, today only 27 per cent. City council may appeal the legality of discriminatory quota to the High Court.

19 August: Israeli and PLO negotiators meeting in Oslo reach final agreed draft of Declaration of Principles (DOP).

9 September: Arafat, in letter to Israeli prime minister, Yitzhak Rabin, recognizes 'the right of the state of Israel to exist in peace and security', and renounces 'the use of terrorism and other acts of violence'.

10 September: Israeli prime minister, Rabin, formally signs letter recognizing PLO as 'the representative of the Palestinian people'.

1995

17 May: US veto (its thirtieth in favour of Israel) prevents the adoption of a UN resolution condemning Israel's confiscation of land in Jerusalem. The fourteen other states that vote approve the resolution.

19 May: Israeli military starts expropriating large tracts of West Bank land to build bypass and security roads (approximately 130 kilometres) for settlers after Israeli redeployment.

2000
25 May: Israeli Army withdraws from south Lebanon.
25 July: End of Camp David talks.
28 September: Sharon visits al-Haram al-Sharif. Start of the al-Aqsa Intifada.
1 October: Start of Israeli police violence, which kills thirteen unarmed protesters.

2003
31 July: Amendment of 1952 Citizenship Law, to deny citizenship to West Bank/Gaza spouses of Israelis.
1 September: Or Commission report published.

2006
25 June: Hamas fighters kidnap Gilad Shalit.
12 July: Israel–Hezbollah war begins.

2010
10 October: Israeli cabinet approves law requiring new non-Jewish citizens to pledge loyalty to Israel as a 'Jewish and democratic state'.
13 December: Hundreds of Israeli police invade Lod, and demolish a large number of Palestinian houses.

2011
17 January: Israeli forces demolish the unrecognized village of al-Araqib for the ninth time.

18 October: Gilad Shalit released in Gaza.

Bibliography

Meron Benvenisti, *Sacred Landscape: The Buried History of the Holy Land since 1948*, California, University of California Press, 2000.

Jonathan Cook, *Blood and Religion*, London, Pluto Press, 2006.

Martin Gilbert, *Israel: A History*, London, Transworld Publishers, 1999.

Sabri Jiryis, *The Arabs in Israel*, Beirut, The Institute for Palestine Studies, 1968.

Walid Khalidi, *All That Remains*, Washington, The Institute of Palestine Studies, 1992.

Saree Makdisi, *Palestine Inside Out*, New York, W. W. Norton & Co., 2008.

Benny Morris, *The Birth of the Palestine Refugee Problem, 1947–1949*, Cambridge, Cambridge University Press, 1988.

Ilan Pappe, *The Ethnic Cleansing of Palestine*, Oxford, Oneworld Publications Ltd, 2006.

Eugene L. Rogan and Avi Shlaim (eds), *The War for Palestine: Rewriting the History of 1948*, Cambridge, Cambridge University Press, 2001.

Andrew Sanger, *The AA Explorer Guide: Israel*, Basingstoke, AA Publishing, 2006.

Tom Segev, *One Palestine Complete*, London, Little, Brown &
Co., 2000.
Leslie Stein, *The Making of Modern Israel: 1948–1967*,
Cambridge, Polity Press, 2009.
Alan R. Taylor, *Prelude to Israel*, London, Dartman,
Longman & Todd, 1959.
R. D. Wilson, *Cordon and Search*, Aldershot, Gale & Polden,
1949.

Fiction

The Palestine National Liberation Movement, Fateh (ed.),
They Claim There Is No Resistance (Palestinian poetry),
c. 1968.
Emile Habiby, trans. Salma Khadra Jayyusi and Trevor
LeGassick, *The Secret Life of Saeed the Pessoptimist*, Zed
Books Ltd, London, 1985.
Ghassan Kanafani, *Palestine's Children* (short stories),
Boulder, Lynne Rienner, 2000.
Elias Khoury, *Gate of the Sun*, London, Vintage, 2006.
S. Yizhar, *Khirbet Khizeh*, London, Granta, 2011.

Websites

A history from the United Nations on the origins and
evolution of the Palestine problem, 1917–1988:
http://unispal.un.org/unispal.nsf/1ce874ab1832a53e852570
bb006dfaf6/57c45a3dd0d46b09802564740045cc0a?
OpenDocument
If Americans Knew: statistics on the Israel Palestine conflict –
though mainly concerned with Palestinians in the Occupied
Territories:
http://www.ifamericansknew.org
Palestine Remembered – for information on the Arab villages
that were destroyed in 1948 and after:
http://www.palestineremembered.com/index.html

IDMC – an organization concerned with internally displaced peoples. There is a section on Palestinians in Israel:
http://www.internal-displacement.org

Sikkuy: a non-partisan NGO in Israel that advances equality between Arab and Jewish citizens of Israel. Its reports give a good overview of relations between the two communities in Israel:
http://www.sikkuy.org.il

Zochrot: a Jewish NGO in Israel aiming to promote understanding of the Nakba to Jewish Israelis:
http://www.zochrot.org

US Department of State – issues human rights reports on many countries. The one for Israel and the Occupied Territories includes sections on the Palestinian citizens of Israel:
http://www.state.gov

Adalah – The Legal Center for Arab Minority Rights in Israel – has reports and active cases:
http://www.adalah.org

Mossawa Centre – The Advocacy Center for Arab Citizens in Israel – has reports and current news of Palestinian issues in Israel:
http://www.mossawacenter.org

The Association for Civil Rights in Israel has an extensive range of reports on civil rights in the country, including Arab rights and the situation in East Jerusalem:
http://www.acri.org.il/en

Acknowledgements

There are many people to whom I owe a great debt of gratitude for their help with this book.

Dozens of Palestinians across Israel and in occupied East Jerusalem have welcomed me into their homes and shared their memories. In cities, villages, shanty-towns and desert encampments, people have opened their hearts and told me their extraordinary personal stories. Only a fraction of the people I interviewed appear in these pages, but the recollections and insights of all those I met have informed and shaped the content of this book. Likewise, many Israeli scholars and activists, both Palestinian and Jewish, have broadened my understanding of the complexity which envelops this part of the world.

There are a number of people I would like to thank individually.

Without Suha Arraf, a Palestinian citizen of Israel and screenwriter, the book simply would not have happened. Her advice and introductions ensured that I met the people and visited the places that would allow me to tell this story. In addition to translating for me, her sympathetic presence enriched many interviews.

Nick Toksvig acted as a sounding board and offered me a calm haven at his home in Jerusalem.

On travels around the region, Geoff Dunlop's experience of and empathy for the Middle East has deepened my own.

Setting out a community's history over a span of more than sixty years, and in many locations, proved a difficult task. I have been fortunate to have some wonderful advisers.

From the outset my mother-in-law and friend, Ann Jasper, has given support and encouragement. Her close and intelligent reading of the various drafts has improved both the writing and the content enormously.

Bill Scott-Kerr and Doug Young offered constant encouragement; their skills and experience as editors helped me define the tone and structure of the book.

Mark Lucas gave me continuous reassurance when I thought there was no way forward through the material. His deft editorial touch reinvigorated many passages.

Sophie Wilson has been an outstanding editor, showing great sensitivity to the stories and displaying real flair in suggesting how best to bring them together. Her involvement and care have been vital.

Hazel Orme worked further wonders as copy editor.

Many thanks must also go to Martin and Laila Asser for all their advice.

Within the context of national and political conflict,

the core theme of this book is the importance of having a home. On a broad level this means having a country where our right to belong is unquestioned, and more locally, a physical place of bricks and mortar that we share with those people closest to us.

In the early chapters of the book I reflect on the way in which thoughts of my home in England sustained me through captivity in Lebanon. I knew I would be safe once I returned there. Above all, thoughts of family and friends, and being confident of their love, gave me a safe mental place to retreat to at times of fear and depression.

Nowadays, a free man again, wherever I might be in the world, I remain safe in the knowledge of my homeland and also can look forward to returning to the home I've made with my family. I thank Anna and Lydia for being there, at home, for me.

Some Other Rainbow

John McCarthy & Jill Morrell

On 17 April 1986 John McCarthy was kidnapped in Beirut. For the next five years he was cut off from everything and everybody he knew and loved, from family, friends, and, perhaps above all, from Jill Morrell, the girl he was going to marry.

For five years, John McCarthy had to endure the deprivation – both physical and psychological – of captivity; the filth and squalor of the cells in which he was kept; the agony of isolation and repeated self-examination; and the pain of ignorance, of not knowing if those he loved even realized he was alive.

For Jill Morrell, the five years of John's captivity were a different kind of hell: the initial shock and disbelief; the gradual acceptance that John had been taken and that her life had changed irrevocably, that all their plans had been shattered.

But Jill refused to give up hope. For five years she and a group of friends worked ceaselessly on behalf of John and all British hostages in the Middle East, until the extraordinary day in August 1991 when John McCarthy stepped down from an aeroplane at RAF Lyneham.

This is their story, a remarkable account of courage, endurance, hope and love.

Between Extremes

Brian Keenan & John McCarthy

From a friendship born out of adversity comes an extraordinary story by two extraordinary men. For four years, Brian Keenan and John McCarthy were incarcerated in a Lebanese dungeon. From the blank outlook of a tiny cell, with just each other and a few volumes of an ancient American encyclopaedia to sustain them, they could only wander the wide open spaces of their imagination. To displace the ugly confines of their existence, they envisaged walking in the High Andes and across the wastes of Patagonia.

Five years after their release, Brian and John chose to travel together again to see how the reality of Chile matched their imagination and to revisit their past experiences. *Between Extremes* is the story of that journey, which once more found them far from home, in an unfamiliar landscape, but which for the first time allowed them to live by their own rules.

A Ghost Upon Your Path

John McCarthy

We all have a need to belong, to have a place and people we feel
tied to: our family, our house, our hometown, our nation. Ever
since he first visited Ireland with his family twenty years ago,
John McCarthy has felt a strong affinity with its people and
landscape. Yet in spite of his Irish name, he never thought of
himself as remotely Irish.

When McCarthy sets up home in a wild and isolated corner of
County Kerry where his ancestors were living a thousand years
before, he realises that he is about to undertake not only a
journey into that small rural community but also into his own
history and his family. What he discovers there reveals a curious
sense of belonging to a place he has never before lived in and
peels back the emotional layers of his own fractured past.

The Lemon Tree

Sandy Tolan

In the summer of 1967, not long after the Six Day War, three young Palestinian men ventured into the town of Ramla in Israel. They were cousins, on a pilgrimage to see their childhood homes, from which they and their families had been driven out nearly twenty years earlier. One cousin had the door slammed in his face, one found that his old house had been converted into a school. But the third, Bashir, was met at the door by a young woman named Dalia, who invited him in . . .

This poignant encounter is the starting point for the story of two families – one Arab, one Jewish – which spans the fraught modern history of the region. In the lemon tree his father planted in the backyard of his childhood home, Bashir sees a symbol of occupation; Dalia, who arrived in 1948 as an infant with her family, as a fugitive from Bulgaria, sees hope for a people devastated by the Holocaust. Both are inevitably swept up in the fates of their people and the stories of their lives form a microcosm of more than half a century of Israeli–Palestinian history.

What began as a simple meeting between two young people grew into a dialogue lasting four decades. *The Lemon Tree* offers a much needed human perspective on this seemingly intractable conflict and reminds us not only of all that is at stake, but also of all that is possible.